The
GOLDEN TOQUE
The Recipe Collection

The
GOLDEN TOQUE
The Recipe Collection

Edited by

MICHAEL MINOR

GEORGIA LOCKRIDGE

VAN NOSTRAND REINHOLD
NEW YORK

Copyright © 1992 by Van Nostrand Reinhold

Library of Congress Catalog Card Number 91-36686
ISBN 0-442-00817-1

Printed in the United States of America

Van Nostrand Reinhold
115 Fifth Avenue
New York, New York 10003

Chapman and Hall
2-6 Boundary Row
London, SE1 8HN, England

Thomas Nelson Australia
102 Dodds Street
South Melbourne 3205
Victoria, Australia

Nelson Canada
1120 Birchmount Road
Scarborough, Ontario MIK 5G4, Canada

16   15   14   13   12   11   10   9   8   7   6   5   4   3   2   1

Library of Congress Cataloging-in-Publication Data
The golden toque recipe collection/[compiled by] Michael Minor,
    Georgia Lockridge.
        p.   cm.
      Includes index.
      ISBN 0-442-00817-1
      1. Cookery. I. Minor, Michael.   II. Lockridge, Georgia.
TX714.G646   1992
641.5—dc20   91-36686
                                                     CIP

CONTENTS

PREFACE

THE Honorable Order of the Golden Toque is an international chefs' honor society dedicated to the pursuit of excellence in the culinary arts and sciences. It was established in 1960 by Pierre J. Bernard and other professional chefs to honor and bring together in a fraternal group some of the best chefs in the United States. The society is limited to one hundred active members and fifteen honorary members, each of whom must have a minimum of twenty-five years of experience, have received numerous culinary honors and awards, and be recognized as an outstanding leader in the profession. A similar professional society of great chefs, called the Black Hat Society, has been in existence for a number of years in France.

Funk and Wagnall's *College Standard Dictionary* defines a *toque* as a small, brimless hat. Originally it was a tall, conical hat worn by the doges of Venice to indicate their rank. In the Middle Ages, toques of various shapes and colors came into being, each designed to distinguish members of the different professions. The color selected by the culinary profession was white, and various shapes indicated rank within the profession. Apprentices wore a plain circular skullcap. *Chefs de parti* wore hats of the same basic shape but added a small puffed flounce; as rank increased, so did the height of this flounced portion. Executive chefs today can be distinguished by their tall hats.

In France black velvet was often a fabric worn by the royalty, and so, when the French wanted to honor their greatest chefs, they created the Black Hat Society, for which the distinguishing hat was a small, black (often velvet) skullcap in the same shape worn by apprentices. In the United States, the professionals forming the Honorable Order of the Golden Toque also chose the toque as its symbol but, instead of black, selected gold, a color often associated with authenticity and premium quality.

The Golden Toque Recipe Collection is unique in that it is the only collection of recipes and information compiled from first and second generations of America's leading chefs available today. Members were asked to submit their best-liked and most useful recipes for inclusion in the book. The recipes were then retested for consumer use by the Culinary Arts Division of Johnson and Wales University. The recipes were then judged for palatability, color, form, ease of preparation, practicality, ingredient availability, and other criteria that would enable the average user to prepare excellent dishes easily and practically. All of the recipes produce small quantities, ranging from two to twelve servings.

Twelve categories of food are covered, from appetizers to desserts, so the book can be used to prepare the menu for a full meal. In addition, much general information on foods, times and temperatures, nutrients, garnishes, and table settings is included. Each recipe lists ingredients and procedures in order of use. Often helpful hints are included to make preparation easier or more understandable. Every food category is prefaced by a bit of helpful technical information, useful for proper recipe preparation.

Because this book is not just a compilation of recipes but contains other material helpful in gaining a knowledge of food preparation, it is an excellent instruction and laboratory manual for food-preparation class. It can also help those people who simply like to cook, as it teaches basic techniques while introducing the user to the realm of the professional chef.

Many chefs tend to guard their recipes closely and try to prevent others from learning their secrets. This is not the case with the members of the Honorable Order of the Golden Toque. They are dedicated professionals, interested in furthering knowledge about fine foods and their preparation. They want to share their extensive knowledge with others. In fact, they look upon this as an obligation—to teach what good foods are all about and how they can lead to better health and a more enjoyable life.

ACKNOWLEDGMENTS

THE Honorable Order of the Golden Toque would like to thank numerous members and individuals for their contributions to this book. First, we are very grateful to the following officers and directors who made this book possible:

OFFICERS

John L. Bandera, *Grand Commander*
Michael L. Minor, *Commander Secretary*
Joe Vislocky, *Commander Treasurer*

DIRECTORS

Commander Robert Nograd
Commander Jean E. Clary
Commander Edward Mauti
Commander Wolfgang A. Bierer
Commander C. Arthur Jones
Commander Oliver Sommer

We want to acknowledge our founder, Honorary Grand Commander Pierre J. Berard, and our past grand commanders, listed below, who have always wanted to see this cookbook published:

Marcel Chabernaud
Ernest Bertschi
John Kempf
Eugene Blumenschein
James H. Edwards
Stanley Nicas

Robert Ehlers made a commitment during his tenure as grand commander to appoint the cookbook committee and retain the services of Georgia D. Lockridge to ensure the realization of the organization's dream of publishing this book.

We are grateful to Commander Michael L. Minor for his leadership as chairman of the cookbook committee and to the following committee members for their dedication to the completion of this book:

Michael L. Minor, Chairman
Dr. Stanley Nicas, Co-chairman
John J. Bowen, Adviser
Robert Nograd
Lendal Kotchevar, Ph.D.
Robert Ehlers
John L. Bandera
Joe Vislocky
Brother Herman Zaccarelli

Also, a very special thanks to all the Honorable Order of the Golden Torque members who contributed money, time, and recipes for the cookbook. Without their contributions, this book would not be possible. We also thank the following major financial contributors to the project: Dr. Lewis J. Minor, the Beringer Vineyards, the L. J. Minor Corporation, and Stouffer Restaurants.

Special thanks to the L. J. Minor Corporation for the use of their facilities, chefs, and support staff, and to Johnson and Wales University for the testing and formulation of recipes by their staff and students.

- *Cookbook coordinator: Georgia D. Lockridge*
- *Photography: Robert Koropp Photography, Denver, Colorado;* Food Preparation and Styling: *Wolfgang A. Bierer, Clarke A. Bernier, John J. Bowen, Michael L. Minor, Robert M. Nograd, Lori Miller, and Richard Coppedge;* Set Design: *Georgia D. Lockridge, Mary Margaret Crews*
- *Preface and chapter introductions: Dr. Lendal Kotschevar*
- *General information (appendixes):* Nutrition: *Lori Miller;* Garnishes: *Alfred Saarne and Carl Richter;* Working a Recipe: *Robert Nelson*
- *Typing: Cheryl Clancy and Pauline Allsworth*

And finally, thanks to Bragard Inc. for providing uniforms for the chefs for the group photograph.

MEMBERS OF THE HONORABLE ORDER OF THE GOLDEN TOQUE

The national officers of the Honorable Order of the Golden Toque are: Grand Commander, John L. Bandera; Commander and Secretary, Michael L. Minor; Commander Treasurer, Joseph Vislocky. Board of Directors: Commander Ex Officio, Robert E. Ehlers; (1 year) Commander C. Arthur Jones and Commander Oliver Sommers; (2 Years) Commander Edward Mauti and Commander Wolfgang A. Bierer; (3 years) Commander Jean E. Clary and Commander Robert Nograd. Past Grand Commanders: Pierre J. Bernard (deceased), Marcel Chabernaud (deceased), Eugene Blumenschein (deceased), Ernest Bertschi (deceased), James H. Edwards, John Kempf, Dr. Stanley J. Nicas, and Robert E. Ehlers.

Active members in the Honorable Order of the Golden Toque include: Paul Amaral, Joseph Amendola, Hideo Aramaki, John Bandera, Jess Barbosa, U. Max Behr, Clark Bernier, Wolfgang Bierer, Richard Bosnjak, John Bowen, Jack Braun, L. Edwin Brown, Raymond Camy, John Carroll, Jean Caubet, Milos Cihelka, Jean Cleary, Nicholas Colletti, Neil Connolly, Lawrence Conti, Noel Cullen, Bert Cutino, Richard Czack, Edward Doucette, Jean-Jacques Dietrich, James Edwards, Robert Ehlers, Siegfried Eisenberger, Paul Elbling, Amato Ferrero, John Folse, Le Roi Folsom, Klaus Friedenreich, Harold Baron Galand, William Gallager, Fred Geissler, Edward Gerstung, Paul Goebel, Louis Gonzales, Jon Greenwalt, Gerhard Grimeissen, Michel Grobon, William Harmon, Thomas J. Hickey, Sr., Socrotes Inonog, James Jenkins, Dr. Jean Joaquin, Arthur Jones, George Karousos, Kamel Kassem, John Kempf, John Kaufmann, Keith Keogh, James Kopcha, James Kosec, Hartmut Handke, Paul Laesecke, Michael Legorgne, Warren Leruth, Ernest Louis, John Lubinski, Romeo Lupinacci, William Lyman, Philip McGuirk, Noble Masi, Edward Mauti, Ferdinand Metz, Walter Meyer, James Miller, Michael Minor, Robert Nelson, Stanley Nicas, Robert Nograd,

Jacques Noe, Paul Pantano, Joseph D. Parratto, Jr., Carl Richter, Rene Roncari, Willy Rossel, Hans Roth, Alfred Saarne, Eugene Scanlan, Hans Schadler, Frank Scherer, Rudolph Soeder, Oliver Sommer, Fritz Sonnenschmidt, Pierre Thomas, Richard Tromposch, Manual Tubio, Bernard Urban, Martial Valentin, Daniel Varano, Joe Vislocky, Clifton Williams, Kenneth Wade, Robert Werth, Roland Zwerger, and Bruno Zuchold.

Senior Active Members include: Paul M. Alexanian, Sr., Adolf Brettschneider, Albert Buda, Harvey Colgin, Charles Finance, Pierre Garbit, Joe Gomez, Aldo Graziotin, Virgilio Rech, Poncho Valez, Arnold Skogstrand, and Louis Traco.

Honorary Members include: George Baggott, Julia Child, Dr. Morris Gaebe, Henry Haller, Dr. Lendal Kotschevar, Herman Leis, Lt. John McLaughlin (retired), Dr. Lewis J. Minor, Hermann Rusch, Joseph Villella, Br. Herman Zaccarelli, Hans Bueschkens, Dr. John Yena, and Dr. Louis Szathmary.

CHAPTER ONE

Appetizers

APPETIZERS should do just what their name implies, whet the appetite. Certain foods do actually increase or heighten one's appetite. For example, as one chews meat, the juices in the meat help to start the flow of saliva and gastric juices, thus increasing hunger. Spicy foods and other food flavors can do the same thing. Alcohol consumed in moderate amounts can increase the appetite, but too much alcohol can destroy it. Eye appeal in itself can heighten interest in food. Salty and acid foods stimulate the appetite, but sweet and oily foods do not.

The variety of foods used in appetizers is almost countless. Vegetables, fruits, meats, poultry, fish, seafood, and even pastas qualify. Appetizers can be hot or cold, liquid or solid. Whatever the case, they should be attractive and highly palatable. Remember this basic rule: hot appetizers should be served *hot* and cold items should be served *cold.* The difference between a piping hot Oysters Rockefeller and a tepid one illustrates this point. Also, with regard to seasonings, remember that heat intensifies flavor while cold reduces it. Therefore, one can add a bit more acid or other flavoring when the product is served cold than when it is served hot.

With the modern trend in dietary patterns, it is wise to select some appetizers that are low in cholesterol, in salt, and in fat. Raw vegetables, for example, offered among the appetizer selections, can win friends.

The professional chef, experienced in using the pastry tube and other equipment can prepare many elaborately decorated appetizers in a fairly short time. A nonprofessional with less practice would require far more time, and for this reason nonprofessionals should usually avoid trying to do too much decoration. Simple things, such as adding a slice of a pimento-stuffed green olive or a carrot curl, can produce a simple, lovely effect. Using a pastry tube to place a tangy star shape in the center of a crisp, round cracker can often provide enough decoration. Judicious combinations of colors and textures can give the desired effect.

Neatness and freshness are absolute requirements for attractive and tasty appetizers. Foods intended to be crisp *must* be served crisp. Heating chips, wafers, crackers, or nuts in a very slow oven can increase their crispness, and serving them slightly warm can add a nice touch.

Keep appetizers simple but good. Don't sacrifice quality for style, and don't try to be too daring.

Appetizers

ESCARGOTS À LA MAISON

MARINATED FRIED SMELTS

MUSSELS IN CREAM SAUCE

OPEN-FACE HOT CRABMEAT AND BACON SANDWICH

TOAST À LA TOSCANA

ENGLISH MUFFIN HORS D'OEUVRES

DEVONSHIRE SANDWICH

CROQUE-MONSIEUR

CHEF'S FAVORITE SANDWICH

SCRAMBLED EGGS, JUMBOTO STYLE

CALAMARI PUFFS

HOT CRAB CANAPÉS

SHRIMP IN BEER

LOBSTER SWISS CHALET

CULTURED ABALONE WITH GINGER SAUCE

LIVER PÂTÉ

LAMB CURRY SALAD

ANTIPASTO CASALINGA

CAJUN CHICKEN SALAD

MOUSSE OF NORWEGIAN SALMON

SWEET-AND-SOUR CHICKEN WINGS

JULIA CHILD'S PISSALADIÈRE (ONION TART)

MARYLAND-STYLE CRAB CAKES

BAKED STUFFED MUSHROOMS SHELBOURNE

MORELS ON TOAST

SPINACH AND SAUSAGE PINWHEELS

CLAMS CASINO

SPINACH AND CHEESE PUFF TRIANGLES

SALMON AND TROUT MOUSSE WITH
CAVIAR AND ASPARAGUS SAUCE

BRANDIED BLUE CHEESE MOLD

QUICHE LORRAINE

HICKORY-SMOKED HAM DIP

LUMP CRABMEAT AND CRAYFISH CARDINAL

ESCARGOTS À LA MAISON

Yield: 2 servings

5 TABLESPOONS SOFT BUTTER
1 TABLESPOON MINCED SHALLOTS
1 DASH HOT PEPPER SAUCE (SUCH AS
  TABASCO)
¼ TEASPOON WORCESTERSHIRE SAUCE
¼ TEASPOON FRESH CHOPPED PARSLEY
1 CLOVE GARLIC, MINCED
¼ TEASPOON FRESHLY SQUEEZED
  LEMON JUICE

1 OUNCE BACON, DICED
2 TABLESPOONS DICED ONIONS
4 OUNCES FRESH SPINACH CHOPPED
  AND STEMMED (APPROXIMATELY
  ½ CUP)
8 MEDIUM MUSHROOM CAPS, STEMS
  REMOVED
SALT AND PEPPER TO TASTE
8 MEDIUM CANNED SNAILS

❖ Whip 4 tablespoons of the butter until soft. Work in the shallots, hot pepper sauce, Worcestershire sauce, parsley, garlic, and lemon juice. Set the butter mixture aside in a small heavy saucepan. Sauté the bacon until crisp, and then add the diced onions. Continue to cook until the onions are transparent. Add the spinach, stir, and remove from the heat. In a separate pan, sauté the mush-

(continued)

rooms in the remaining tablespoon of butter for 2 to 3 minutes until firm. Season with salt and pepper if desired. Remove the mushroom caps to individual serving plates. Spoon the butter mixture into each cap. Top each with a snail and then with the spinach mixture.

Note: A gratinée of 1 tablespoon breadcrumbs and Parmesan cheese and ⅛ teaspoon paprika can be added for a nice variation. Once topped, just pop the appetizers under the broiler until brown, or bake for a few minutes in a very hot oven.

MARINATED FRIED SMELTS

Yield: 6 servings

2 POUNDS FRESH SMELTS
6 TABLESPOONS FLOUR
VEGETABLE OIL FOR FRYING
SALT AND PEPPER TO TASTE
1 MEDIUM ONION, DICED FINE
1 CLOVE GARLIC, CRUSHED

1 TABLESPOON OLIVE OIL
1 SMALL RED PEPPER, DICED FINE
1 SMALL GREEN PEPPER, DICED FINE
1 TABLESPOON CHOPPED FRESH BASIL
½ CUP WINE VINEGAR

❖ Gut and wash the smelts, and pat dry with paper towels. Dredge them in the flour, and fry in vegetable oil in a skillet over medium heat until golden brown. Remove and drain on paper towels. Sprinkle with salt and pepper while still hot. Place the fried fish in a glass or china casserole, and set aside. Sauté the onion and garlic in the olive oil in a skillet for 3–4 minutes; do not brown. Add the diced red and green peppers and the basil. Pour in the wine vinegar, and bring to a simmer. Remove from the heat. Pour this marinade over the fried smelts, and cool. Marinate for 2 hours. Serve cold, with the marinade spooned over the smelts.

MUSSELS IN CREAM SAUCE

Yield: 6 servings

1 CUP WHITE WINE
2 TABLESPOONS DICED SHALLOTS
¼ TEASPOON CRUSHED BLACK PEPPER
1 BAY LEAF
4 DOZEN MUSSELS, WELL CLEANED
3 EGG YOLKS, BEATEN

1 CUP HEAVY CREAM
1 PARSLEY SPRIG, CHOPPED
1 TABLESPOON FINELY CHOPPED CHIVES
12 SLICES GARLIC TOAST (USING FRENCH
   BREAD)

✤ In a shallow casserole, combine the wine, shallots, pepper, bay leaf, and mussels. Cover, and steam until the mussels open. Strain the liquid into a saucepan, and reduce it by two-thirds. Whisk together the eggs and cream, mixing well. Temper this liaison by gradually adding a bit of the hot mussel liquid; add the tempered liaison to the sauce. Bring the sauce to a simmer over medium heat, stirring constantly with a wooden spoon; simmer for 2 minutes (do not boil, or the eggs will curdle). Remove and discard the top shells of the mussels, and arrange the steamed mussels on a serving dish. Sprinkle the chopped parsley and chives on the mussels. Coat each mussel with sauce, and serve with the garlic toast.

OPEN-FACE HOT CRABMEAT AND BACON SANDWICH

Yield: 16 pieces

1 POUND CANNED PASTEURIZED BACK-
   FIN LUMP CRABMEAT
4 OUNCES ICEBERG LETTUCE, MINCED
3 OUNCES MAYONNAISE

8 SLICES BREAD, LIGHTLY TOASTED
2 TABLESPOONS BUTTER
8 BACON STRIPS, FRIED AND HALVED
   (8 OUNCES)

✤ Combine the crabmeat and lettuce with the mayonnaise. Spread each piece of toast evenly with butter and then with the crabmeat mixture. Criss-cross 2 bacon halves on each sandwich. Warm in the oven for 10 minutes at 375°F.

TOAST À LA TOSCANA

Yield: 6 servings

12 OUNCES CHICKEN LIVERS
1 GARLIC CLOVE, CRUSHED
½ MEDIUM ONION, CHOPPED
4 TABLESPOONS BUTTER

SALT, PEPPER, AND SAGE TO TASTE
3 OUNCES CAPERS, DRAINED AND FINELY
   CHOPPED
12 SLICES FRENCH BREAD, TOASTED

(continued)

❖ Clean and finely chop the chicken livers. Sauté the garlic and onion in the butter for 3 to 4 minutes. Add the livers, and sauté until their color changes. Season with the salt, pepper, and sage. Stir well, and add the capers. Cook and stir until well mixed into a paste. Spread the paste on the toasted bread, and serve hot.

ENGLISH MUFFIN HORS D'OEUVRES

Yield: 40 appetizers

¾ CUP GRATED CHEDDAR CHEESE
¾ CUP CHOPPED RIPE OLIVES
⅓ CUP DICED ONIONS

⅓ CUP MAYONNAISE
¼ TEASPOON CURRY POWDER
5 ENGLISH MUFFINS, HALVED

❖ Combine the cheese, olives, onions, mayonnaise, and curry powder. Spread on halved english muffins. Cook in a 350°F oven until light brown. Quarter and serve.

DEVONSHIRE SANDWICH

Yield: 6 servings

6 SLICES WHITE TOAST
18 CRISP-COOKED BACON STRIPS
9 OUNCES SLICED COOKED TURKEY OR
   CHICKEN BREAST

2½ CUPS MORNAY SAUCE (SEE RECIPE
   IN CHAPTER 3)
3 OUNCES GRATED ROMANO CHEESE

❖ On each slice of toast, place 3 slices of bacon and 1½ ounces of sliced turkey or chicken. Top with the Mornay sauce, and sprinkle with the grated cheese. Bake in a preheated 350°F oven for about 10 minutes, until the cheese is melted.

CROQUE-MONSIEUR

Yield: 12 appetizers

6 SLICES SANDWICH BREAD
2 OUNCES SOFT BUTTER
3 SLICES HAM, PRESSED
3 SLICES GRUYÈRE CHEESE, THINLY CUT

PEPPER TO TASTE
2 EGGS, BEATEN
OIL FOR FRYING

❖ Set the slices of bread on a cutting board. Spread each with thin layer of the butter. Place a slice of ham on three of the buttered slices, and cover with a thin slice of Gruyère. Add pepper to taste from a peppermill. Cover each with a second slice of buttered bread. Press each sandwich along its entire length with the flat of your hand. Heat the oil to 350°F. Dip each sandwich into the beaten eggs, and fry to a golden brown. Cut the sandwiches into quarters.

CHEF'S FAVORITE SANDWICH

Yield: 1 sandwich

1 ENGLISH MUFFIN
1 TEASPOON BUTTER
3 OUNCES COOKED TURKEY BREAST,
   THINLY SHAVED
2 TABLESPOONS SOUR CREAM
2 TABLESPOONS GUACAMOLE

2 TOMATO SLICES (1 OUNCE EACH)
2 CRISP BACON SLICES
3 SLICES MONTEREY JACK CHEESE
   (½ OUNCE EACH)
1 TABLESPOON CRUMBLED BLUE CHEESE

❖ Split the english muffin in half. Butter each half, then broil in a pan until toasted. Set the two halves, toasted side up, next to each other on a dinner plate. Spread the thinly shaved turkey evenly over both halves. Spread the sour cream evenly over the turkey. Spread the guacamole on each, and top with the tomato slices. Lay the bacon on top of the tomato slices, extending the length of both halves. Fan or overlap the Monterey Jack slices to cover the entire sandwich. Sprinkle the crumbled blue cheese evenly over the Monterey Jack. Place the sandwich under a broiler, and cook until the cheese is well melted.

SCRAMBLED EGGS, JUMBOTO STYLE

Yield: 8 to 10 servings

¼ CUP VEGETABLE OIL
½ CUP CHOPPED ONIONS
1 CUP DICED GREEN PEPPERS
1 CUP SLICED MUSHROOMS
1 CUP SLICED PEPERONI

½ CUP DICED FRESH TOMATOES
   (OPTIONAL)
15 EGGS, BEATEN
SALT AND PEPPER TO TASTE

✤ Heat the vegetable oil in a 2-quart skillet, add the onions, and cook until wilted. Add the green peppers, mushrooms, peperoni, and tomatoes. Cook for 8 minutes, or until all the vegetables are tender. Add the beaten eggs, and cook to the desired consistency. Serve immediately.

CALAMARI PUFFS

Yield: 6 servings

12 OUNCES SQUID
6 OUNCES SEASONED BREADCRUMBS
   (SEE RECIPE BELOW)
3 EGGS

2 TABLESPOONS MILK
3 OUNCES FLOUR
OIL FOR FRYING

✤ Clean the squid, and grind finely. Add 3 ounces of the seasoned breadcrumbs and 2 eggs to the ground squid. Mix well. Let stand for 15 minutes. Beat the remaining egg with the milk. Roll the squid mixture into ½-ounce balls. Dredge the balls in the flour, dip them in the eggwash, and roll them in the breadcrumbs. Deep-fry in 350°F oil until golden brown. Drain and serve.

SEASONED BREADCRUMBS

6 OUNCES BREADCRUMBS (FROM
   SANDWICH BREAD)
½ TABLESPOON CHOPPED PARSLEY
½ TEASPOON MINCED GARLIC

¼ TEASPOON FRESH SWEET BASIL
½ TABLESPOON MINCED ONION
DASH OF SALT AND PEPPER

✤ Combine all ingredients.

HOT CRAB CANAPÉS

Yield: 48 puffs

¾ CUP MAYONNAISE
2 TEASPOONS CRAB BASE*
¼ CUP COOKED CRABMEAT, DRAINED
   WELL AND FLAKED

1 TABLESPOON LEMON JUICE
⅛ TEASPOON GROUND RED PEPPER
2 EGG WHITES
48 SLICES PARTY RYE BREAD

❖ In a medium mixing bowl, combine the mayonnaise, crab base, crabmeat, lemon juice, and red pepper. Mix until well blended. In a small mixing bowl, beat the egg whites until stiff. Fold into the crab mixture. Spoon ½ tablespoon of the mixture onto each bread slice. Place the canapés on a lightly greased baking sheet, and broil until lightly browned, about 5 minutes. Serve immediately.

Variation: Shrimp Puffs: Substitute 1 cup of finely chopped cooked shrimp for the crabmeat, and use either shrimp base or crab base.

* For information about this base, see chapter 3.

SHRIMP IN BEER

Yield: 8 to 10 servings

2 POUNDS RAW SHRIMP, SHELLED AND
   DEVEINED
3 TABLESPOONS MINCED ONIONS
4 TABLESPOONS BUTTER
1½ TEASPOONS SALT
¼ TEASPOON HOT PEPPER SAUCE
   (TABASCO)

2 TABLESPOONS FLOUR
1 CUP BEER OR ALE
3 TABLESPOONS LEMON JUICE
1 BAY LEAF
½ TEASPOON THYME
2 TEASPOONS MINCED PARSLEY

❖ Wash and dry the shrimp. Sauté the shrimp and onions in the butter for 2 minutes, turning the shrimp halfway through. Add the salt, hot pepper sauce, beer, and lemon juice. Heat to boiling, stirring constantly. Add the bay leaf and thyme; cook over low heat for 5 minutes. Discard the bay leaf. Sprinkle with the parsley, and serve with toothpicks.

LOBSTER SWISS CHALET

Yield: 6 servings

12 OUNCES MAYONNAISE
12 OUNCES SOUR CREAM
1 TABLESPOON LEMON JUICE
¼ TABLESPOON FINELY CHOPPED GARLIC
1 OUNCE RIPE BLACK OLIVES, SLICED
4 PIMENTOS, DICED
2 OUNCES FROZEN GREEN PEAS,
  THAWED

12 OUNCES COOKED LOBSTER, CUT IN
  1-INCH DICE
12 OUNCES GRATED SWISS CHEESE
3 OUNCES BUTTER
1 TABLESPOON SWEET PAPRIKA

❖ Mix the mayonnaise, sour cream, lemon juice, garlic, olives, pimentos, peas, lobster, and 8 ounces of the Swiss cheese in a bowl, and chill for 2 hours. Divide the lobster mixture into six individual buttered casseroles, and top with the remaining grated Swiss cheese and the paprika. Bake in a 350°F oven until bubbly and brown.

CULTURED ABALONE WITH GINGER SAUCE

Yield: 4 servings

SAUCE

1 TABLESPOON FRESH GINGER
1 TEASPOON CHOPPED SHALLOTS (NOT
  PEELED)
½ CUP CHICKEN STOCK

½ CUP DRY WHITE WINE
1 OUNCE MUSHROOMS, SLICED
1 PINT HEAVY CREAM
8 OUNCES SWEET BUTTER, CUBED

❖ In a medium saucepan, combine the ginger, shallots, stock, wine, and mushrooms. Cook over medium heat until the liquid is reduced by one-half. Add the heavy cream, and reduce by about two-thirds. Remove from the heat, and stir in the butter cubes, whipping constantly until the sauce has a nice texture. Keep the sauce warm, but do not allow it to boil.

ABALONE
1 CUP FLOUR
SALT AND PEPPER TO TASTE

2 TABLESPOONS OLIVE OIL
4 TO 6 OUNCES ABALONE

❖ Lightly flour the abalone on each side. Season with salt and pepper. Sauté in the oil over medium-high heat, no longer than 30 seconds per side. Transfer the abalone to serving plates, and serve with the sauce. Use the small abalone shells as a garnish.

LIVER PÂTÉ

Yield: Approximately 3 pounds

8 OUNCES BACON, DICED
2 POUNDS CALF'S OR CHICKEN LIVER, DICED
1 BONELESS CHICKEN BREAST, DICED
2 ONIONS, CHOPPED
1 CELERY STALK, DICED
1 CARROT, DICED

1½ CUPS SOFT BUTTER
¼ CUP COGNAC
1 CUP HEAVY CREAM
DASH OF NUTMEG
SALT AND PEPPER TO TASTE
1 CUP CHICKEN BROTH

❖ Sauté the bacon only until half done (still whitish). Add the liver, chicken breast, onions, celery, and carrots. Bake in a 350°F oven until brown, about 30 to 45 minutes. Cool the mixture, and pass it through a grinder. Place in mixing bowl. Slowly add the soft butter, Cognac, cream, nutmeg, and seasonings.* (If the mixture becomes too heavy, thin with the chicken broth.) Place the pâté in a mold, and chill.

* Instead of salt, Minor's chicken base can be used (see chapter 3).

LAMB CURRY SALAD

Yield: 6 servings

3 LARGE MCINTOSH APPLES, CORED,
  PEELED, AND SLICED
¼ CUP WHITE WINE
¼ CUP WATER
10 OUNCES MAYONNAISE
1 TABLESPOON MADRAS CURRY
SALT AND PEPPER TO TASTE

2 MANGOES, CUT INTO JULIENNE
24 OUNCES RAW LAMB, COOKED AND
  CUT INTO JULIENNE
6 LETTUCE LEAVES
1 TABLESPOON SHREDDED COCONUT
1 TABLESPOON SLIVERED ALMONDS,
  TOASTED

❖ Combine the sliced apples, wine, and water in a saucepan. Cook over medium heat until soft, about 20 minutes. Pour into a blender, and puree until smooth; set aside. In a bowl, mix the mayonnaise with the curry, salt, and pepper. Fold in the applesauce, mangoes, and lamb. Divide the salad among six Champagne glasses, and decorate with the lettuce leaves, shredded coconut, and almonds.

ANTIPASTO CASALINGA

Yield: 8 servings, 4 ounces each

¼ CUP OLIVE OIL
1 OUNCE ONIONS, CHOPPED
1 OUNCE CARROTS, CRINKLE-CUT
3 CELERY STALKS, CHOPPED
1 OUNCE GREEN PEPPERS, NEATLY CUT
1 OUNCE TINY ARTICHOKE HEARTS
1 OUNCE CAULIFLOWER FLORETS
6 SMALL MUSHROOMS
1 TABLESPOON LEMON JUICE
1 TABLESPOON WINE VINEGAR
20 OUNCES CANNED TOMATO PASTE
1 TABLESPOON CHILI SAUCE
2 GARLIC CLOVES, CRUSHED
WHITE PEPPER TO TASTE
1 BAY LEAF
¼ TEASPOON OREGANO, CRUSHED

¼ TEASPOON MARJORAM, CRUSHED
¼ TEASPOON THYME, CRUSHED
¼ TEASPOON DRIED CHILI PEPPERS
SALT TO TASTE
2 HEADS BIBB LETTUCE
12 OUNCES CANNED WATER-PACKED
  TUNA
8 ANCHOVY FILLETS
16 SLICES MILANO SALAMI
8 PARSLEY SPRIGS
8 LEMON WEDGES
6 SMALL STUFFED OLIVES
6 SMALL PICKLED PEPPERS
1 TEASPOON CAPERS
1 PEARL ONION

✤ Heat the oil in a large sautoir. Sauté the onions for 2 to 3 minutes, then add the carrots, celery, peppers, artichokes, cauliflower, and mushrooms, and continue cooking for about 10 minutes, stirring often. Add lemon juice and wine vinegar, then blend in the tomato paste and chili sauce. Add the garlic, pepper, bay leaf, oregano, marjoram, thyme, dried chili peppers, and salt. Cover and simmer very slowly for about 30 minutes. Add the olives, pickled peppers, capers, and pearl onion and shake the pan gently so antipasto is evenly mixed. Bring again to a simmer, and remove from the heat.

Place the antipasto in a suitable earthen crock, and cool. When cooled, place in the refrigerator, and chill until needed. Serve in neat lettuce cups, enhance with a piece of tuna, an anchovy fillet, and 2 Milano salami slices, rolled cornet fashion. Garnish with a parsley sprig and a lemon wedge.

CAJUN CHICKEN SALAD

Yield: 6 servings

⅔ CUP MAYONNAISE
⅓ CUP SOUR CREAM
SALT AND PEPPER TO TASTE
¼ TEASPOON HOT PEPPER SAUCE
    (TABASCO)
1 TEASPOON LEMON JUICE
4 CUPS DICED COOKED CHICKEN MEAT
½ CUP DICED CELERY

¼ CUP DICED ONIONS
¼ CUP DICED RED PEPPERS
½ CUP QUARTERED PECANS
3 ANCHOVY FILLETS, MASHED
2 TABLESPOONS CAPERS, CHOPPED FINE
1 TABLESPOON DICED JALAPEÑO
    PEPPERS

✤ In a bowl, mix the mayonnaise with sour cream, salt, pepper, hot pepper sauce, and lemon juice. Fold in the chicken, celery, onions, red peppers, pecans, anchovy fillets, capers, and jalapeño peppers. Chill and serve.

MOUSSE OF NORWEGIAN SALMON

Yield: 8 molds, 3 ounces each

12 OUNCES SALMON, BONED, SKINNED,
   AND COOKED
½ CUP MAYONNAISE
¼ CUP DRY WHITE WINE
JUICE OF 1 LEMON
1 TEASPOON PAPRIKA

SALT AND PEPPER TO TASTE
1 TEASPOON CHOPPED CHIVES
4 TEASPOONS GELATIN, DISSOLVED IN
   ¾ CUP WARM WATER
¾ CUP UNSWEETENED WHIPPED CREAM
½ HEAD ICEBERG LETTUCE, SHREDDED

✤ Flake the salmon and combine it with the mayonnaise, white wine, lemon juice, paprika, salt, pepper, and chives. Pass the mixture through a fine meat grinder twice. Mix well, add the gelatin, and fold in the unsweetened whipped cream. Season to taste. Spoon the mixture into eight oiled 3-ounce molds, and chill for a few hours. Unmold, place atop the shredded lettuce, and serve cold.

SWEET-AND-SOUR CHICKEN WINGS

Yield: 4 servings

20 CHICKEN WINGS
2 CUPS WATER
SALT TO TASTE
3 EGGS
1 CUP CORNSTARCH
½ CUP VEGETABLE OIL

2 TABLESPOONS FINELY CHOPPED
   GARLIC
½ CUP CATSUP
1 TABLESPOON SOY SAUCE
1 CUP SUGAR
½ CUP CIDER VINEGAR

✤ Cut the tips from the chicken wings, and set the wings aside. Simmer the tips in the water to make a broth; add salt to taste. Strain the broth after cooking for 20 minutes; there should be 1 cup of broth.

Beat the eggs to make an eggwash. Dip the reserved wings in the eggwash and then in the cornstarch. Heat the oil in a sauté pan. Add the garlic and cook until the garlic begins to color. Fry the wings in the garlic and oil until brown. Remove to a large baking dish.

Combine the chicken broth, catsup, soy sauce, sugar, and vinegar. Pour the mixture over the chicken wings. Bake in a 350°F oven until tender, about 15 minutes.

JULIA CHILD'S PISSALADIÈRE (ONION TART)

Yield: 12-inch free-form-tart, serving at least 6

6 CUPS SLICED ONIONS
¼ TO ⅓ CUP OLIVE OIL OR GOOD
　　COOKING OIL
1 POUND BEST-QUALITY PIE DOUGH
2 OUNCES FLAT ANCHOVIES PACKED IN
　　OLIVE OIL
1 TABLESPOON WHITE VERMOUTH
SALT AND PEPPER TO TASTE

DRIED HERBS, SUCH AS OREGANO OR
　　ITALIAN HERB SEASONING, TO TASTE
12 CHERRY TOMATOES
6 TO 8 SMALL BLACK OLIVES
2 TABLESPOONS GRATED PARMESAN
　　CHEESE (OR OTHER GRATED HARD
　　CHEESE)

❖ Cook onions slowly in 3 to 4 tablespoons of olive oil in a large covered pan for about 20 minutes, until thoroughly tender. Uncover when tender to color them lightly. They must be meltingly tender before they are placed on the tart, because they hardly cook in the oven.)

Meanwhile, roll out the dough about ⅛ inch thick, and cut it into a circle 13 inches in diameter. Roll the circle up on your pin, and unroll onto a buttered baking sheet (the kind with no edges, or at least with a flat edge, for easy transferring after baking). Turn up the edge against the body of the dough to make an edged circle about 12 inches in diameter. Prick with a fork all over at ½-inch intervals, to prevent the dough from rising during baking. Chill for 20 to 30 minutes. Preheat the oven to 425°F.

Puree 4 anchovies with 1 teaspoon of olive oil, the white vermouth, and a pinch of pepper and herbs. Brush the puree over the inner surface of the dough. If the cooked onions are still warm, stir them over cold water to cool; otherwise, they will soften the pastry. Spread the onions in the tart shell. Arrange the remaining anchovies over the onions, like the spokes of a wheel. Halve the tomatoes, season them lightly with the salt, pepper, and herbs plus a few drops of oil, and arrange them and the olives over the onions with decorative abandon. Sprinkle the surface with a dusting of herbs and with the grated cheese. Drizzle a little oil over all.

Bake on the lower rack of the preheated oven for 20 to 30 minutes, until the bottom of the pastry has browned lightly (lift it gently with a spatula to peek). Slide the tart onto a serving board. Serve hot, warm, or cold; it is best eaten the day it is baked.

MARYLAND-STYLE CRAB CAKES

Yield: 25 cakes, 1 ounce each

4 SLICES BREAD
2 EGGS
1 POUND CRABMEAT, CLEANED AND
  CHOPPED
2 TABLESPOONS CHOPPED FRESH
  PARSLEY

1 TEASPOON SALT
2 DROPS HOT PEPPER SAUCE (TABASCO)
OIL FOR DEEP FRYING

✤ Soak the bread in the eggs. Mix all the ingredients (except the oil) and refrigerate for 2 hours. Using a small ice-cream scoop, form the mixture into small 1-ounce balls. Heat the oil in a deep fryer, and fry a sample ball; test for flavor and texture and adjust ingredients as necessary. Deep-fry the remaining balls until golden, drain, and serve immediately.

Note: To serve as an entrée, make 2½-ounce balls (this recipe will yield 10 entrée-size cakes).

BAKED STUFFED MUSHROOMS SHELBOURNE

Yield: 4 servings

4 OUNCES CHICKEN LIVERS, MARINATED
1¾ CUPS MADEIRA WINE
20 LARGE, FLAT MUSHROOM CAPS (NO
  STEMS)
1 TABLESPOON LEMON JUICE
SALT TO TASTE
1 SHALLOT
1 GARLIC CLOVE, CHOPPED
PINCH OF THYME
PINCH OF NUTMEG
CRACKED BLACK PEPPER TO TASTE

1 OUNCE BUTTER
2 OUNCES SPINACH, BLANCHED
¼ CUP HEAVY CREAM
2 TABLESPOONS CHOPPED CHIVES
1 CUP WHITE BREADCRUMBS
½ CUP CHOPPED GRATED CHEDDAR
  CHEESE
2 TABLESPOONS CORNSTARCH
2 TABLESPOONS COLD WATER
¼ CUP HALF-AND-HALF CREAM

✤ Combine the chicken livers with 1 cup of the Madeira, cover, chill, and marinate for 1 hour. Blanch the mushroom caps in the lemon juice, remaining ¾ cup of Madeira and salt. Remove the caps, and keep warm. Strain the blanching liquid, and set aside. Drain the chicken livers, and sauté with the shallot, garlic, thyme, nutmeg, and pepper for 2 minutes. Allow to cool. Blend the livers in a food processor with the butter, spinach, cream, chives, and salt to taste. Fill the mushroom caps with the mixture. Top with the crumbs and cheese. Bake for 5 minutes at 400°F.

Stir the cornstarch into the water until well dissolved. Bring the reserved blanching liquid to a simmer. Add the cornstarch/water mixture and return to a simmer, stirring constantly. Cook and stir for 2 minutes over medium heat. Gradually stir in the half-and-half; simmer for 2 minutes. Spoon the sauce onto serving plates, top with the stuffed mushrooms, and serve.

MORELS ON TOAST

Yield: 6 servings

24 OUNCES FRESH MOREL MUSHROOMS
2 TABLESPOONS CLARIFIED BUTTER
¼ CUP FINELY MINCED SHALLOTS
2 TABLESPOONS PALE DRY SHERRY
¼ CUP HEAVY CREAM
1½ CUPS SOUR CREAM
2 TABLESPOONS FINELY CHOPPED
   PARSLEY

SALT TO TASTE
FRESHLY GROUND WHITE PEPPER TO
   TASTE
6 SLICES TOAST WITH CRUSTS TRIMMED
6 DILL SPRIGS

❖ Wash the morels carefully, and cut off the ends of the stems. Slice the morels into ½- to ¾-inch chunks. Heat the clarified butter in a skillet until moderately hot. Add the shallots and sauté briefly; do not let them brown. Add the morels and sherry; cook over high heat until dry. Reduce the heat, add the cream and sour cream, and simmer gently, stirring constantly, until the mixture is smooth and lightly thickened. Stir in the chopped parsley; season with salt and pepper. Place the toast pieces on heated plates. Spoon the mushrooms over the toast, and garnish each plate with a sprig of dill.

Variations: The mushrooms can be spooned into a prebaked tartlet crust, instead of onto toast. The morels can also be replaced by any other mushroom, in the same quantity.

SPINACH AND SAUSAGE PINWHEELS

Yield: 25 pinwheels

1 PUFF PASTRY DOUGH SHEET
  (PREPARED, FROZEN PRODUCT)
1 EGG
¼ CUP WATER
12 OUNCES PACKAGED FROZEN SPINACH
  SOUFFLÉ, THAWED

8 OUNCES SAUSAGE, COOKED AND
  CRUMBLED
8 OUNCES GRATED CHEESE (BLUE
  CHEESE WORKS WELL)
8 OUNCES PARMESAN OR ROMANO
  CHEESE, GRATED

❖ Thaw the dough sheet, flat, on a floured surface. Roll slightly, just to make the dough pliable, not to thin it.

Beat the egg with the water. Brush the entire dough surface with the eggwash. Spread the spinach soufflé onto the dough in a ⅛-inch-thick layer, leaving 1½-inch border on one edge of long side of the dough. Sprinkle the sausage over the spinach, then sprinkle on both cheeses.

Roll the dough, jelly-roll fashion, toward the 1½-inch border. Brush the log with the remaining eggwash, and freeze for several hours or overnight. (It can be wrapped at this point and kept frozen for up to one month.)

Preheat the oven to 350°F. Cut the log into ¼-inch-thick slices. Lay the slices on a lightly greased baking sheet, and bake until golden brown, about 7 to 10 minutes.

CLAMS CASINO

Yield: 25 clams

25 CHERRYSTONE CLAMS, 2½ TO
  3 INCHES EACH
2 CANS CHOPPED CLAMS, 6½ OUNCES
  EACH
3 OUNCES BUTTER
10 OUNCES ONIONS, CUT IN ¼-INCH
  DICE
10 OUNCES GREEN PEPPERS, CUT IN
  ¼-INCH DICE

10 OUNCES RAW BACON, CUT IN ½-INCH
  DICE
2 TEASPOONS CLAM BASE*
2 TEASPOONS GARLIC BASE*
1 TEASPOON ONION BASE*
½ CUP ITALIAN-STYLE BREADCRUMBS
3 FLUID OUNCES DRY WHITE WINE

❖ Wash the cherrystone clams. Cover with water, and simmer until the clam shells open (discard any that remain closed). Drain, remove the meat, and chop. Wash and reserve the shells. Drain the canned clams, and add them to the chopped clam meat; mix until blended. Arrange the shells on a baking sheet. Place ½ teaspoon of clam meat in each shell.

Melt the butter in a sauté pan. Add the onions and peppers, and sauté for 5 minutes. Add the bacon, and sauté for 10 minutes. Add the clam, garlic, and onion bases, and stir well. Simmer for 3 minutes. Top each clam with 1 teaspoon (1 ounce) of the vegetable-bacon mixture. Sprinkle the breadcrumbs over the vegetable-bacon topping, and sprinkle the wine over all. Bake in a 400°F oven for 15 minutes, or until nicely browned. Serve hot.

* For information about these bases, see chapter 3.

SPINACH AND CHEESE PUFF TRIANGLES

Yield: Approximately 40 triangles

1 SMALL ONION, MINCED
2 TABLESPOONS OLIVE OIL
8 OUNCES FETA CHEESE, DRAINED AND FINELY CRUMBLED
10 OUNCES SPINACH LEAVES, STEMMED AND FINELY CHOPPED
3 EGGS, BEATEN

½ CUP CHICKEN OR VEAL VELOUTÉ (SEE NOTE BELOW)
1 TEASPOON WHITE PEPPERCORNS, FRESHLY GROUND
SALT TO TASTE
8 OUNCES PHYLLO PASTRY SHEETS
8 OUNCES BUTTER, MELTED

❖ Sauté the onions in the olive oil until transparent. Add the feta cheese, stirring to evaporate water. Add the spinach, and let the mixture cool. Add the beaten eggs, chicken or veal velouté, white pepper, and salt. Taste, and adjust the seasonings. Working with only two of the phyllo sheets at a time (keep the remaining sheets covered), brush the pastry with the melted butter. Stack the two sheets, and cut into 3-inch strips. Place 1 tablespoon of the filling at one end of each strip; fold to a triangle shape. Brush each triangle with melted butter. Repeat for all the pastry sheets. Bake at 425°F for 15 minutes, or until puffed and golden. Serve immediately.

Note: Undiluted canned cream of chicken soup may be substituted for the velouté.

SALMON AND TROUT MOUSSE WITH CAVIAR AND ASPARAGUS SAUCE

Yield: 12 servings

⅔ CUP COLD CONSOMMÉ
3½ FLUID OUNCES FISH VELOUTÉ
3½ OUNCES POACHED SALMON PIECES
SALT AND FRESHLY GROUND WHITE
   PEPPER TO TASTE
4 TEASPOONS GELATIN, DISSOLVED IN
   ¼ CUP WARM WATER

1 CUP WHIPPED CREAM
5½ OUNCES SMOKED OZARK TROUT
2 OUNCES BLACK, GOLDEN, OR RED
   CAVIAR
1 PINT ASPARAGUS SAUCE (SEE RECIPE
   IN CHAPTER 3)

❖ Put half of the consommé and half of the velouté in a blender. Add the poached salmon pieces, and blend until smooth. Strain by rubbing through a sieve. Add the salt and pepper, then add half of the warm soaked gelatin. Mix well. Fold in half of the whipped cream.

Repeat the procedure for the trout mousse, using the remaining consommé, velouté, gelatin, and whipped cream and substituting the trout for the salmon.

Line a 1-quart mold with plastic wrap, and fill about half full with salmon mousse. Make a hole in the center, and fill it with the caviar. Fill in the remainder of the mold with trout mousse. Chill overnight, covered with plastic wrap.

The following day, remove the mousse from the mold, slice, and serve on plates napped with asparagus sauce.

Note: Undiluted canned cream of chicken soup may be substituted for the velouté.

BRANDIED BLUE CHEESE MOLD

Yield: 1 mold, of 1 quart

1 POUND BLUE CHEESE
5 OUNCES CREAM CHEESE, AT ROOM
   TEMPERATURE
⅔ CUP MAYONNAISE
⅓ CUP BRANDY

1¼ TABLESPOONS GELATIN, DISSOLVED
   IN ⅔ CUP WATER
⅔ CUP WHIPPED CREAM
1 TEASPOON CHOPPED CHIVES
CRACKERS AS NEEDED

✤ Combine the cheeses, mayonnaise, and brandy. Blend well until smooth, or pass the mixture through a fine grinder or sieve. Add the dissolved gelatin, and mix well. Fold in the whipped cream and chives. Place in an oiled 1-quart mold, and chill for a few hours. Unmold on a platter, and surround with the crackers.

Variation: Sherry may be substituted for the brandy.

QUICHE LORRAINE

Yield: 1 tart

4 OUNCES BACON, CUT IN MEDIUM DICE
4 OUNCES ONION, CUT IN MEDIUM DICE
4 OUNCES COOKED HAM, CUT IN
    MEDIUM DICE
4 OUNCES GRUYÈRE, DICED
1 CUP MILK
1 CUP WHIPPING CREAM
3 EGGS

2 OUNCES FRESH PARMESAN CHEESE,
    GRATED
DASH OF SALT
DASH OF FRESHLY GROUND BLACK
    PEPPER
DASH OF FRESHLY GRATED NUTMEG
DOUGH FOR ONE (9–10-INCH) PIE SHELL
    (SEE RECIPE IN CHAPTER 11)

✤ In a heavy 2-quart saucepan over medium heat, sauté the bacon until crisp; *do not* drain. Stir in the onions, and sauté until glazed. Stir in the ham and sauté for 1 minute. Remove from the heat, and chill. Add the Gruyère after completely chilled. In a separate bowl, whisk together the milk, cream, eggs, Parmesan cheese, salt, pepper, and nutmeg.

Line a 9- or 10-inch round pie pan with the pie dough. Pierce the dough with a fork before baking to prevent the dough from shrinking. Partially bake in a 350°F oven for 12 to 15 minutes. Add the meat and cheese mixture to the partially baked crust; gradually pour in the milk mixture. Bake at 350°F for approximately 30 to 40 minutes, until the custard is firm and resilient to the touch.

HICKORY-SMOKED HAM DIP

Yield: 1 pound

8 OUNCES CREAM CHEESE, SOFTENED
8 OUNCES SOUR CREAM

4 TEASPOONS HAM BASE*

❖ Combine all the ingredients, mixing well. Cover and chill for at least 1 hour. Serve with crackers, chips, or crisp fresh vegetables.

* For information about this base, see chapter 3.

LUMP CRABMEAT AND CRAYFISH CARDINAL

Yield: 6 servings

2 SHALLOTS, FINELY CHOPPED
4 TABLESPOONS BUTTER
¼ CUP WHITE WINE
¼ CUP TOMATO SAUCE
1½ CUPS THICK BÉCHAMEL SAUCE (SEE
   RECIPE IN CHAPTER 3)
½ POUND LUMP CRABMEAT

1 POUND COOKED AND PEELED
   CRAYFISH TAILS
¼ CUP CRAYFISH FAT
SALT AND RED PEPPER TO TASTE
TOASTED FRENCH BREAD SLICES
CHOPPED PARSLEY FOR GARNISH

❖ Sauté the shallots in the butter for 3 minutes over medium heat. Add the white wine and tomato sauce, and reduce for 5 minutes, by one-third. Add the béchamel sauce, and return to a boil. Add the crabmeat, crayfish, and fat. Season to taste. Return to a boil, stirring gently. Spread on the toasted french bread slices. Sprinkle with the chopped parsley, and serve warm.

CHAPTER TWO

Salads and Salad Dressings

Depending on the menu, the salad may be served at the beginning of the meal, following the appetizer, or, more traditionally, between the entrée and the dessert. Many advocate the last, as the salad tends to provide a transition between the meat and the sweet. Regardless of when the salad is served, it is very important to keep the overall menu in mind when selecting the salad ingredients and their dressing.

If the salad is to be served as the first course to a heavy meal, choose a light salad, such as a tart green salad, being certain that the salad does not compete with the main course. If the salad is served between the entrée and the dessert, it too must not compete with the meal and must not be heavy. Often, a salad functions as the main course for an informal luncheon or light supper, and in this case, a variety of ingredients can be used to construct the salad; for example, a chef salad combining greens, cheeses, and meats, can be served, or the cook may choose a shrimp, lobster, crab, roast beef, or chicken salad as the featured attraction.

A wide variety of greens are available in most supermarkets and grocery stores, and one should not be afraid to experiment with different types. For optimal flavor, choose seasonal varieties when possible. Available greens include iceburg, bibb, oakleaf, and Boston lettuces, curly endive, leaf lettuce, romaine, red-leaved chicory, spinach, and watercress, to name just a few. Hydroponic greens (grown in water, rather than soil) are now available in some supermarkets and specialty produce markets. Always wash the greens with cold water, and be sure the leaves are well chilled, crisp, and dry before preparing the salad. For a tossed salad, always tear the greens rather than cutting them.

Salad dressings are almost always added immediately before serving and must never overpower the salad or "drown" it. There are many kinds and varieties of dressings to choose from; always select a dressing that will enhance the salad by bringing out its special flavors and textures, as well as enhance the meal, rather than compete with the other courses. Various herbs and spices can be used, but they should be chosen with care. Remember, fresh herbs are always best, but if they are unavailable, dried can be used. You need only about one-third as much dried herbs as you would fresh.

Salads and Salad Dressings

PLAZA SALAD

MEDITERRANEAN SALAD

TURKEY AND PASTA SALAD

CARROT SALAD

CHATEAU SPA SALAD

CUCUMBER SALAD ON TOMATOES

VERMICELLI SALAD WITH SHRIMP

CHEDDAR WALDORF SALAD

HOT CHICKEN SALAD

POTATO SALAD WITH A FLAIR

PESTO CRAB SALAD

SAUTÉED MARINATED SEA SCALLOPS WITH
PINEAPPLE-AVOCADO RELISH AND
SALAD GREENS

HAM PASTA SALAD

HONEY MUSTARD DRESSING

MIAMI MUSTARD SAUCE

HONEY AND LIME DRESSING

GINGER DRESSING

ITALIAN DRESSING

BUTTERMILK DRESSING

COLE SLAW DRESSING

GREEN GODDESS DRESSING

ROQUEFORT DRESSING

THOUSAND ISLAND DRESSING

VINAIGRETTE DRESSING

PLAZA SALAD

Yield: 6 servings

2 WHOLE EGGS
2 TEASPOONS OREGANO
2 TEASPOONS MINCED GARLIC
1 OUNCE SUGAR
1½ CUPS VEGETABLE OIL
¼ CUP WINE VINEGAR
JUICE OF 1 LEMON
SALT AND WHITE PEPPER TO TASTE
12 OUNCES SHRIMP, COOKED
　(26–30-PER-POUND SIZE)

1 SMALL ONION, CUT IN JULIENNE
4 OUNCES RED PEPPER (ABOUT
　½ MEDIUM PEPPER), CUT IN JULIENNE
4 OUNCES PEA PODS (24–30), CUT ON
　THE BIAS
4 OUNCES BLACK OLIVES, CUT
　LENGTHWISE
3 OUNCES BEAN SPROUTS (OPTIONAL)

✣ Beat the eggs, and stir in the oregano, garlic, and sugar. Add the oil, whipping to emulsify. Add the vinegar, lemon juice, salt, and pepper. Toss together the shrimp, onions, red peppers, pea pods, and olives. Pour the dressing onto the salad, mix well, and marinate in the refrigerator for a few hours before serving. The bean sprouts may be used as a garnish.

MEDITERRANEAN SALAD

Yield: 6 servings

3 ITALIAN FRYING PEPPERS
1 RED BELL PEPPER
3 LARGE TOMATOES
1 CUCUMBER
1 BUNCH SCALLIONS
1 PACKET RADISHES (6 OUNCES)

3 DILL PICKLES
2 GARLIC CLOVES, MINCED
¼ CUP OLIVE OIL
JUICE OF 1 LEMON
SALT AND PEPPER TO TASTE
½ BUNCH CHOPPED PARSLEY

✣ Chop the peppers, tomatoes, and cucumber into a ¼-inch dice. Chop the scallions, using all white and part of green portion. Halve the radishes, and slice thinly. Chop the dill pickles into a small dice. Place all these vegetables and the garlic into large bowl and refrigerate until ready to serve. Just before serving, add the oil, lemon juice, salt, and pepper. Toss, and sprinkle the parsley over the top.

Note: Leftover salad can be saved by draining and mixing with mayonnaise.

TURKEY AND PASTA SALAD

Yield: 6 servings

8 OUNCES PASTA
1½ CUPS MAYONNAISE
⅓ CUP BUTTERMILK
1 TEASPOON ITALIAN SEASONING
20 OUNCES TURKEY MEAT, COOKED AND
    CUT INTO STRIPS

3 OUNCES PEA PODS (ABOUT 18–20),
    BLANCHED AND CUT IN JULIENNE
2 OUNCES BLACK OLIVES, SLICED
    LENGTHWISE
4 OUNCES CHERRY TOMATOES (ABOUT
    12–15), HALVED

❖ Cook the pasta until about three-quarters done. Chill. Combine the mayonnaise, buttermilk, and Italian seasonings; mix well. Add the turkey, pea pods, black olives, and cherry tomatoes. Toss lightly with the pasta. Serve chilled.

CARROT SALAD

Yield: 6 servings

1 POUND CARROTS (ABOUT 4 MEDIUM),
    SCRAPED AND SHREDDED
2 APPLES, SHREDDED
½ TEASPOON LEMON JUICE
¼ TEASPOON SALT
¼ TEASPOON FRESHLY GROUND PEPPER

1–2 TABLESPOONS HONEY (OPTIONAL)
¼ CUP ALMONDS SLIVERED AND
    TOASTED (OPTIONAL)
¼ CUP MAYONNAISE
¼ CUP SOUR CREAM

❖ Mix the carrots and apples with the lemon juice. Add the salt and pepper. If salad does not seem sweet enough, add the honey. Mix in the almonds if desired. Combine the mayonnaise and sour cream, and add to the salad, mixing to coat all the ingredients.

Variations: The following can also be added to this salad: 4 ounces seedless raisins or 2 sliced bananas or 2 segmented oranges.

CHATEAU SPA SALAD

Yield: 6 servings

1 HEAD ROMAINE LETTUCE
6 OUNCES ALFALFA SPROUTS
6 OUNCES RADISHES
6 OUNCES GRUYÈRE CHEESE
6 OUNCES SHARP CHEDDAR CHEESE

6 MUSTARD-GREEN LEAVES
1 MEDIUM CARROT
¼ CUP VINAIGRETTE (OIL AND VINEGAR
   DRESSING)

✤ Wash, dry, and shred the lettuce; chill. Wash, drain, and chill the sprouts. Slice radishes very thinly (there should be about 1½ cups). Slice the gruyère and Cheddar cheeses into julienne. Line each chilled salad plate with a mustard-green leaf (romaine may be used instead). Shred the carrot. Toss the shredded romaine, alfalfa sprouts, radishes, Gruyère, and Cheddar. Place the tossed salad on top of the mustard greens. Garnish with the shredded carrot. Drizzle with the vinaigrette.

CUCUMBER SALAD ON TOMATOES

Yield: 6 servings

3 MEDIUM CUCUMBERS
SALT AS NEEDED
1 CUP SOUR CREAM
1 TEASPOON DILL

1 OUNCE CHIVES, CHOPPED
3 TOMATOES
6 PARSLEY SPRIGS
½ CUP DICED PIMENTOS

✤ Peel the cucumbers, and halve lengthwise. Scoop out the seeds with a spoon. Slice thinly, and place in a bowl. Pour on enough salt to cover the cucumbers, mix well, and let stand in the refrigerator for about 2 hours. Wash the cucumbers in cold water to remove the salt, and press out the excess water. Mix with the sour cream, dill, and chopped chives. Thinly slice the tomatoes, and place on serving plates. Top with the cucumber salad. Garnish with a sprig of parsley and the diced pimentos.

VERMICELLI SALAD WITH SHRIMP

Yield: 8 servings

1 POUND VERMICELLI, BROKEN INTO
  2-INCH PIECES AND COOKED AL DENTE
1 POUND COOKED PINK SHRIMP
1 CUP CHOPPED CELERY
1 CUP CHOPPED ONION
2 CUPS MAYONNAISE
½ CUP WELL-DRAINED, CHOPPED SOUR
  PICKLES
2 OUNCES CAPERS, FINELY CHOPPED
1 TABLESPOON FINE HERBS
1 TABLESPOON DIJON-STYLE MUSTARD
LETTUCE LEAVES TO GARNISH

✤ In a large bowl, combine the vermicelli, shrimp, celery, and onion. Toss well, and set aside. In a medium bowl, combine the mayonnaise, pickles, capers, fine herbs, and mustard. Stir to mix well. Combine with the vermicelli mixture. Toss the salad until the vermicelli and shrimp are coated. Serve very cold on the lettuce leaves.

Note: If the salad seems dry, add additional mayonnaise. The mustard can be replaced with ½ teaspoon freshly ground white pepper.

CHEDDAR WALDORF SALAD

Yield: 4 servings

¾ CUP MAYONNAISE
1½ TABLESPOONS MILK
1 TEASPOON LEMON JUICE
SALT AND PEPPER TO TASTE
3 LARGE RED APPLES, CORED AND
  COARSELY CHOPPED
3 LARGE CELERY RIBS, THINLY SLICED
12 OUNCES CHEDDAR CHEESE, CUT IN
  ½-INCH CUBES
½ CUP COARSELY CHOPPED WALNUTS
4 LETTUCE CUPS
¼ CUP HALVED WALNUTS

✤ Mix the mayonnaise, milk, lemon juice, salt, and pepper in a medium bowl. Add the apples, celery, Cheddar, and chopped walnuts; toss. Refrigerate for 1 hour. Serve in the lettuce cups, decorated with the walnut halves.

HOT CHICKEN SALAD

Yield: 6 servings

10½ OUNCES CANNED CONDENSED
   CREAM OF CHICKEN SOUP
¼ CUP WATER
¾ CUP MAYONNAISE
1 TABLESPOON LEMON JUICE
2 CUPS COOKED, DICED CHICKEN
1 CUP DICED CELERY

2 HARD-BOILED EGGS, CHOPPED
2 TABLESPOONS MINCED ONIONS
½ CUP SLIVERED ALMONDS
1½ CUPS COOKED RICE
½ TABLESPOON SALT
½ TABLESPOON PEPPER
1 CUP CRUSHED POTATO CHIPS

❖ Combine the chicken soup, water, mayonnaise, and lemon juice in a large bowl. Add the chicken, celery, eggs, onions, almonds, rice, salt, and pepper, and mix well. Spread in an 8- by 11-inch baking pan. Top with the potato chips. Bake at 350°F for 20 to 25 minutes, until heated thoroughly; the celery should remain crunchy. Cut into squares, remove with a spatula, and serve immediately.

POTATO SALAD WITH A FLAIR

Yield: 6 servings

⅓ CUP OIL
2 TABLESPOONS VINEGAR
½ TEASPOON SALT
¼ TEASPOON FRESHLY GROUND PEPPER
3 CUPS SLICED PARBOILED POTATOES
   (DON'T OVERCOOK)
½ CUP PEELED, SEEDED, AND SLICED
   CUCUMBERS

1 TEASPOON LEMON JUICE
¾ CUP MAYONNAISE
3 TABLESPOONS CREAM
3 TABLESPOONS MINCED ONION
1½ TEASPOONS DRIED BASIL

❖ Combine the oil, vinegar, salt, pepper, potatoes, and cucumber. Marinate overnight; drain. Combine the lemon juice, mayonnaise, cream, onion, and basil. Fold the potatoes and cucumbers into the dressing. Refrigerate, covered, for several hours before serving.

PESTO CRAB SALAD

Yield: 12 servings

1½ CUPS OLIVE OIL
3 TABLESPOONS LEMON JUICE
¼ CUP GRATED PARMESAN CHEESE
3 TABLESPOONS FROZEN CHOPPED
   SPINACH, THAWED, AND WELL
   DRAINED
2 TABLESPOONS SLIVERED ALMONDS
2 TABLESPOONS DRIED SWEET BASIL
1 TABLESPOON CRAB BASE*
¼ TEASPOON GARLIC BASE*

½ TEASPOON BLACK PEPPER
½ HEAD ICEBERG LETTUCE, BROKEN
   INTO BITE-SIZE PIECES
1 SMALL BUNCH RED LEAF LETTUCE,
   TORN INTO BITE-SIZE PIECES
2 SMALL TOMATOES, CUT INTO WEDGES
1 SMALL CUCUMBER, SLICED ⅛-INCH
   THICK
12 OUNCES FROZEN CRABMEAT, THAWED
   AND WELL DRAINED

✤ Combine the olive oil, lemon juice, Parmesan, spinach, almonds, basil, crab and garlic bases, and pepper in a blender container; process at high speed until smooth. Chill well.

   Wash, rinse, and dry the lettuce, tomatoes, and cucumber. Place in a large bowl and toss. In each salad bowl, place 1 cup chilled salad; sprinkle each with 3 tablespoons (1 ounce) crabmeat. Shake or stir the chilled dressing, and spoon 3 tablespoons over each salad.

* For information about these bases, see chapter 3.

SAUTÉED MARINATED SEA SCALLOPS WITH PINEAPPLE-AVOCADO RELISH AND SALAD GREENS

Yield: 8 servings

2 TABLESPOONS CHOPPED FRESH DILL
1 TABLESPOON CHOPPED FRESH BASIL
½ CUP LIME JUICE
9 FLUID OUNCES OLIVE OIL
SALT AND PEPPER TO TASTE
32 LARGE SEA SCALLOPS
1½ CUPS DICED PINEAPPLE
1 CUP DICED AVOCADO
1 TABLESPOON FRESH GINGER, CUT IN A
   FINE BRUNOISE

3 OUNCES RED ONIONS, CUT IN A FINE
   BRUNOISE
1½ TABLESPOON SHREDDED CILANTRO
3 TABLESPOONS RICE-WINE VINEGAR
¼ CUP PEANUT OIL
3 HEADS RED-OAK LETTUCE
2 HEADS BIBB LETTUCE
¼ CUP BALSAMIC VINEGAR
1 TABLESPOON DIJON MUSTARD

❖ Combine the dill, basil, lime juice, 1 cup olive oil, salt, and pepper. Add the scallops and marinate for at least 2 hours.

Mix the diced pineapple, avocado, ginger, onions, cilantro, rice-wine vinegar, and peanut oil, and reserve.

Clean, wash, and spin-dry the lettuce. Combine the remaining 1 fluid ounce (2 tablespoons) olive oil, balsamic vinegar, Dijon mustard, and salt and pepper to taste into a vinaigrette. Just before serving, toss the lettuce with the vinaigrette.

Sauté the scallops on both sides in a hot skillet for 2 minutes. For each serving, spread 2 tablespoons of pineapple-avocado relish on one-third of a large plate. Top the relish with sautéed scallops. Fill the remainder of the plate with the vinaigrette-dressed salad greens, and serve immediately.

HAM PASTA SALAD

Yield: 6 servings

1 CUP MAYONNAISE
¼ CUP CULTURED SOUR CREAM
1 TABLESPOON HAM BASE*
1½ TEASPOONS BROWN SUGAR
¼ TEASPOON CHILI POWDER
½ CUP MEDIUM-DICED TOMATOES

½ CUP SMALL-CUBED BOILED HAM
⅓ CUP SMALL-DICED CELERY
⅓ CUP KIDNEY BEANS, RINSED AND
   DRAINED
¼ CUP SMALL-DICED GREEN PEPPERS
6 CHERRY TOMATOES, HALVED

❖ In a blender or food processor, mix the mayonnaise, sour cream, ham base, brown sugar, and chili powder on medium speed until well blended, about 3 to 4 minutes. In a large mixing bowl, combine this dressing with the diced tomatoes, ham, celery, kidney beans, and peppers. Toss lightly. Chill well, and serve garnished with the cherry tomato halves.

* For information on this base, see chapter 3.

HONEY MUSTARD DRESSING

Yield: Approximately 1 pint

1¼ CUPS MAYONNAISE
½ CUP VEGETABLE OIL
¼ CUP HONEY
3 TABLESPOONS DIJON MUSTARD
½ CUP FINELY CHOPPED ONIONS

1 TEASPOON FINELY CHOPPED PARSLEY
2 TEASPOONS LEMON JUICE
⅛ TEASPOON GARLIC BASE *
2 DROPS HOT PEPPER SAUCE (TABASCO)

✤ Combine all the ingredients in a large china or stainless-steel bowl. Mix well and refrigerate until needed. This dressing will keep for up to seven days under refrigeration.

* For information about this base, see chapter 3.

MIAMI MUSTARD SAUCE

Yield: Approximately 1 pint

2 OUNCES DRY MUSTARD
¼ CUP WHITE WINE
2 CUPS MAYONNAISE

½ CUP WHIPPING CREAM
½ TEASPOON HOT PEPPER SAUCE
  (TABASCO)

✤ Mix the dry mustard with the white wine, and let stand for 30 minutes. Add the mayonnaise, cream, and hot pepper sauce, and mix well. Chill and serve with boiled seafood (it is especially good with crab claws).

HONEY AND LIME DRESSING

Yield: 1 quart

1 CUP OLIVE OIL
2 TEASPOONS ONION JUICE
1 CUP SUGAR
1 TEASPOON PAPRIKA
1 TEASPOON CELERY SEED

½ TEASPOON SALT
½ CUP VINEGAR
1 TEASPOON DRY MUSTARD
1¼ CUPS HONEY
JUICE OF 4 LIMES

✤ Combine all the ingredients in a blender container, and process until thoroughly mixed. Refrigerate overnight. This dressing will keep indefinitely when refrigerated. It is an excellent dressing, especially good on a spinach salad.

GINGER DRESSING

Yield: 1½ quarts

2 CUPS SALAD OIL
1 CUP SESAME OIL
3 CUPS SEASONED RICE-WINE VINEGAR
1 TABLESPOON MINCED GARLIC
2 TABLESPOONS GRATED FRESH GINGER

8 TABLESPOONS GRATED DAIKON
  RADISHES
1 CUP SOY SAUCE
6 TABLESPOONS SESAME SEEDS

✤ Combine all the ingredients in a food processor and process for 2 minutes. Serve at room temperature.

ITALIAN DRESSING

Yield: Approximately 1 pint

6 GARLIC CLOVES, CHOPPED
½ TEASPOON OREGANO
PINCH OF RED PEPPER FLAKES
½ CUP WHITE VINEGAR

9 FLUID OUNCES CORN OIL
1 TEASPOON SALT
1 TABLESPOON SUGAR
3 FLUID OUNCES WATER

✤ Place all the ingredients in a bottle, and shake well. Refrigerate overnight. Shake well before serving.

Variation: Italian Gorgonzola Dressing: Add 2 ounces of crumbled Gorgonzola cheese to the above recipe.

BUTTERMILK DRESSING

Yield: Approximately 1 pint

1 CUP MAYONNAISE
1 CUP BUTTERMILK
½ TEASPOON ONION SALT
½ TEASPOON GARLIC SALT
1 TEASPOON COARSELY GROUND BLACK
   PEPPER

½ TEASPOON PARSLEY FLAKES
2 TABLESPOONS FINELY CHOPPED
   ONIONS

✤ Combine all the ingredients in a bowl, stir well, and refrigerate. Serve chilled.

COLE SLAW DRESSING

Yield: Approximately 1 pint

1 EGG
½ CUP WHITE VINEGAR
⅔ CUP SUGAR
2 TABLESPOONS PREPARED MUSTARD
1 TEASPOON SALT

2 TABLESPOONS FINELY CHOPPED ONION
1 CUP CORN OIL
¼ TEASPOON HOT PEPPER SAUCE
   (TABASCO)
½ TEASPOON CELERY SEEDS (OPTIONAL)

✤ Place all the ingredients except the celery seeds in blender container, and mix for 1 minute on medium speed. Add the celery seeds if desired. Chill.

GREEN GODDESS DRESSING

Yield: Approximately 2½ cups

1 CUP MAYONNAISE
1 CUP SOUR CREAM
½ CUP WHIPPING CREAM
5 PARSLEY SPRIGS, CHOPPED
3 SCALLIONS, CHOPPED (GREEN PART
   ONLY)

1 TABLESPOON ANCHOVY PASTE
1 TEASPOON SALT
½ TEASPOON WHITE PEPPER

✤ Combine all the ingredients in a bowl, stirring to mix thoroughly. Refrigerate.

ROQUEFORT DRESSING

Yield: Approximately 1 pint

1 CUP MAYONNAISE
2 TABLESPOONS SOUR CREAM
2 TABLESPOONS BUTTERMILK
¼ TEASPOON WORCESTERSHIRE SAUCE

¼ TEASPOON WHITE PEPPER
½ TEASPOON SALT
2–3 OUNCES ROQUEFORT CHEESE, CRUMBLED

✤ Combine all the ingredients in a bowl; stir well. Refrigerate.

THOUSAND ISLAND DRESSING

Yield: Approximately 2½ cups

1 CUP MAYONNAISE
½ CUP CATSUP
¾ CUP SWEET PICKLE RELISH

½ TEASPOON WORCESTERSHIRE SAUCE
2 HARD-BOILED EGGS, CHOPPED
DASH OF HOT PEPPER SAUCE (TABASCO)

✤ Combine all the ingredients in a bowl; stir well. Refrigerate.

VINAIGRETTE DRESSING

Yield: 1½ quarts

3 CUPS OLIVE OIL
1 CUP VINEGAR
¼ CUP MUSTARD
½ CUP MINCED ONIONS
½ CUP MINCED PICKLES
½ CUP CHOPPED CAPERS

1 CUP CHOPPED PARSLEY
½ CUP CHOPPED PIMENTOS
3 HARD-BOILED EGGS, CHOPPED
1 TABLESPOON SALT
1 TABLESPOON SUGAR
DASH OF HOT PEPPER SAUCE (TABASCO)

✤ Emulsify the oil and vinegar with the mustard by beating together with a wire whisk. Add the remaining ingredients, and mix well. Refrigerate.

CHAPTER THREE

Soups and Sauces

Essential in many kitchens is the ability to produce good stocks, which can, in turn, serve as the bases of soups, sauces, and gravies. Good stocks are also used in the production of many main dishes. However, they require hours of cooking and skimming, and time is often at a premium in professional as well as home kitchens. Fortunately, available on the market are powdered products that are simply added to water to make a stock. Many chefs today use these bases—and are proud to use them—because they do a job that once required many hours of work to accomplish. Chefs can then concentrate on items that they feel need more of their attention. In this book you will find many recipes using these bases. They have become standard items in many kitchens, just as other commercially made items, such as butter and ice cream, have. Quality food bases are an essential culinary tool in a number of today's kitchens.

Many of the recipes in this book call for commercially prepared bases, which are readily available to the professional chef but may not be available to the consumer in your area. Check with your local supermarket or gourmet shop for the availability of these bases. If you are unable to acquire them through local retail outlets, you may wish to contact the L. J. Minor Corporation for information on obtaining bases. Minor's products are used extensively in the foodservice industry. Once available only to professional chefs, they are now available to consumers. For more information on how you can obtain these bases for home use, please call or write:

The L. J. Minor Corporation
Home Collection
30003 Bainbridge Road
Solon, OH 44139
(800) 441–5914

SOUPS

The soup served at any meal should be well suited to that meal. As a great French gourmand once said, "The soup, like an overture to an opera, should indicate what is to follow." A modern rule in determining the soup to serve is:

serve a heavy soup if the meal is to be light; serve a light soup to introduce a more elaborate meal.

Thus, soups can run the gamut from very light consommés to the heavy peasant soups that are in themselves a hearty meal. The purpose of the light soup is like that of appetizer: to whet the appetite, not suppress it. Often a soup with meat flavors or other appetizing ingredients is introduced to start the flow of gastric juices and stimulate the appetite. Such is the case with a light consommé, bouillon, or broth; light cream soups, bisques, and purees are also suitable for this purpose. A soup served with a sandwich for lunch may be heavier. And, of course, soups that are intended as an almost complete meal should be far more substantial.

SAUCES

Sauces are thickened stocks flavored with concentrated meat essences and other ingredients. They are intended to complement other foods, not dominate them. Sauces should enhance flavor rather than overwhelm it. Today's diners prefer lighter foods, and sauces therefore now tend to include less fat such as butter, animal fat, or oil. The sauce should not drench its accompaniment; often it is placed under it or covering just a part of it. Sauce is increasingly served on the side, allowing the individual diner to select the amount desired.

The most common thickener of sauces is a *roux,* an equal mixture of fat and flour, which thickens when in the presence of moisture and heat. For some roux, the flour may be lightly browned to give some extra color and also impart a slightly toasted flavor. Some roux are made with more heavily browned flour. Because browning destroys some of the thickening power of the flour, more roux must be used to thicken as much as an unbrowned roux can.

Chefs are careful to cook a roux until it bubbles and cooks for the appropriate amount of time. They also often follow the principle of adding a cold roux to a warm liquid and a warm roux to a cold liquid. Stir all sauces well as the roux or thickener is added and continue to stir after it has been added. After the roux or any other starch thickener is added to a sauce, the sauce is usually cooked for about ten minutes, to ensure that all the starch has been gelatinized, eliminating any starchy taste from the sauce.

Chefs usually prefer to use a roux for thickening, but other starch thickeners, such as a water and flour mixed until smooth, will also thicken a sauce. The resulting thickened product, however, is not as smooth tasting or as attractive as that made with a roux.

Eggs can also be used as thickeners. They must be added carefully, as they can cook and curdle a mixture if not properly incorporated. Often, some of the hot sauce or mixture to be thickened is added to beaten eggs or egg yolks and blended quickly. This mixture is, in turn, thoroughly stirred into the hot mixture to be thickened, with care taken to prevent the mixture from boiling. Eggs will cook thoroughly in a sauce below the boiling point.

Soups and sauces are often given a finishing touch with a liaison—a mixture of egg yolks and cream—or with cream or melted butter. These give a more delicate flavor to the sauce. A liaison will also thicken the sauce somewhat. A mixture of butter and flour kneaded together (*beurre manié*) can also be used as a finisher and will add some thickening. This final treatment of a sauce or soup is called "finishing."

Soups and Sauces

COLD VEGETABLE SOUP

COLD SENEGALESE SOUP

COLD CUCUMBER SOUP

VICHYSSOISE

WATERCRESS SOUP

VELOUTÉ OF SQUASH

LOUISIANA GUMBO

MINESTRONE

RED BEAN SOUP

AUTUMN BISQUE

SPRINGTIME CHOWDER

CREAM OF TOMATO SOUP

NEW ENGLAND CLAM CHOWDER

MARCIE'S OYSTER SOUP

BAVARIAN LENTIL SOUP

BLACK BEAN SOUP

BOOKBINDERS SOUP

CHAMPAGNE ONION SOUP

BLACK BEAN SOUP, RIO GRANDE

(continued)

Soups and Sauces (continued)

CABBAGE AND POTATO SOUP
SCALLOP SOUP
POLISH-STYLE BORSCHT
HUNGARIAN GOULASH SOUP
CREAM OF AVOCADO SOUP, ANDALOUSE
BASIC BROWN STOCK
BASIC BROWN SAUCE (SAUCE ESPAGNOLE)
DEMI-GLACE
RED WINE SAUCE I
RED WINE SAUCE II
MADEIRA SAUCE
HUNTER SAUCE
BROWN MUSHROOM SAUCE
BROWN DEVILED SAUCE
BROWN MUSTARD SAUCE
BROWN SAUCE, GYPSY STYLE
BASIC WHITE STOCK
BASIC WHITE SAUCE (VELOUTÉ)
BASIC WHITE OR CREAM SAUCE
SUPRÊME SAUCE
BÉCHAMEL SAUCE
MORNAY SAUCE
CHEESE SAUCE
ALFREDO SAUCE
WHITE MUSHROOM SAUCE
WHITE CAPER SAUCE
WHITE HORSERADISH SAUCE

FENNEL SAUCE

WHITE FISH SAUCE (NORMANDE SAUCE)

NEWBURG SAUCE

LOBSTER SAUCE

TOMATO SAUCE

TOMATO BASIL SAUCE

SAUCE WITH TOMATOES AND GARLIC

HOLLANDAISE SAUCE

MOCK HOLLANDAISE SAUCE

BÉARNAISE SAUCE

PESTO

ASPARAGUS SAUCE

POLYNESIAN BARBECUE SAUCE

TERIYAKI STEAK SAUCE

COCKTAIL SAUCE

COLD VEGETABLE SOUP

Yield: 4 servings

2 CUPS TOMATOES
1 CUCUMBER, PEELED, SEEDED, AND DICED
¼ CUP CHOPPED ONIONS
2 GARLIC CLOVES, CRUSHED
¾ CUP DICED GREEN PEPPERS
¾ CUP DICED RED PEPPERS
1 CUP FRESH WHITE BREADCRUMBS
⅓ CUP RED-WINE VINEGAR
½ CUP CHICKEN STOCK
6 TABLESPOONS OLIVE OIL
12 FRESH BASIL LEAVES

2 TEASPOONS DRIED OREGANO
1 TEASPOON SALT
⅛ TEASPOON FRESHLY GROUND BLACK PEPPER
½ CUP LIGHT CREAM
4 TEASPOONS PEELED, SEEDED, AND SMALL-DICED TOMATOES
4 TEASPOONS PEELED AND SMALL-DICED CUCUMBER
4 TEASPOONS FINELY CHOPPED SCALLIONS

(continued)

✣ Combine the tomatoes, cucumber, onions, garlic, peppers, and breadcrumbs in a large bowl. Add the vinegar, chicken stock, olive oil, 6 of the basil leaves, oregano, salt, and pepper. Mix thoroughly. Chill in the refrigerator for at least 12 hours. Puree in a blender or food processor. Cut the remaining 6 basil leaves into a fine julienne. Mix the cream into the soup and serve cold, topped with the chopped basil and diced tomatoes, cucumbers, and scallions.

Note: A drop or two of hot pepper sauce (Tabasco) or cayenne pepper may be added as desired.

COLD SENEGALESE SOUP

Yield: 8 servings

1 MEDIUM ONION, CHOPPED
1 CARROT, DICED
1 CELERY STALK, SLICED
3 TABLESPOONS BUTTER
2 TABLESPOONS CURRY POWDER
2 TABLESPOONS FLOUR
1 TABLESPOON TOMATO PASTE
1½ QUARTS CHICKEN STOCK

8 OUNCES UNCOOKED CHICKEN BREAST,
    BONED AND SKINLESS
10 WHOLE CLOVES
1 CINNAMON STICK
1½ CUPS HEAVY CREAM
2 TABLESPOONS RED CURRANT JELLY
SALT TO TASTE

✣ In a large saucepan, sauté the onions, carrots, and celery in the butter for 5 minutes. Remove from the heat, and stir in the curry powder and flour until well blended. Add the tomato paste, and cook for 1 minute. Add the chicken stock and bring to a boil, stirring constantly. Add the chicken breast, cloves, and cinnamon stick. Simmer, covered, for 30 minutes. Remove and reserve the chicken breast. Strain the soup. Blend in the cream, currant jelly, and salt. Chill thoroughly. Remove the fat from chilled soup. Dice the reserved chicken breast, add to the soup, and serve cold.

COLD CUCUMBER SOUP

Yield: 6 servings

1 LARGE ONION, FINELY DICED
2 GARLIC CLOVES, MINCED
3 MEDIUM CUCUMBERS, PEELED,
   SEEDED, AND SLICED
3 TABLESPOONS SALTED BUTTER
4 TABLESPOONS FLOUR
3 CUPS CHICKEN STOCK

1 CUP MILK OR HALF-AND-HALF
SALT TO TASTE
WHITE PEPPER TO TASTE
1 MEDIUM CUCUMBER, SEEDED AND
   JULIENNED
1 CUP SOUR CREAM
1 TABLESPOON CHOPPED FRESH DILL

✤ Sauté the onions, garlic, and sliced cucumbers in the butter until glazed. Add the flour, and cook for 3 minutes. Add the chicken stock, and bring to boil; add the milk or half-and-half, and simmer, covered, until the cucumbers are tender. Remove from the heat, puree, and season with salt and white pepper. Return the soup to the stove, add the julienned cucumbers, and simmer, covered, for 5 minutes. Remove and chill. Before serving, add the sour cream, and sprinkle with the chopped dill.

VICHYSSOISE

Yield: 6 servings

6 TABLESPOONS BUTTER
½ CUP SLICED LEEKS
½ CUP DICED ONIONS
1½ POUNDS POTATOES, PEELED AND
   DICED (ABOUT 2 MEDIUM POTATOES)

1 QUART CHICKEN BOUILLON OR BROTH
SALT AND PEPPER TO TASTE
1 TABLESPOON CHOPPED CHIVES
½ CUP HALF-AND-HALF

✤ Heat the butter in a large saucepan. Add the leeks and onions, and cook slowly for 20 minutes, or until tender. Add the potatoes and chicken broth; cook until the potatoes are very tender. Season with salt and pepper. Pass the mixture through a fine-mesh strainer; cool. Add the half-and-half and chives, and serve chilled. Cold vichyssoise should not be too thick.

(continued)

Variations: Vichyssoise with Curry (Senegalese): To the recipe above, sauté 2 tablespoons of curry in 1 tablespoon of butter, and add after the chives.

Vichyssoise with Avocado: To the recipe above, add ¼ cup of finely pureed avocado. The soup should be light green.

Vichyssoise Portugaise: To the recipe above, add ¼ cup of freshly made tomatoes concassé with a touch of garlic; puree until very fine. The soup should be light red or pink.

Vichyssoise with Cucumbers: To the recipe above, add 1 cup peeled, seeded, and finely diced cucumbers with the potatoes. Garnish the soup with diced cucumbers and chives.

WATERCRESS SOUP

Yield: 6 servings

2 BUNCHES WATERCRESS
2 MEDIUM ONIONS, THICKLY SLICED
1 CELERY RIB (3 INCHES LONG), DICED
1 TABLESPOON CORNSTARCH
1 TABLESPOON SUGAR

3 CUPS CHICKEN STOCK
1½ CUPS HALF-AND-HALF
2 TABLESPOONS BUTTER
SALT TO TASTE

❖ Remove the stems from the watercress. Place the watercress leaves, onions, celery, cornstarch, sugar, and 2 cups chicken stock in a blender, and puree until smooth. Place the mixture in a saucepan, add the remaining 1 cup of stock, and bring the mixture to a boil. Reduce the heat, and simmer uncovered for 10 minutes, stirring constantly. Add the half-and-half and butter, and simmer for 5 minutes longer. Season with the salt, and serve.

VELOUTÉ OF SQUASH

Yield: 6 servings

1 LARGE SQUASH (SEE NOTE BELOW)
¼ CUP BUTTER, MELTED
¼ CUP CHOPPED ONIONS
¼ CUP SLICED LEEKS, WHITES ONLY
2 CUPS RICH CHICKEN STOCK
SALT, WHITE PEPPER, AND NUTMEG TO
    TASTE

1 CUP SOUR CREAM
2 TABLESPOONS LEMON JUICE
3 TABLESPOONS COLD BUTTER
3 TABLESPOONS SLICED ALMONDS

❖ Cut a "lid" in the squash; remove and discard the seeds. Place the squash in 350°F oven for approximately 40 minutes (depending on size), until the flesh becomes tender. Scoop out and reserve the flesh; there should be 2 cups. (Reserve the shell if you wish to serve the soup in it.)

Over medium heat, sauté the onions and leeks in butter until translucent. Add the squash, chicken broth, salt, pepper, and nutmeg. Bring to a boil, then reduce the heat and simmer, uncovered, for 20 minutes. Remove the mixture from the heat, puree it, and strain. Return it to the stove. Whip the sour cream into the soup. Bring it to a simmer, *do not boil*. Simmer for about 1 minute, until heated through. Just before serving, add the lemon juice, cold butter, and almonds.

If you wish, preheat the squash shell by filling it with boiling water. After about 1 minute, pour the water out. Place the shell on a serving platter, fill with the soup, replace the lid, and serve.

Note: Various types of squash are suitable, such as hubbard, butternut, pepper, and sweet dumpling, as is pumpkin. Not suitable are zucchini, summer, scallop, spaghetti, vegetable marrow, and turban squash.

LOUISIANA GUMBO

Yield: 6 servings

6 OUNCES BACON, DICED
3 GARLIC CLOVES
1 CUP DICED ONIONS
½ CUP DICED CELERY
2 TABLESPOONS FLOUR
PINCH OF CELERY SALT
½ BAY LEAF, CRUSHED
¼ TEASPOON WHITE PEPPER
1 TEASPOON CAYENNE PEPPER
1 DROP HOT PEPPER SAUCE (TABASCO)
1 TEASPOON WORCESTERSHIRE SAUCE

1 OUNCE FISH BASE*
1 TABLESPOON LEMON JUICE
1½ OUNCES FILÉ POWDER
20 OUNCES CANNED TOMATOES, DICED
½ CUP UNCOOKED RICE
1 QUART WATER
1 CUP SLICED OKRA
8 OUNCES SHRIMP (WITH SHELLS)
6 OYSTERS
12 OUNCES FRESH FISH, DICED
1 TABLESPOON SHERRY

❖ Sauté the bacon until crisp. Add the garlic, onions, celery, flour, celery salt, crushed bay leaf, white pepper, cayenne, hot pepper sauce, Worcestershire sauce, fish base, lemon juice, filé powder, diced tomatoes, rice, and water. Boil for 30 minutes. Add the okra, shrimp, oysters, and fish; simmer for 10 minutes. Add the sherry. Taste, and adjust the seasonings as desired.

* For information about this base, see the introduction to this chapter.

MINESTRONE

Yield: 16 servings

¾ CUP DRIED GREAT NORTHERN BEANS
5½ QUARTS HOT WATER
1½ TEASPOONS SALT
6 TABLESPOONS BUTTER
1 MEDIUM ONION, CUT IN ½-INCH DICE
½ CUP DICED GREEN PEPPERS
4 GARLIC CLOVES, FINELY MINCED
1 CUP DICED CELERY (½-INCH DICE)
2 MEDIUM CARROTS, CUT IN
   ½-INCH DICE
⅓ CUP BEEF BASE*
¾ CUP CRUSHED TOMATOES IN PUREE

½ CUP DITALINI (OR ELBOW MACARONI)
2¼ CUPS DICED CABBAGE (½-INCH DICE)
1¾ CUPS PARED AND CUBED POTATOES
   (½-INCH CUBES)
1½ TEASPOONS PARSLEY FLAKES
¼ TEASPOON SWEET BASIL, CRUSHED
¼ TEASPOON DRIED THYME LEAVES,
   CRUSHED
1 TEASPOON SUGAR
SALT AND FRESHLY GROUND PEPPER TO
   TASTE

❖ Sort and rinse the beans. Cover them with cold water, to 2 inches above the height of the beans. Either soak the beans in the cold water overnight, or boil the beans for 2 minutes, remove from the heat, and soak for 1 hour. Drain the beans, and discard water. Combine the soaked beans, 2½ quarts of hot water, and salt. Heat to boiling, reduce the heat, and gently simmer for 1½ to 2 hours, until the beans are tender. Drain the beans, reserving the broth. Melt the butter in an 8-quart heavy stockpot. Add the onions, green peppers, garlic, celery, and carrots. Sauté over medium heat until almost tender, about 15 to 20 minutes. Add the drained cooked beans, 1 cup of the reserved bean broth, the remaining 3 quarts of hot water, the beef base, tomatoes, ditalini, cabbage, potatoes, parsley flakes, sweet basil, thyme, and sugar. Heat to boiling. Reduce the heat, and simmer for 20 minutes, until the ditalini and vegetables are tender. Add salt and pepper, and serve hot.

* For information about this base, see the introduction to this chapter.

RED BEAN SOUP

Yield: 12 servings

2 TABLESPOONS DICED ONIONS
½ CUP DICED CELERY
2 TABLESPOONS OIL
2 TABLESPOONS FLOUR
1½ QUARTS HOT CHICKEN STOCK
2 TABLESPOONS TOMATO PUREE

3 CUPS KIDNEY BEANS, COOKED
2 TABLESPOONS FINELY DICED BACON
1 CUP (LARGE) PASTA BOW TIES
    (*FARFALLE*)
SALT AND PEPPER TO TASTE

❖ Sauté the diced onions and celery in the oil in 4-quart pot until light brown. Add the flour, and cook for 3 minutes, stirring continuously. Add the chicken stock, tomato puree, kidney beans, and bacon. Stir well, and simmer for 10 to 15 minutes. Add the bow ties, and simmer until they are tender. Add the salt and pepper, and serve hot.

AUTUMN BISQUE

Yield: 6 servings

1 BUTTERNUT SQUASH (1 POUND)
2 GRANNY SMITH APPLES
1 MEDIUM ONION, CHOPPED
1 MEDIUM POTATO, PEELED AND
   COARSELY DICED
PINCH OF GROUND ROSEMARY
PINCH OF GROUND THYME
PINCH OF GROUND BAY LEAF
3 CUPS CHICKEN STOCK

SALT AND PEPPER TO TASTE
1 EGG YOLK
⅓ CUP MEDIUM CREAM
1 CARROT, CUT JULIENNE, BLANCHED
   AL DENTE
1 TURNIP, CUT JULIENNE, BLANCHED
   AL DENTE
1 TABLESPOON CHOPPED CHIVES,
   BLANCHED AL DENTE

❖ Cut and seed the butternut squash, and remove its skin. Peel, core, and coarsely chop the apples. Combine the squash, apples, onions, potatoes, rosemary, thyme, bay leaf, chicken stock, salt, and pepper in a heavy saucepan. Bring to a boil, reduce the heat, and simmer uncovered until the vegetables are tender. Puree the soup in a blender until smooth. Return the soup to the saucepan; bring back to a simmer, stirring occasionally. Beat the egg yolk and cream in a bowl with a wire whisk. Whisk 1 cup of hot soup slowly into the egg mixture. Remove the soup from the heat, and slowly stir the egg mixture into the soup. (Do not boil the soup if reheating.) Adjust the seasonings, and garnish with the carrots, turnips, and chives.

Variation: As an alternative garnish, mix 2 tablespoons of apple sauce with 1 cup of whipped cream, and pipe a rosette of the mixture on top of each serving of soup.

SPRINGTIME CHOWDER

Yield: 6 to 8 servings

1 CUP DICED PORK
1 CUP DICED ONIONS
1 CUP DICED LEEKS (⅜-INCH DICE)
½ CUP DICED CARROTS
1 CUP DICED CELERY (⅜-INCH DICE)
3 CUPS CHICKEN BROTH
1 MEDIUM BAY LEAF

¼ CUP CORNMEAL
1½ CUPS CORN
2 CUPS HOT MILK
⅛ TEASPOON FRESHLY GROUND WHITE
   PEPPER
CHOPPED PARSLEY TO GARNISH

✤ Place the salt pork in a saucepan, and cover with cold water. Bring to boil, and cook for a few seconds. Drain and rinse the salt pork well with cold water. Place the salt pork in 4-quart stockpot or marmite, and render over medium heat, do not let brown. Add the onions, and sauté until glossy but not brown. Add the leeks and repeat. Add the carrots and celery, blend in well, and then add the chicken broth and bay leaf. Bring to a boil; add the cornmeal in a slow stream, stirring occasionally. Add the corn kernels and return to a boil. Turn off the heat, cover the pot, and let the mixture stand for 30 minutes. Just before serving, remove the bay leaf and add the hot milk and pepper. Serve sprinkled with the chopped parsley.

Variations: For a richer soup, substitute some of the milk with half-and-half and/or blend a tablespoon of butter into the soup just before serving.

The salt pork may be replaced by cooked chicken meat. Other vegetables can also be added to taste.

CREAM OF TOMATO SOUP

Yield: 8 servings

5 TABLESPOONS BUTTER
1 CUP CHOPPED ONIONS
½ CUP CHOPPED CELERY
⅔ CUP ALL-PURPOSE FLOUR
1¾ QUARTS HOT WATER
3½ TABLESPOONS CHICKEN BASE*
6 OUNCES TOMATO PASTE

1 LARGE TOMATO, CORED AND CHOPPED
   (OR ⅔ CUP CANNED WHOLE
   TOMATOES, CHOPPED)
3½ TABLESPOONS SUGAR
SALT TO TASTE
½ CUP HOT HEAVY CREAM

✤ In a heavy stockpot, melt the butter over low heat. Add the onions and celery, and sauté until tender but not brown, about 10 minutes. Blend in the flour with a wire whisk. Stir over low heat until well blended, evenly cooked, and bubbly, about 2 to 3 minutes. Remove from the heat. Add the hot water gradually, mixing well. Stir in the chicken base, tomato paste, tomatoes, and sugar; season with salt to taste. Simmer for 10 minutes, stirring occasionally. Strain the soup, discarding the vegetables, and return it to the pot. Blend in the hot cream, and serve.

* For information about this base, see the introduction to this chapter.

NEW ENGLAND CLAM CHOWDER

Yield: 8 servings

1½ CUPS PARED AND CUBED POTATOES
  (½-INCH CUBES)
5 TABLESPOONS BUTTER
½ CUP CHOPPED ONIONS
½ CUP ALL-PURPOSE FLOUR
2½ CUPS HOT WATER

1½ TABLESPOONS CLAM BASE*
1½ TEASPOONS PORK BASE*
13 OUNCES CANNED, UNDRAINED
  CHOPPED OR MINCED CLAMS
2½ CUPS HOT HALF-AND-HALF CREAM
SALT AND WHITE PEPPER TO TASTE

✤ In a 1-quart saucepan, cover the potatoes with cold water, and heat to boiling. Reduce the heat, cover, and simmer for 10 to 12 minutes, until almost tender. Drain the potatoes, and set aside. In a 4-quart stockpot, melt the butter over low heat. Add the onions, and sauté until tender but not brown, about 10 minutes. Blend in the flour with a wire whisk. Stir over low heat until well blended, evenly cooked, and bubbly, about 2 to 3 minutes. Remove from the heat. Add hot water gradually, mixing well. Stir in the clam base and pork base and the clams with their juice. Heat to boiling over medium heat, stirring constantly. Boil and stir for 1 minute. Reduce the heat, and simmer for 10 minutes, stirring occasionally. Add the potatoes and hot cream, stirring gently. Taste, and adjust the seasonings.

Note: For best results, use new or waxy potatoes.

* For information about these bases, see the introduction to this chapter.

MARCIE'S OYSTER SOUP

Yield: 10 servings

1 BUNCH SCALLIONS, CHOPPED
1 MEDIUM ONION, CHOPPED
2 GARLIC CLOVES, CHOPPED
1 CELERY HEART, FINELY CHOPPED
½ CUP BUTTER
¾ CUP FLOUR

4 DOZEN OYSTERS, SHELLED
2 QUARTS OYSTER LIQUID AND WATER
SALT AND RED AND BLACK PEPPER TO
  TASTE
1 CUP WHIPPING CREAM
½ BUNCH PARSLEY, CHOPPED

✤ Sauté the chopped scallions, onions, garlic, and celery heart in the butter until tender. Stir in the flour to make a smooth paste. Add the oysters and oyster liquid. Bring to boil, and season with the salt and peppers to taste. Add the cream and parsley. Heat to 170°F; do *not* boil.

BAVARIAN LENTIL SOUP

Yield: 10 servings

3 OUNCES BACON FAT
⅓ CUP FINELY CHOPPED CARROTS
⅓ CUP FINELY CHOPPED ONIONS
⅓ CUP FINELY CHOPPED CELERY
10 OUNCES LENTILS, WASHED AND
   SOAKED IN WATER FOR SEVERAL
   HOURS
2 LARGE RAW POTATOES, DICED
1 HAM BONE
1 TEASPOON MARJORAM

2 BAY LEAVES
2 QUARTS HOT BEEF OR CHICKEN STOCK
¼ CUP FLOUR
2 TABLESPOONS WHITE VINEGAR
SALT AND FRESHLY GROUND WHITE
   PEPPER TO TASTE
WORCESTERSHIRE SAUCE TO TASTE
6 OUNCES FRANKFURTERS, THINLY
   SLICED

✤ Melt the bacon fat in a stockpot. Add the chopped carrots, onions, and celery, and smother. Add the soaked and drained lentils, diced potatoes, ham bone, marjoram, and bay leaves. Add the hot stock. Stir to mix thoroughly, and bring to a boil. Reduce the heat, and simmer slowly, stirring frequently, until the lentils are soft. Remove the ham bone. Mix the flour with enough water to make a smooth paste, and stir the mixture into the soup. Continue to cook for another 10 minutes. Add the vinegar, salt, pepper, and Worcestershire sauce. Heat the sliced frankfurters separately in water, drain, and add to the soup just before serving.

BLACK BEAN SOUP

Yield: 6 servings

8 OUNCES DRIED BLACK BEANS
5 CUPS BOUILLON OR SOUP STOCK
2 TABLESPOONS LARD OR SHORTENING
1 CUP CHOPPED ONIONS
1 GARLIC CLOVE, MINCED
¾ CUP DICED SMOKED HAM (¼-INCH DICE)
1 CUP PEELED, SEEDED, AND DICED TOMATOES

¼ TEASPOON GROUND CUMIN SEED
1 TABLESPOON MALT VINEGAR
SALT AND FRESHLY GROUND PEPPER TO TASTE
3–6 DROPS HOT PEPPER SAUCE (TABASCO)
¼ CUP PEELED AND DICED LEMON
1 CUP COOKED WHITE RICE
½ CUP DRY SHERRY

❖ Sort the beans, wash thoroughly, and place them with the cold stock into 4-quart stockpot or marmite. Bring to a boil, skim any scum from the surface, and simmer partially covered for 1 to 1¼ hours, until the beans are tender (cooking time may vary, depending on the age of the beans). Remove 1 cup of the beans from the liquid, and set aside. Puree the remaining soup in a blender or food processor, and reserve in a bowl. In a stew pan, heat the lard or short-ening, and sauté the onions and the garlic until transparent. Mix in the ham, tomatoes, cumin, and vinegar, and cook for 5 minutes over medium heat. Add the pureed beans and the reserved whole beans. Bring the soup to a boil, reduce the heat, and simmer for 15 minutes. Season with salt, pepper, and hot pepper sauce to taste. Serve each portion with 2 to 3 tablespoons of rice, a few dices of lemon, and a dash of sherry.

This soup tastes even better when reheated the next day and can easily be stored in the refrigerator for 3 days. Always be sure to properly heat before serving.

BOOKBINDERS SOUP

Yield: 6 servings

5 TABLESPOONS BUTTER
1 CUP FINELY CHOPPED ONIONS
1 CUP FINELY CHOPPED GREEN PEPPERS
1 CUP FINELY CHOPPED CELERY
1½ TEASPOONS FISH BASE *
2 TEASPOONS BEEF BASE *
1 CUP TOMATO PUREE

4 CUPS WATER
2 TABLESPOONS FLOUR
1 CUP CHOPPED RAW RED SNAPPER (½-INCH PIECES)
⅓ CUP DRY SHERRY
SALT AND PEPPER TO TASTE

❖ Heat 3 tablespoons of butter in a sauté pan, add the onions, peppers, and celery, and sauté until tender. In a bowl, dissolve the fish base, beef base, and tomato puree in the water. Melt the remaining 2 tablespoons of butter in a saucepan, add the flour, and cook for 2 minutes. Add the liquid mixture, and cook for 3 minutes. Add the sautéed vegetables, and simmer for 10 minutes. Add the red snapper, and simmer for 5 minutes. Add the sherry, taste, and season if needed.

* For information about these bases, see the introduction to this chapter.

CHAMPAGNE ONION SOUP

Yield: 8 to 10 servings

3 CUPS FINELY CHOPPED WHITE ONIONS	3 TABLESPOONS BEEF BASE*
4 TABLESPOONS BUTTER	2 CUPS CHAMPAGNE
5 CUPS WATER	PEPPER TO TASTE

❖ In a large sauté pan, cook the onions in the butter until soft. Put the onions in a large pot, add the water, beef base, Champagne, and pepper. Bring to a boil; lower the heat and simmer, covered, for 3 minutes. Serve with buttered toast, alongside or au gratin in the traditional way. You may substitute 5 cups of beef stock for the beef base and water.

* For information about this base, see the introduction to this chapter.

BLACK BEAN SOUP, RIO GRANDE

Yield: 3 quarts

¾ CUP DRIED BLACK BEANS	½ BAY LEAF
1 QUART COLD WATER	2½ CUPS HOT WATER
½ TABLESPOON VEGETABLE OIL	2½ TABLESPOONS HAM BASE*
¼ CUP DICED CARROTS	1 SMALL TOMATO, CORED AND
¼ CUP DICED CELERY	DICED SMALL
¼ CUP DICED ONIONS	½ CUP DRY RED WINE
1 SMALL GARLIC CLOVE, MINCED	SOUR CREAM TO GARNISH
1 JALAPEÑO PEPPER, SEEDED AND	COLBY CHEESE, GRATED, TO GARNISH
DICED SMALL	

(continued)

❖ Sort and wash the beans well. Combine the beans and the cold water in a 3-quart saucepan. Heat to boiling over medium-high heat. Boil for 2 minutes. Remove from the heat, cover, and let stand for 1 hour. Drain and set aside. In a heavy 2- or 3-quart saucepan, heat the oil over medium heat. Add the carrots, celery, onions, garlic, pepper, and bay leaf. Sauté over low heat for 5 to 8 minutes, until the onions are tender. Stir in the water, ham base, tomatoes, and cooked black beans. Heat to boiling, stirring occasionally. Reduce the heat and cover loosely; simmer for 1 hour, stirring occasionally. Stir in the wine and continue to simmer, loosely covered, for approximately 20 minutes, until the beans are tender. Remove and discard the bay leaf. Puree the soup in blender or food processor. Serve hot, garnished with sour cream and grated Colby cheese.

* For information about this base, see the introduction to this chapter.

CABBAGE AND POTATO SOUP

Yield: 3 quarts

2 OUNCES BACON, MEDIUM DICE (ABOUT 2 SLICES)
½ CUP MEDIUM-DICE ONIONS
½ CUP SLICED CARROTS (⅛-INCH THICK)
½ CUP MEDIUM-DICE CELERY
1 SMALL GARLIC CLOVE, MINCED
2 QUARTS HOT WATER
2 CUPS SLICED CABBAGE (2- BY ¼-INCH STRIPS)
1 OUNCE HAM BASE*
1 OUNCE CHICKEN BASE*
14½ OUNCES CANNED WHOLE TOMATOES, DRAINED AND DICED SMALL

¼ TEASPOON SALT
⅛ TEASPOON WHITE PEPPER
1⅓ CUPS LARGE-DICED UNPEELED RED POTATOES
1 CUP PEELED AND GRATED RED POTATOES
3 OUNCES COOKED HAM, CUT IN 1–1½-INCH-LONG JULIENNE
1 CUP CHOPPED FRESH PARSLEY

✤ In a heavy 8-quart saucepan, fry the bacon over medium-high heat until lightly browned, about 5 minutes, stirring occasionally. Add the onions, carrots, celery, and garlic. Sweat the vegetables, stirring over low heat until they are tender, about 10 to 15 minutes. Add the water, cabbage, ham base, chicken base, tomatoes, salt, and pepper. Heat to boiling over medium heat, stirring frequently. Add the diced potatoes, and simmer over medium heat for 15 minutes, stirring occasionally. Remove from the heat. Cover, and let stand for 30 minutes. Add the grated potatoes and ham. Heat to boiling, stirring frequently. Reduce the heat, and simmer for 5 minutes. Serve hot, garnished with the chopped parsley.

* For information about these bases, see the introduction to this chapter.

SCALLOP SOUP

Yield: 4 servings

5 OUNCES YOUNG SPINACH LEAVES
   (1 BUNCH)
1 MEDIUM TOMATO
1 SHALLOT
1 TEASPOON BUTTER
8 OUNCES SMALL SCALLOPS
½ CUP COCONUT MILK
3 CUPS CHICKEN CONSOMMÉ OR FRESH
   FISH CONSOMMÉ

½ TEASPOON MASHED GARLIC
¼ TEASPOON SAFFRON
½ TEASPOON FRESHLY GROUND WHITE
   PEPPER
½ TEASPOON SALT
¾ CUP HEAVY CREAM
4 EGG YOLKS

✤ Clean the spinach, shred it roughly, and blanch. Blanch the tomato, then peel, seed, and dice it. Finely dice the shallot. Heat the butter, and sauté the diced shallot until golden. Add the scallops, coconut milk, consommé, mashed garlic, and saffron; simmer for 10 minutes. Add the tomato, spinach, pepper, and salt. Fold in the heavy cream and egg yolks, and heat to 190°F for 2 minutes (do *not* boil). Serve hot, in cups.

Note: Use scallops with roe if available.

POLISH-STYLE BORSCHT

Yield: 6–8 servings

3 QUARTS WATER
1 POUND DUCK, DISJOINTED AND
  BROWNED
1 POUND CHUCK BEEF
1½ OUNCES FENNEL
2 CLOVES
1 BAY LEAF
2 CUPS JULIENNED LEEKS
2⅓ CUPS JULIENNED SAVOY CABBAGE
1½ CUPS JULIENNED CANNED RED
  BEETS, WITH JUICE
1 MEDIUM POTATO, PEELED AND CUT IN
  JULIENNE
1 SMALL ONION, CUT IN JULIENNE

2 MEDIUM CELERY STALKS, CUT IN
  JULIENNE
2 MEDIUM PARSLEY ROOTS, CUT IN
  JULIENNE
4 TABLESPOONS BUTTER
7 OUNCES BACON, DICED (ABOUT 7
  STRIPS)
10 OUNCES POLISH SAUSAGE, SLICED
2 OUNCES BEEF BASE*
2 OUNCES CHICKEN BASE*
1 CUP SOUR CREAM
SALT AND PEPPER TO TASTE
2 OUNCES HAM BASE*

❖ In a stockpot, heat the water, duck, chuck beef, fennel, cloves, and bay leaf to a boil; cook until tender. Remove from the heat, and let set for 15 to 20 minutes. Remove the meat, slice into portions, and return to the soup. Remove and discard the bay leaf. Sauté the leeks, cabbage, beets (reserve the juice), potatoes, onions, celery and parsley in the butter until tender. Cook the bacon until crisp, add the sausage, and cook together for 3 minutes; drain off the fat. Stir the sautéed vegetables and sausage and bacon into the soup. Stir in the beef and chicken bases. Add the reserved beet juice (1¼ cups), and fold in the sour cream (the sour cream can be served on the side instead if desired). Taste, and season with salt and pepper. If a smokier flavor is desired, add the ham base. Serve hot. (The meat can be removed and served separately if desired.)

* For information about these bases, see the introduction to this chapter.

HUNGARIAN GOULASH SOUP

Yield: 10 servings

4 OUNCES BACON, MINCED (ABOUT 4
  STRIPS)
3 MEDIUM ONIONS, PARED AND DICED
4 GARLIC CLOVES, MINCED
2 POUNDS BEEF SHANK, CUT IN ½-INCH
  CUBES
3 OUNCES TOMATO PUREE
2 TABLESPOONS HUNGARIAN PAPRIKA

½ CUP FLOUR
2 QUARTS BEEF STOCK
2 POUNDS POTATOES, CUT IN ½-INCH
  DICE (ABOUT 3 MEDIUM POTATOES)
1 TEASPOON CHOPPED CARAWAY SEEDS
1 TEASPOON MARJORAM
1 TEASPOON SALT

DUMPLINGS
1 CUP FLOUR
2 EGGS
½ CUP WATER

2 TABLESPOONS OIL
⅓ TEASPOON SALT

❖ In a 4-quart stockpot, fry the bacon until crisp. Add the diced onions and garlic, and sauté for 5 to 7 minutes. Add the beef cubes, and sauté until the meat shrinks. Add the tomato puree and paprika, and continue to sauté for 5 minutes. Add the flour, and sauté for 2 more minutes. Add the stock, bring to a boil, and cook until meat is browned. Add the potatoes, caraway, marjoram, and salt, and continue cooking until the meat and potatoes are tender. About 20 minutes before serving, mix the flour, eggs, water, oil, and salt to form a light dough. Pass the mixture through a large-hole colander into the boiling soup. Cook for approximately 10 to 12 minutes.

Note: For additional flavor, green pepper rings can be added, and the tomato puree can be replaced with fresh tomatoes. Additional salt, garlic, and caraway seeds can also be added at the end, to taste.

CREAM OF AVOCADO SOUP

Yield: 6 servings

¼ CUP BUTTER
1 CUP CHOPPED ONIONS
1 LEEK (WHITE ONLY), SLICED
1 CELERY STALK, CHOPPED
¾ POUND POTATOES, DICED (ABOUT 1
    MEDIUM POTATO)
1 BAY LEAF

1 TEASPOON SALT
½ TEASPOON WHITE PEPPER
5 CUPS CHICKEN STOCK
½ CUP HEAVY CREAM
½ TABLESPOON CHOPPED CHIVES
1 TABLESPOON WORCESTERSHIRE SAUCE
1 RIPE AVOCADO

✤ Melt the butter in a large saucepan. Add the onions, leeks, celery, potatoes, bay leaf, salt, pepper, and stock. Cook for 1¼ hours over low heat. Remove the bay leaf. Remove from the heat, and puree the mixture. Return it to the stove, and heat to a boil. Stir in the cream, chives, and Worcestershire sauce; remove from the heat and chill.

Peel the avocado, and cut it into small pieces. Place in a blender, and process into a paste. Add 1 cup cold soup, bit by bit, mixing well. Add the thinned paste to the remainder of the soup, and mix well. Serve cold. (This soup may also be served hot.)

BASIC BROWN STOCK

Yield: 2 quarts

4 POUNDS BONES (BEEF, GAME,
    CHICKEN, VEAL)
1 GALLON COLD WATER
2 OUNCES OIL OR FAT
1 ONION, CHOPPED
4 CELERY STALKS
2 CARROTS

20 OUNCES CANNED TOMATOES, PEELED
2 OUNCES TOMATO PUREE
2 BAY LEAVES
¼ TEASPOON MARGARINE
½ TEASPOON THYME
4 PEPPERCORNS, CRUSHED
1 GARLIC CLOVE

✤ Place the bones in a roasting pan, and brown in a 375°F oven until evenly browned (do not burn). Remove to a stockpot. Add the cold water, and bring to a boil. Deglaze the roasting pan with a little water to dissolve all the sticky residue, and add to the bones in pot. Add the remaining ingredients, and simmer for 2½ to 3 hours, skimming any foam and fat that rises to the top. The best-suited bones are neck or rib bones, chopped into small pieces.

BASIC BROWN SAUCE (SAUCE ESPAGNOLE)

Yield: 1 quart

2 OUNCES BEEF, CHICKEN, OR
    OTHER FAT
1 ONION, DICED
1 CARROT, SLICED
2 CELERY STALKS, CHOPPED
⅓ CUP FLOUR

1 BAY LEAF
1 GARLIC CLOVE
¼ CUP (SCANT) TOMATO PUREE
1 QUART BROWN STOCK (SEE
    PRECEDING RECIPE)
SALT AND PEPPER TO TASTE

❖ Heat the fat in a saucepan, add the onions, and sauté for 5 minutes. Add the carrots and celery, and continue sautéing for 5 minutes. Add the flour, and cook until slightly brown. Add the bay leaf, garlic, tomato puree, and stock. Simmer for 1½ to 2 hours, being careful not to scorch. Strain, taste, and adjust the seasonings.

DEMI-GLACE

Yield: 2 cups

2 CUPS SAUCE ESPAGNOLE (BASIC
    BROWN SAUCE—SEE PRECEDING
    RECIPE)

2 CUPS BROWN STOCK (SEE RECIPE
    EARLIER IN THIS CHAPTER)
2 TEASPOONS SHERRY.

❖ Combine the brown sauce and stock in a saucepan. Reduce by half. Stir in the sherry, and serve.

RED WINE SAUCE I

Yield: 1 pint

½ CUP RED BORDEAUX WINE
1 FRESH THYME SPRIG
1 BAY LEAF
1 TEASPOON CHOPPED SHALLOTS

1 PINT BASIC BROWN SAUCE (SEE
    RECIPE EARLIER IN THIS CHAPTER)
SALT AND WHITE PEPPER TO TASTE

(continued)

❖ Place the wine, thyme, bay leaf, and shallots in a pot. Bring to a boil, and reduce by half. Add the basic brown sauce, and bring to a short boil. Strain. Adjust the seasonings. Serve with braised beef, broiled steaks, or sautéed dark meats.

Note: In classical preparation, this sauce is garnished with poached bone marrow.

RED WINE SAUCE II

Yield: 1 pint

2 TABLESPOONS BUTTER
1 TABLESPOON CHOPPED SHALLOTS
½ CUP SLICED MUSHROOMS
1 BAY LEAF
1 PEPPERCORN, CRUSHED

1 PARSLEY SPRIG
½ CUP RED BURGUNDY WINE
1 PINT BASIC BROWN SAUCE (SEE
   RECIPE EARLIER IN THIS CHAPTER)
SALT AND WHITE PEPPER TO TASTE

❖ Heat the butter in a saucepan, add the shallots, mushrooms, bay leaf, peppercorn, and parsley and sauté for 5 minutes. Add the burgundy, and reduce by half. Add the basic brown sauce, and simmer for 5 minutes. Strain, and adjust the seasonings. Serve with sautéed beef or chicken.

MADEIRA SAUCE

Yield: 2 cups

1¾ CUPS LUKEWARM WATER
3 TABLESPOONS BROWN SAUCE PREP*

2 TABLESPOONS MADEIRA WINE

❖ In a heavy 1-qt. saucepan, blend the water with the brown sauce prep, mixing well with a wire whisk. Stir in the wine. Heat to boiling over medium heat, stirring constantly. Reduce the heat, and simmer for 5 minutes, stirring occasionally. Serve hot over beef entrées.

* For information about this preparation, see the introduction to this chapter.

HUNTER SAUCE

Yield: 1 pint

1 PINT BASIC BROWN SAUCE (SEE
   RECIPE EARLIER IN THIS CHAPTER)
½ CUP TOMATO SAUCE
2 TABLESPOONS BUTTER
½ CUP SLICED MUSHROOMS
1 TABLESPOON CHOPPED SHALLOTS

¼ CUP WHITE WINE
¼ TEASPOON DRIED CHERVIL
½ TEASPOON DRIED TARRAGON
SALT AND WHITE PEPPER TO TASTE
1 TABLESPOON CHOPPED PARSLEY

❖ Combine the basic brown sauce and tomato sauce in a saucepan, and bring to a simmer. In a separate pan, heat the butter, add the mushrooms and sweat. Add the shallots, and cook until translucent. Add the wine, chervil, and tarragon, and reduce by half. Add the mushroom reduction to the brown sauce, and continue reducing until 1 pint remains. Taste, and season with salt and pepper. Add the chopped parsley as a garnish. Serve with sautéed chicken or beef.

Note: The tomato sauce can be replaced with peeled, chopped tomatoes, which are sautéed with the mushrooms and shallots.

BROWN MUSHROOM SAUCE

Yield: 1 quart

4 TABLESPOONS BUTTER
½ CUP CHOPPED MUSHROOMS (STEMS
   MAY BE USED)
¼ CUP RED MADEIRA WINE
1 CUP SLICED MUSHROOMS (LARGE
   CAPS)

1½ CUPS BASIC BROWN SAUCE (SEE
   RECIPE EARLIER IN THIS CHAPTER)
SALT AND WHITE PEPPER TO TASTE

❖ Heat 2 tablespoons of the butter in a saucepan, add the chopped mushrooms, and sauté for 3 to 4 minutes. Add the Madeira, and reduce by half. Strain; there should be ¼ cup.

Sauté the sliced mushrooms in the remaining 2 tablespoons of butter. Add the mushroom/Madeira reduction, and bring to a boil. Add the brown sauce, and simmer for 5 minutes. Taste and season. Serve with sautéed chicken, veal, or braised beef.

BROWN DEVILED SAUCE

Yield: 1 pint

½ CUP WHITE WINE
1 TEASPOON WHITE VINEGAR
1 TABLESPOON CHOPPED SHALLOTS
1 THYME SPRIG
1 BAY LEAF

¼ TEASPOON FRESHLY GROUND BLACK
  PEPPER
1 PINT BASIC BROWN SAUCE (SEE
  RECIPE EARLIER IN THIS CHAPTER)
SALT AND CAYENNE PEPPER TO TASTE

❖ In a saucepan, bring the wine, vinegar, shallots, thyme, bay leaf, and black pepper to a boil; reduce by half. Meanwhile, in a separate saucepan, bring the brown sauce to a simmer. Add the reduction to the simmering brown sauce, and continue simmering until reduced to 1 pint. Taste, and season with salt and cayenne. Remove and discard the bay leaf. Serve with roast or broiled chicken or sautéed émincé of veal.

BROWN MUSTARD SAUCE

Yield: 1 pint

2 TABLESPOONS BUTTER
2 TABLESPOONS FINELY MINCED ONIONS
¼ CUP WHITE WINE

1 PINT BASIC BROWN SAUCE (SEE
  RECIPE EARLIER IN THIS CHAPTER)
1 TABLESPOON MILD MUSTARD

❖ Heat the butter in a saucepan. Add the onions, and sauté for 5 minutes. Add the wine. Simmer until reduced by half. Add the brown sauce, and cook for 5 minutes. Dilute the mustard with a little of the sauce, then add to sauce, and mix well. Do not boil after mustard has been added. This sauce usually is served only with roast pork or broiled pork chops.

Note: To make the sauce more tart, some white vinegar can be added along with the wine.

BROWN SAUCE, GYPSY STYLE

Yield: 1 pint

2 TABLESPOONS BUTTER
¼ CUP SLICED MUSHROOMS
1 OUNCE SMOKED HAM, CUT IN
    JULIENNE
1 OUNCE SMOKED TONGUE, CUT IN
    JULIENNE

1 OUNCE DILL PICKLES, CUT IN JULIENNE
1 TABLESPOON TOMATO PUREE
1 PINT BASIC BROWN SAUCE (SEE
    RECIPE EARLIER IN THIS CHAPTER)
SALT AND CAYENNE PEPPER TO TASTE

❖ Heat the butter in a saucepan, add the mushrooms, ham, tongue, and pickles, and sauté for 2 to 3 minutes. Add the tomato puree, and sauté for 1 minute. Add the brown sauce; bring to a boil. Simmer for 5 minutes. Taste, and season with salt and cayenne. Serve with braised chicken, roast veal steaks, or veal or turkey roulades.

Note: Do not add salt before tasting, as the ham, tongue, and pickles are salted.

BASIC WHITE STOCK

Yield: 2 quarts

4 POUNDS BONES (BEEF, GAME,
    CHICKEN, VEAL; SEE NOTE BELOW)
1 GALLON COLD WATER
2 ONIONS
1 LEEK

4 CELERY STALKS
2 BAY LEAVES
6 PEPPERCORNS
1 GARLIC CLOVE

❖ Wash the bones, and cover with the water in a suitable pot. Bring to a boil, reduce the heat, and begin to simmer. When foam floats on surface, skim it off using a perforated spoon or ladle. Simmer for 2 hours. Add the onions, leek, celery, bay leaves, peppercorns, and garlic, and continue simmering for at least 2 more hours. When the desired strength is achieved, strain and chill. This basic white stock can be used for soups or light-colored sauces such as veloutés. To produce a stronger flavor, return the stock to a boil and reduce until the desired flavor is achieved.

Note: The type of bone used will dictate the flavor of the stock.

BASIC WHITE SAUCE (VELOUTÉ)

Yield: 1 quart

6 TABLESPOONS BUTTER
2½ OUNCES FLOUR (ABOUT ½ CUP)

1 QUART WHITE CHICKEN STOCK (SEE
  PRECEDING RECIPE)

✤ Melt the butter in a stainless-steel pot. Add the flour, and make a white roux. Add the white chicken stock, and cook for 3 to 5 minutes. Strain.

BASIC WHITE OR CREAM SAUCE

Yield: 1 pint

3½ TABLESPOONS SAUCE/SOUP
  THICKENER *
½ CUP COLD WATER

1½ CUPS HOT MILK OR HALF-AND-HALF
½ TEASPOON SALT

✤ In a heavy 1-quart saucepan, blend the sauce/soup thickener with the cold water until smooth, using a wire whisk (only tiny butter particles will remain). Whisk the hot milk into the smooth paste. Stir in the salt. Heat to boiling over medium heat, stirring continuously. Boil and stir for 1 minute. Serve hot, or chill and reheat as needed.

* For information about this thickener, see the introduction to this chapter.

SUPRÊME SAUCE

Yield: Approximately 1 quart

1 QUART VELOUTÉ (SEE RECIPE EARLIER
  IN THIS CHAPTER)
¼ CUP HEAVY CREAM

4 TABLESPOONS BUTTER
1 TABLESPOON LEMON JUICE
SALT AND WHITE PEPPER TO TASTE

✛ Bring the velouté to a boil in a stainless-steel pot. Stir a bit of the hot velouté into the heavy cream, and stir this tempered cream into the velouté. Add the butter, lemon juice, and seasonings. Cook for 5 minutes. This sauce can be used as a sauce itself or as a base for other white sauces.

BÉCHAMEL SAUCE

Yield: 1 quart

6 TABLESPOONS BUTTER
⅔ CUP FLOUR
1 QUART MILK
1 ONION CLUTE (ONION STUDDED WITH
   CLOVES)

¼ TEASPOON GRATED NUTMEG
SALT AND WHITE PEPPER TO TASTE

✛ Melt the butter in a stainless-steel pot. Add the flour, and make a white roux. Add the milk, and bring to a boil. Add the onion clute. Cook for 15 minutes. Season with the nutmeg, salt, and pepper. Strain, and use whenever white sauce is needed.

MORNAY SAUCE

Yield: 2½ cups

4 TABLESPOONS SHORTENING
4 TABLESPOONS FLOUR
2 CUPS SCALDED MILK
SALT AND PEPPER TO TASTE

2 EGG YOLKS
½ CUP GRATED GRUYÈRE CHEESE
3 TABLESPOONS COLD BUTTER

✛ Heat the shortening in a saucepan until melted, and add the flour to make a roux. Stir well, cooking the roux for 3 minutes over low heat. Add the scalded milk, and stir until smooth. Season with salt and pepper, and cook for 4 minutes, stirring constantly. Remove from the heat, add the egg yolks and cheese, and mix well. Dot with the butter. Allow the sauce to set until needed.

CHEESE SAUCE

Yield: 2 cups

3½ TABLESPOONS SAUCE/SOUP
   THICKENER*
¼ CUP LUKEWARM WATER
1¼ CUPS HOT MILK

½ TEASPOON SALT
4 OUNCES SHARP CHEDDAR CHEESE,
   SHREDDED (ABOUT 1 CUP)

✣ In a heavy 1-quart saucepan, blend the sauce/soup thickener with the luke-warm water until smooth, using a wire whisk. Add the milk and salt. Heat to boiling over medium heat, stirring continuously. Boil and stir for 1 minute, until thickened. Remove from the heat. Add the cheese, mixing well. Heat to a simmer, stirring continuously, and cook until the cheese is melted. Serve hot over pasta, cooked vegetables, or tortilla chips topped with sliced chili peppers and chopped onions.

* For information about this thickener, see the introduction to this chapter.

ALFREDO SAUCE

Yield: 4½ cups

5 TABLESPOONS SAUCE/SOUP
   THICKENER*
1 CUP LUKEWARM WATER
1½ TEASPOONS SALT
¼ TEASPOON DRY MUSTARD

⅛ TEASPOON BLACK PEPPER
3 CUPS HOT MILK
1 CUP GRATED PARMESAN CHEESE
¼ CUP GRATED ROMANO CHEESE

✣ In a heavy 2-quart saucepan, blend the sauce/soup thickener with the water until smooth, using a wire whisk. Add the salt, dry mustard, pepper, and milk. Heat to boiling over medium heat, stirring continuously. Boil and stir for 1 minute, until thickened. Remove from the heat, and stir in the cheeses, mixing until well blended. Serve tossed with cooked fettucini.

* For information about this thickener, see the introduction to this chapter.

WHITE MUSHROOM SAUCE

Yield: 1 pint

2 TABLESPOONS BUTTER
1 TABLESPOON FINELY CHOPPED
  SHALLOTS
1 CUP SLICED MUSHROOMS

¼ TEASPOON GRATED NUTMEG
1½ CUPS SUPRÊME SAUCE (SEE RECIPE
  EARLIER IN THIS CHAPTER)
SALT AND PEPPER TO TASTE

❖ Heat the butter in a sauté pan, add the shallots, and sauté for 2 to 3 minutes. Add the mushrooms, and sauté for 1 minute. Sprinkle with the nutmeg. Add the mushroom mixture to the suprême sauce. Bring to a short boil. Taste, and adjust the seasonings. Serve with boiled or poached meat or vegetables.

WHITE CAPER SAUCE

Yield: 1 pint

1½ CUPS SUPRÊME SAUCE (SEE RECIPE
  EARLIER IN THIS CHAPTER)

1 OUNCE CAPERS
½ CUP HEAVY CREAM

❖ Bring the suprême sauce to a boil. Add the capers. Add a bit of the hot sauce to the heavy cream, and stir this tempered cream into the sauce. Serve with boiled or poached chicken.

Note: Because capers are pickled in brine, which is salty, this sauce may have a saltier flavor than desired. To reduce the saltiness, wash the capers in cold water before adding.

WHITE HORSERADISH SAUCE

Yield: 1 Pint

½ HORSERADISH ROOT
¼ CUP SEMISWEET WHITE WINE
1½ CUPS BÉCHAMEL SAUCE (SEE RECIPE
   EARLIER IN THIS CHAPTER)

¼ CUP HEAVY CREAM
¼ TEASPOON CAYENNE PEPPER
SALT TO TASTE

❖ Soak the horseradish in water overnight. Peel and grate. Place in a small pot, add the wine and simmer until all the wine is evaporated. Add the béchamel sauce, and bring to a simmer. Add a bit of the sauce to the heavy cream, and add it to the simmering sauce. Add the cayenne pepper and salt. Serve with boiled brisket of beef, short ribs of beef, or roast beef. Always serve this sauce separately in a saucier (sauceboat).

Note: This sauce can also be flavored just before serving with vinegar and sugar to taste, as in some European countries.

FENNEL SAUCE

Yield: 1 quart

1 MEDIUM SHALLOT, FINELY MINCED
1 TABLESPOON BUTTER
1 TEASPOON CHOPPED FENNEL SEED
½ CUP DRY WHITE WINE
2 CUPS GOOD WHITE VEAL STOCK

2 CUPS HEAVY CREAM
2 TEASPOONS SWEET BUTTER
SALT AND WHITE PEPPER TO TASTE
½ CUP WHIPPED CREAM

❖ Sauté the shallots in the tablespoon of butter until glazed. Add the chopped fennel seed, deglaze the pan with the white wine, and reduce by one-half. Add the veal stock. Bring to boil, then simmer for approximately 30 minutes. Add the heavy cream, and simmer 10 minutes. Whisk in the sweet butter, and salt and pepper. (If a thicker sauce is desired, reduce at this point to the desired consistency. Puree the sauce in a blender, and strain. Fold in the whipped cream just before serving.

WHITE FISH SAUCE (NORMANDE SAUCE)

Yield: 1 pint

10 TABLESPOONS BUTTER
½ CUP FLOUR
1 QUART FISH STOCK

¼ CUP HEAVY CREAM
SALT AND CAYENNE PEPPER TO TASTE

❖ Melt 6 tablespoons of butter in a stainless-steel pot. Add the flour, and make a white roux. Add the fish stock, and simmer for 30 minutes. Strain, and return to a simmer. Add a bit of the hot sauce to the heavy cream, and stir this tempered cream into the simmering sauce. Thinly shave the remaining 4 tablespoons of butter with a knife, and swirl into the sauce. Add flaked butter, season to taste with the salt and cayenne. Serve with poached fish, sautéed shellfish, fish vol-au-vents, or other seafood dishes.

NEWBURG SAUCE

Yield: 1 quart

4 TABLESPOONS BUTTER
⅔ CUP CHOPPED ONIONS OR LEEKS
1 CUP CHOPPED CELERY
¾ CUP DICED CARROTS
2 POUNDS LOBSTER AND SHRIMP
    SHELLS

1 QUART NORMANDE SAUCE (SEE
    PRECEDING RECIPE)
¾ CUP DRY SHERRY WINE
6 TABLESPOONS BRANDY
½ CUP HEAVY CREAM
SALT AND CAYENNE PEPPER TO TASTE

❖ Heat the butter in a saucepan; add the onions, celery, and carrots, and sauté for 5 minutes. Add the covered seafood shells; and sauté until they turn pink/red. Add the normande sauce, and bring to a boil. Reduce the heat and simmer for 30 minutes. Strain, and return to a simmer. Place the sherry and brandy in a small pan, bring to boil; and reduce by two-thirds. Add the spirits to the sauce. Add a bit of the hot sauce to the heavy cream; add this tempered cream to the simmering sauce. Taste and season with salt and cayenne pepper. Serve with poached fish or seafood stew.

LOBSTER SAUCE

Yield: 1 pint

1 TABLESPOON BUTTER
¼ CUP ALL-PURPOSE FLOUR
1½ CUPS HOT WATER

1 TABLESPOON LOBSTER BASE*
½ CUP HOT CREAM
1 TABLESPOON PALE DRY SHERRY

❖ Melt the butter over low heat. Blend in flour, using a wire whip. Stir the roux over low heat for 1 to 2 minutes, until bubbly and well blended. Remove from the heat, and add the hot water gradually, mixing well. Stir in the lobster base. Heat the sauce to boiling, stirring constantly; boil and stir for 1 minute. Add the hot cream and dry sherry, mixing well. Hold in a hot-water bath until ready to serve.

* For information about this base, see the introduction to this chapter.

TOMATO SAUCE

Yield: 1 quart

2 CUPS BOILING WATER
3 TABLESPOONS PASTA N' PIZZA
   SAUCE PREP*

2 TABLESPOONS VEGETABLE
   OR OLIVE OIL
12 OUNCE CANNED TOMATO PASTE

❖ In a medium mixing bowl, combine the water, pasta 'n pizza sauce prep, and oil, mixing well with a wire whisk. Add the tomato paste, and continue to mix until thoroughly blended.

* For information about this sauce prep, see the introduction to this chapter.

TOMATO BASIL SAUCE

Yield: 6 servings

1 TABLESPOON OLIVE OIL
½ CUP FINELY CHOPPED YELLOW
  ONIONS
2 GARLIC CLOVES, PEELED AND CRUSHED
16 OUNCES CANNED ITALIAN PLUM
  TOMATOES, DRAINED AND CHOPPED
1 TEASPOON SALT

1 TEASPOON SUGAR
¼ TEASPOON FRESHLY GROUND
  WHITE PEPPER
3 TABLESPOONS CHOPPED FRESH BASIL
1½ TEASPOONS CORNSTARCH
½ CUP WATER

❖ Heat the olive oil in a saucepan; add the chopped onions, and cook until tender. Add the crushed garlic and tomatoes, and simmer for 5 minutes. Stir in the salt, sugar, pepper, and basil. Mix the cornstarch with the water and slowly add to the tomato mixture. Simmer for 5 minutes, stirring constantly. Remove from the heat, adjust the seasonings, and serve. This sauce is excellent with veal chops.

SAUCE WITH TOMATOES AND GARLIC

Yield: 1 pint

3 TABLESPOONS OIL
¼ CUP FINELY DICED ONIONS
½ CUP PEELED AND CHOPPED
  TOMATOES
3 GARLIC CLOVES, MINCED
1 TEASPOON PAPRIKA

¼ CUP WHITE WINE
1½ CUPS BASIC BROWN SAUCE (SEE
  RECIPE EARLIER IN THIS CHAPTER)
SALT AND BLACK PEPPER TO TASTE
1 TABLESPOON CHOPPED PARSLEY

❖ Heat the oil in a saucepan, add the onions, and sauté for 5 minutes. Add the tomatoes, garlic, and paprika, and continue sautéing for 3 minutes. Add the white wine and brown sauce, and bring to a short boil. Taste, season, and add the parsley. Serve with sautéed chicken or veal, baked fish, eggs en cocotte, omelets, or braised vegetables.

HOLLANDAISE SAUCE

Yield: Approximately 1 pint

1 POUND BUTTER
5 EGG YOLKS
3 TEASPOONS WATER
4 TEASPOONS LEMON JUICE

¼ TEASPOON HOT PEPPER SAUCE
(TABASCO)
¼ TEASPOON WORCESTERSHIRE SAUCE
¼ TEASPOON SALT

✛ Melt the butter over medium heat, and set aside for 10 minutes. Skim and discard the foam from the top, and strain the clear yellow liquid into a bowl, leaving behind the milky particles in the pot. There should be 1½ cups of yellow liquid (clarified butter). Combine the egg yolks, 1½ teaspoons of water, the lemon juice, hot pepper sauce, Worcestershire sauce and salt in a round-bottomed stainless-steel bowl. Set the bowl over a pot of simmering water. Beat the mixture with a wire whip until it thickens and adheres to the whip (do not overcook the eggs). Gradually add the clarified butter ½ cup at a time. After each ½ cup of butter is added, mix in ½ teaspoon of water. Continue until all the butter and water have been used. Adjust seasonings to taste

MOCK HOLLANDAISE SAUCE

Yield: 1 quart

3 CUPS LUKEWARM WATER
1½ OUNCES SAUCE/SOUP THICKENER*
2 TEASPOONS SALT
⅛ TEASPOON CAYENNE PEPPER

2 TABLESPOONS LEMON JUICE
6 DROPS YELLOW FOOD COLORING
8 EGG YOLKS
1 OUNCE BUTTER

✛ In a 2-quart saucepan, combine the lukewarm water, sauce/soup thickener, salt, cayenne pepper, lemon juice, and yellow food coloring with a wire whip. Heat to boiling over medium heat, stirring constantly. Reduce the heat, and simmer for 2 minutes, stirring occasionally. Remove from heat. Beat the egg yolks vigorously in a mixing bowl with a wire whip. Gradually add half of the hot sauce to the beaten yolks while continuing to beat. Add the egg-yolk mixture to the remaining sauce. Bring to a boil, stirring constantly. Reduce the heat, and simmer for 1 minute stirring constantly. Swirl in the butter to finish the sauce.

* For information about this thickener, see the introduction to this chapter.

BÉARNAISE SAUCE

Yield: 2½ cups

2 CUPS HOT HOLLANDAISE SAUCE (SEE
   RECIPE EARLIER IN THIS CHAPTER)
2 TABLESPOONS TARRAGON VINEGAR

⅛ TEASPOON CRUSHED BLACK PEPPER
1 TEASPOON CHOPPED DRY TARRAGON
¼ TEASPOON CRUSHED THYME

❖ Combine all the ingredients, mixing well. Serve over broiled steaks and chops.

PESTO

Yield: 1 pint

2 CUPS FRESH BASIL LEAVES,
   THOROUGHLY WASHED AND
   PATTED DRY
4 LARGE GARLIC CLOVES, PEELED
   AND CHOPPED
½ CUP SHELLED WALNUTS
½ CUP PINE NUTS

1 CUP OLIVE OIL
1 CUP FRESHLY GRATED PARMESAN
   CHEESE
¼ CUP FRESHLY GRATED ROMANO
   CHEESE
SALT AND FRESHLY GROUND PEPPER
   TO TASTE

❖ Combine the basil, garlic, walnuts, and pine nuts in the bowl of a food processor, and chop. With the processor running, add the olive oil in a slow, steady stream. Shut the processor off, add the cheeses, a pinch of salt, and a liberal grinding of pepper. Process briefly to combine; scrape into a bowl, and cover until needed.

Note: If a food processor is unavailable, the recipe can be halved and prepared in a blender.

ASPARAGUS SAUCE

Yield: 3 cups

1 CUP PLUS 2 TABLESPOONS
  MAYONNAISE
9 OUNCES GREEN ASPARAGUS, DICED
1 CUP BEEF CONSOMMÉ

4 EGG YOLKS
SALT, PEPPER, LEMON JUICE, AND
  SUGAR TO TASTE

✤ Mix all the ingredients in a blender for 5 minutes, until an emulsion is formed.

POLYNESIAN BARBECUE SAUCE

Yield: Approximately 1 pint

1¼ CUPS CATSUP
½ CUP FIRMLY PACKED BROWN SUGAR
2 TEASPOONS MOLASSES
1 TEASPOON SOY SAUCE

1½ TEASPOONS CIDER VINEGAR
½ TEASPOON WHOLE CLOVES
4 TEASPOONS CRUSHED PINEAPPLE

✤ Combine the catsup and brown sugar, blending well until all the sugar is dissolved. Stir in the molasses, soy sauce, cider vinegar, and whole cloves; mix with a mixer for 10 minutes. Add the crushed pineapple and mix well.

Note: For more flavor and aroma, add 2 minced garlic cloves and 1 tablespoon hoisin sauce. Refrigerated, this sauce will keep indefinitely.

TERIYAKI STEAK SAUCE

Yield: Approximately 1 pint

1 CUP SOY SAUCE
2 GARLIC CLOVES, CRUSHED
2 TEASPOONS CRUSHED FRESH GINGER

1 TEASPOON CIDER VINEGAR
1⅓ CUPS FIRMLY PACKED BROWN
  SUGAR

✤ Combine the soy sauce, garlic, ginger, and cider vinegar in a mixing bowl. Add the brown sugar slowly, mixing well. Strain and serve. This sauce is excellent with broiled steaks and chicken.

Note: For additional flavor, add 2 tablespoons sweet sakē (Mirin).

COCKTAIL SAUCE

Yield: Approximately 1 pint

½ CUP CATSUP
½ CUP CHILI SAUCE
3 TABLESPOONS HORSERADISH
½ TEASPOON WORCESTERSHIRE SAUCE

¼ TEASPOON HOT PEPPER SAUCE
  (TABASCO)
JUICE OF 1 LEMON
1 TABLESPOON OLIVE OIL

✤ Combine all the ingredients in a bowl; stir well. Refrigerate.

CHAPTER FOUR

Beef

Obtaining optimum tenderness is usually the most important goal in the cooking of any meat. Tenderness is affected by the cooking method used, but other factors, such as the age of the animal, the feed used and the length of time the animal is fed, the location of the cut in the carcass, the amount of marbling in the meat, and the quality grade (prime, choice, select) of the animal are also factors influencing tenderness. Young animals are more tender than older ones; thus, veal is usually more tender than beef. The parts of the carcass that receive more exercise, the forequarters and the hindquarters (the chuck and the round primal cuts), are less tender than the parts of the carcass that get less exercise, the middle part of the carcass (the rib and loin primal cuts).

Preparation is a most important factor in tenderness. The proteins in meat can be divided into two general categories: red skeletal muscle tissue and connective tissue between the muscle fibers. There are two types of connective tissue, collagen and elastin. Collagen is often called the white connective tissue and can be changed by moist-heat cooking into gelatin and water. Adding a bit of acid with the moisture helps speed this change. This is one of the key reasons that stews are cooked in water and meats are braised. Moist-heat cooking over a prolonged period of time breaks down the connective tissue and makes the item tender. The more tender cuts with less connective tissue can be cooked using dry-heat methods, such as broiling or roasting. It is possible, however, to toughen a tender piece of meat by overcooking it or subjecting it to heat that is too high.

The other connective tissue, elastin, often called yellow connective tissue, cannot be changed by cooking. It remains tough. To tenderize meat with a great deal of elastin, the elastin must be broken up by such methods as pounding, cubing, or grinding. Another way of destroying elastin is to add a meat tenderizer containing an enzyme such as papain (derived from papaya), which actually dissolves the connective tissue. "Tenderized steaks" are examples of meat tenderized with enzymes.

Retention of flavor and moisture in meats is also very important. Animal flesh is composed of a large percentage of water. If the moisture—the juices—are lost in cooking, much of the flavor is also lost. Unfortunately, the old belief that high heat sears meat and thus locks in the juices is not true. Searing can add a desirable flavor by carmelizing some of the outer surface, but scientific tests show that high heat actually causes meat to lose more moisture than low heat does. An exception is broiling, which is done at a high temperature but for a short period of time, which reduces moisture loss.

The flavor of meat comes from the flesh as well as the fat. Fat can also help contribute moistness to meat. Meat that is well marbled tends to be more moist than leaner meats. Roast meats, such as sirloin or rib roasts, should be cooked with the fat side up, so that the fat melts in cooking and runs down over the meat, thus basting it. Because fat is high in calories and excess consumption can increase the risk of heart disease, much of it is often trimmed prior to cooking.

Beef is typically cooked rare to medium; pork and veal, well-done; and lamb, medium or medium rare. Meat is considered rare at 125°F, medium at 140 to 160°F, and well-done at 170°F. To determine degree of doneness of roast meat, insert a meat thermometer into the deepest part of the meat, being careful not to touch any bone. The meat should be removed from the oven a short time before it reaches the desired temperature, as it will continue to cook somewhat after it is removed from the heat. For example, if a rib roast is to be served rare to medium rare, it should be taken out of the oven at about 130°F; as it sets up, it will reach the desired internal temperature. The roast should be allowed to set or rest in a warm place for fifteen to twenty minutes before carving. This procedure will firm the roast, retain more of its juices, and make it easier to carve. When carving, always carve against the grain for optimum tenderness.

Nutritionally, beef is comparable to other protein sources in calories, cholesterol, protein, and fat content, and lean beef fits easily into a well-balanced diet. Beef and other red meats are nutrient-dense foods: they supply a large amount of necessary nutrients without a lot of calories. Beef, pork, and lamb are some of the best sources of iron, zinc, B vitamins, and protein in the diet.

Beef

PEPPERED STRIP STEAK

SIRLOIN STEAK BRITTANY

BEEF FUNGHETTO

BEEF SIRLOIN TIPS, ESTONIAN STYLE

ORIENTAL BEEF STIR-FRY

STEAK DIANE WITH WILD RICE

TOURNEDOS ROSSINI

TOURNEDOS ALEXANDER

BEEF À LA DEUTSCH

BEEF TENDERLOIN À LA BLACKSTONE

BEEF BEACHCOMBER

CARBONNADE OF BEEF TENDERLOIN

STEAK VALEZ

PEPPERED RIB-EYE

MARINATED FLANK STEAK

STUFFED FLANK STEAK

BEEF TENDERLOIN POINTS MARINATED WITH
LAUREL LEAVES

GLAZED CORNED BEEF

BRAISED STEAK

BRAISED BEEF, PIEMONTESE STYLE

SHORT RIBS OF BEEF

HUNGARIAN BEEF GOULASH

BEEF STROGANOFF, COUNTRY STYLE

BEEF ROULADES BOURGUIGNONNE

SAUERBRATEN

BEEF BRISKET WITH HERB MUSTARD SAUCE

CHILI CON CARNE

ALL-PURPOSE MEATBALLS

BEEF AND MACARONI WITH TOMATOES

MEAT LOAF

PEPPERED STRIP STEAK

Yield: 6 servings

6 CHOICE-GRADE STRIP STEAKS,
  8 OUNCES EACH
1½ TEASPOONS SALT
1 TABLESPOON CRUSHED BLACK
  PEPPERCORNS
2 TABLESPOONS BUTTER, MELTED
2 TABLESPOONS FINELY CHOPPED
  SHALLOTS

1 TABLESPOON SPICED BUTTER (SEE
  RECIPE BELOW)
1½ TEASPOONS LEMON JUICE
1½ CUPS RED WINE
¾ TEASPOON WORCESTERSHIRE SAUCE
½ CUP BRANDY

✤ Season the steaks with the salt and pepper. Pan-fry the steak in the butter. Pour off the excess butter. Add the shallots and sauté but do not brown; Add the spiced butter, lemon juice, wine, and Worcestershire. Bring to a boil, and reduce by one-third. Remove the steaks to serving plates, pour the sauce over them, sprinkle with the brandy, flame, and serve.

SPICED BUTTER
¼ CUP BUTTER
⅜ TEASPOON GROUND PEPPER
1 TEASPOON CHOPPED CHIVES

¾ TEASPOON CHOPPED SHALLOTS
1/16 TEASPOON CHOPPED GARLIC

✤ Combine all the ingredients. This recipe yields about 4 tablespoons.

SIRLOIN STEAK BRITTANY

Yield: 4 servings

6 TABLESPOONS OLIVE OIL
4 SIRLOIN STEAKS, 8 OUNCES EACH
2 TEASPOONS SEASONED SALT
2 CUPS SLICED MUSHROOMS
1 TEASPOON CHOPPED SHALLOTS
1 TEASPOON CHOPPED GARLIC
¾ CUP BEEF CONSOMMÉ

½ CUP MADEIRA
½ CUP BRANDY
¾ CUP HEAVY CREAM
1½ OUNCES BUTTER
2 TEASPOONS CHOPPED PARSLEY
4 WATERCRESS SPRIGS

❖ Heat the olive oil in a pan until almost smoking. Add the sirloin steaks, and brown as desired. Sprinkle the steaks with the seasoned salt, and remove from the pan. Lightly sauté the mushrooms, shallots, and garlic in the same pan. Add the consommé, Madeira, and brandy, and reduce to the desired consistency. Add the heavy cream, return the steaks to the sauce, and heat briefly. Add the butter, stirring until melted. Serve immediately, garnished with parsley and watercress.

BEEF FUNGHETTO

Yield: 6 servings

6 SIRLOIN STEAKS, 6 OUNCES EACH
¼ CUP BUTTER
24 WHOLE PEELED CANNED ONIONS
PINCH OF CHOPPED GARLIC
1 CUP BURGUNDY WINE

2 CUPS CANNED CONDENSED
   MUSHROOM SOUP
1½ CUPS HALF-AND-HALF CREAM
2 TEASPOONS CHOPPED PARSLEY

❖ Pound the steaks until thin. Heat the butter in a sauté pan over high heat until bubbly and foaming. Sauté the steaks on both sides to the desired degree of doneness, about 4 to 5 minutes (medium rare is recommended). Add the onions, garlic, wine, mushroom soup, cream, and parsley. Swirl all the ingredients together, and serve immediately.

BEEF SIRLOIN TIPS, ESTONIAN STYLE

6 servings

2 POUNDS BEEF SIRLOIN TIPS
SALT AND BLACK PEPPER TO TASTE
FLOUR FOR DREDGING
½ CUP SOFT BUTTER
1 ONION, DICED
¼ CUP DICED SHALLOTS
1 CUP DICED MUSHROOMS
2 TABLESPOONS TOMATO PASTE

1 TEASPOON HOT MUSTARD
½ CUP WHITE WINE
½ CUP DEMI-GLACE (SEE RECIPE IN
   CHAPTER 3)
2 CUPS WHIPPING CREAM, REDUCED TO
   1 CUP
   OR 1 CUP SOUR CREAM
¼ TEASPOON NUTMEG

(continued)

✤ Dredge the beef in the flour, salt, and pepper. Heat half of the butter in a heavy skillet, and quickly sauté the beef in it until brown. Set aside. In a separate pan, sauté the onions, shallots, and mushrooms in the remaining butter for 4 to 5 minutes. Add the tomato paste, mustard, wine, and demi-glace. Add the beef, and cook until heated through. Finish by swirling in the cream and nutmeg. This dish goes well with rice or noodles.

ORIENTAL BEEF STIR-FRY

Yield: 4 servings

2 TEASPOONS BUTTER
1 POUND BEEF SIRLOIN TIPS
2 CUPS JULIENNE OF CELERY
1½ CUPS JULIENNE OF ONIONS
½ CUP CHOPPED GREEN PEPPERS
½ CUP SLICED MUSHROOMS
1 CUP SLICED CARROTS

½ CUP SLICED WATER CHESTNUTS
½ CUP SOY SAUCE
1 TEASPOON MINCED GARLIC
1 TEASPOON MINCED OREGANO
¼ CUP FLOUR
1 CUP BEEF BROTH
SALT AND PEPPER TO TASTE

✤ Melt the butter in a wok or skillet. Add the beef and sauté until brown; remove and keep warm. Add the celery, onions, peppers, mushrooms, carrots, water chestnuts, soy sauce, garlic, and oregano. Sauté until the vegetables are tender-crisp. Stir in the flour, and sauté for 1 minute. Add the beef broth. Return the meat to the pan and bring to a short boil. Taste, and season as needed.

STEAK DIANE WITH WILD RICE

Yield: 6 servings

6 CUPS COOKED WILD RICE (SEE NOTE
    BELOW)
9 OUNCES BUTTER
SALT AND PEPPER TO TASTE
18 ROUNDED SLICES OF BEEF
    TENDERLOIN 2 OUNCES EACH

3 TABLESPOONS CHOPPED SHALLOTS
1½ CUPS FRESH SLICED MUSHROOMS
⅔ CUP SHERRY
¾ CUP BROWN SAUCE (SEE RECIPE IN
    CHAPTER 3)
¼ CUP BRANDY

❖ Sauté the precooked wild rice in 3 ounces of the butter with salt and pepper. Set aside.

Melt 6 tablespoons of the butter in a frying pan or chafing dish. When hot, cook the tenderloin slices until brown on both sides. Remove the beef from the pan, and place it atop the wild rice. Add the remaining 6 tablespoons of butter, chopped shallots, sliced mushrooms, and sherry to the frying pan. Cook until the mushrooms are tender. Add the sauce, and reduce by one-quarter. Pour the mushrooms over the sliced steak. In the same frying pan, pour the brandy, and ignite when hot. Pour the flaming brandy over the steak and serve.

Note: A combination of white and wild rice can be substituted. Chopped scallions can also be added with the wild rice when sautéing.

TOURNEDOS ROSSINI

Yield: 4 servings

4 BEEF FILETS, 4 TO 5 OUNCES EACH
¼ CUP BUTTER
4 PIECES TOAST, TRIMMED OF CRUSTS
1 SLICE PÂTÉ DE STRASBOURG (FOIE
  GRAS) ⅛ INCH THICK, CUT INTO
  4 SQUARES (SEE NOTE BELOW)

1 TEASPOON CHOPPED SHALLOTS
1 TABLESPOON CHOPPED TRUFFLES
⅔ CUP SHERRY
1 CUP BROWN GRAVY

❖ Sauté the filets in the butter until cooked to the desired degree of doneness. Place the filets (also known as tournedos) on the toast. Top the tournedos with the foie gras. Using the same pan, slightly braise the shallots; add the truffles and sherry, and reduce by half. Add the brown gravy; simmer for few minutes. Pour the sauce over the tournedos, and serve.

Note: Commercial goose-liver pâté can also be used.

TOURNEDOS ALEXANDER

Yield: 6 servings

12 BABY CARROTS, PEELED
12 BABY CORNS
12 NEW POTATOES
1 CUP BABY GREEN BEANS
12 BUTTON MUSHROOMS, SAUTÉED IN
  BUTTER
6 FILETS OF BEEF, 6 OUNCES EACH
SALT AND FRESHLY GROUND PEPPER TO
  TASTE

2 TABLESPOONS OIL
2 TABLESPOONS CABERNET SAUVIGNON
2 CUPS DEMI-GLACE (SEE RECIPE IN
  CHAPTER 3; ALSO, SEE NOTE BELOW)
1 TABLESPOON CHOPPED FRESH
  TARRAGON
6 TABLESPOONS SWEET BUTTER

✤ Steam the carrots, corn, potatoes, green beans, and mushrooms until tender-crisp. Cool in ice water, drain, and pat dry. Season the filets. Heat the oil in a sauté pan, add the beef, and sauté to the desired degree of doneness. Remove the meat from the pan; keep warm. Degrease the pan, deglaze with the Cabernet Sauvignon. Add the demi-glace, tarragon, and 2 tablespoons of the sweet butter. Shake the pan to swirl in the butter. Heat the vegetables and mushrooms in the remaining ¼ cup (4 tablespoons) of butter, and season. Place the meat in the middle of a plate and surround with the vegetables. Spoon the sauce over the meat, and serve.

Note: The demi-glace can be replaced with commercial beef gravy or Minor's Espagnole Sauce made according to label instructions.

BEEF À LA DEUTSCH

Yield: 6 servings

2 POUNDS BEEF TENDERLOIN,
  WELL-TRIMMED
4 TABLESPOONS BUTTER
½ TEASPOON SALT
1 TEASPOON PAPRIKA
2 MEDIUM ONIONS, CUT INTO ½ TO
  ¾-INCH DICE
2 GREEN PEPPERS, DICED

8 OUNCES FRESH MUSHROOMS, WASHED
  AND SLICED ¼ INCH THICK
4 TABLESPOONS BROWN SAUCE
  (ESPAGNOLE) BASE*
1⅔ CUPS LUKEWARM WATER
⅓ CUP RED BURGUNDY WINE
COOKED RICE OR NOODLES

✤ Cut the tenderloin lengthwise with the grain into 1-inch strips. Then cut crosswise, across the grain, into slices about ¼ inch wide by 1½ to 2 inches long. In a large heavy skillet, melt 2 tablespoons of the butter over medium-high heat. Add the tenderloin strips, tossing until well coated with butter. Sprinkle the salt and paprika evenly over the meat. Sauté and stir until browned, about 5 to 10 minutes. Remove the meat from the pan and set aside.

In the same skillet, melt the remaining 2 tablespoons of butter over medium-high heat. Add the onions, green peppers, and mushrooms. Sauté, stirring until tender-crisp, about 7 to 10 minutes. Remove from the heat and set aside.

In a 1-quart saucepan, blend the brown sauce base with a small amount of lukewarm water, using a wire whisk to make a smooth paste. Mix in the remaining water and Burgundy. Heat to boiling over medium heat, stirring constantly. Reduce the heat, and simmer for 5 minutes, stirring occasionally.

Combine the sautéed vegetables with the beef and the Burgundy brown sauce. Simmer for 5 minutes over medium heat, stirring occasionally. Serve hot over rice or noodles.

* For information about this base, see chapter 3.

BEEF TENDERLOIN À LA BLACKSTONE

Yield: 8 servings

2½ POUNDS BEEF TENDERLOIN, SLICED
2 TABLESPOONS SALAD OIL
2 TABLESPOONS BUTTER
1 GREEN PEPPER, SLICED IN JULIENNE
1 ONION, THINLY SLICED
½ POUND MUSHROOMS, SLICED
1 GARLIC CLOVE, FINELY CHOPPED

1 CUP CANNED TOMATOES
1 CUP BROWN GRAVY
½ CUP MADEIRA OR SHERRY WINE
SALT AND PEPPER TO TASTE
2 POUNDS NOODLES, COOKED AND
 BUTTERED

✤ In a skillet, sauté the beef in the oil until rare; remove the beef and set aside. To the same skillet, add the butter, peppers, onions, mushrooms, and garlic, and sauté until tender but not brown. Add the tomatoes, brown gravy, wine, and beef, and bring to a boil. Season. Remove, and serve over the hot buttered noodles.

BEEF BEACHCOMBER

Yield: 4 servings

1 TEASPOON SALT
PINCH OF WHITE PEPPER
½ TABLESPOON SOY SAUCE
¼ CUP SHERRY WINE
14 OUNCES FLANK STEAK, THINLY
   SLICED
2 TABLESPOONS OIL
1 TEASPOON MINCED FRESH GINGER

2 TABLESPOONS CHOPPED WHITE
   ONIONS
½ FRESH PINEAPPLE, CUT INTO CHUNKS
3 OUNCES ALMONDS, SLICED AND
   TOASTED
4 OUNCES FRESH PEAPODS
2 TABLESPOONS CORNSTARCH
¼ CUP BEEF BROTH

✤ Combine the salt, pepper, soy sauce, and sherry. Pour over the sliced flank steak, and marinate for approximately 30 minutes. Remove the meat from the marinade, and place on paper towels to dry. Reserve the marinade. Heat the oil in a frying pan. When very hot, add the ginger and onions, and cook for 1 minute; then add the meat and sauté briefly. Add the pineapple, almonds, and peapods at once. Simmer for a minute, then pour in the marinade. Dissolve the cornstarch in the beef broth, stir in, and cook for an additional 2 to 3 minutes. Serve at once over fluffy rice.

CARBONNADE OF BEEF TENDERLOIN

Yield: 6 servings

2 TABLESPOONS OIL
½ CUP BUTTER
1 POUND ONIONS, THINLY SLICED
1 TABLESPOON CHOPPED GARLIC
6 TABLESPOONS FLOUR

SALT AND PEPPER TO TASTE
1 TABLESPOON MARJORAM
1 PINT BEER
2½ POUNDS BEEF TENDERLOIN, CUBED

✤ Heat 1 tablespoon of the oil and 3 tablespoons of the butter in a sauté pan, add the onions and garlic, and sauté until translucent; set aside. Combine the flour, salt, pepper, and marjoram and dredge the cubed meat in the flour mixture. Heat the remaining tablespoon of oil and 3 tablespoons of butter in another sauté pan, and brown the meat. Add the onions and garlic; mix together, and sauté for 2 minutes. And the beer, and simmer for 3 minutes. Knead the remaining 2 tablespoons of butter with the flour to make a smooth paste. Add to the pan, and cook for 5 to 7 minutes. Serve with boiled potatoes sprinkled with chives.

STEAK VALEZ

Yield: 6 servings

6 STRIP SIRLOIN STEAKS, 5 OUNCES
    EACH
6 GARLIC CLOVES, FINELY CHOPPED
¾ CUP BUTTER
1 TEASPOON SALT

½ TEASPOON FRESHLY GROUND BLACK
    PEPPER
6 MEDIUM ONIONS, CUT INTO RINGS
3 TABLESPOONS CIDER VINEGAR

❖ Rub the steaks with the garlic. Heat the butter in a skillet, add the steaks, and sauté to the desired degree of doneness. Remove from the pan and season with salt and pepper. Sauté onions in the same pan, until translucent. Return the meat to the pan. Top with the onions. When hot, pour in vinegar, ignite, and serve.

PEPPERED RIB-EYE

Yield: 8 servings

1 RIB-EYE STEAK, 5 TO 6 POUNDS
½ CUP COARSELY CRACKED BLACK
    PEPPER
½ TEASPOON GROUND CARDAMOM
1 CUP SOY SAUCE
¾ CUP WHITE VINEGAR

1 GARLIC CLOVE, MINCED
1 TABLESPOON TOMATO PASTE
1 TEASPOON PAPRIKA
2 CUPS BEEF STOCK, SEASONED
1 TABLESPOON CORNSTARCH

(continued)

✧ Trim the fat from the steak. Combine the cracked black pepper and the cardamom and sprinkle over the steak. Combine the soy sauce, vinegar, garlic, tomato paste, and paprika to make a marinade. Place the steak in a shallow dish, and cover with the marinade. Cover the dish, and chill in the refrigerator for 24 hours, basting the steak occasionally with the marinade.

Remove the meat from the refrigerator; drain and reserve the marinade. Let the meat stand at room temperature for 1 hour. Wrap meat securely in foil, place it in a roasting pan, and roast in a 325°F oven for 1 hour. Remove from the oven. Open the foil, and drain and reserve the juices. Raise the oven temperature to 400°F, and brown the rib-eye, uncovered, for 10 minutes. Remove the steak from the oven, place on a serving platter, and keep warm.

Skim the fat from the reserved pan juices, combine the pan juices with ¼ cup of the reserved marinade, and add the beef stock. Heat. Mix the cornstarch with a small amount of water, and add to the simmering stock. Simmer for 2 minutes, or until clear. Remove from the heat and serve the sauce with the sliced steak.

MARINATED FLANK STEAK

Yield: 4 servings

¾ CUP DRY RED WINE	1½ POUNDS FLANK STEAK, TRIMMED
4 TEASPOONS SOY SAUCE	SALT AND BLACK PEPPER, TO TASTE
¼ TEASPOON DRIED OREGANO	1 OUNCE BEEF BASE*
¼ TEASPOON DRIED SWEET BASIL	1 PINT HOT WATER
½ TEASPOON DRIED ROSEMARY	8 SLICES RYE BREAD
¼ TEASPOON DRIED THYME	2 TABLESPOONS BUTTER, MELTED

✧ Combine the red wine, soy sauce, oregano, sweet basil, rosemary, thyme, salt, and pepper to make a marinade. Add the flank steak, making sure it is entirely covered with the marinade. Marinate for 12 hours or overnight.

Remove the flank steak from the marinade, and broil for about 4 minutes on each side (flank steak should be pink in the center). Slice the broiled steak into thin slices at a sharp angle across the grain. Strain the marinade mixture, discarding the herbs. Mix together the beef base, hot water, and strained marinade. Bring to a boil, and remove from the heat; keep warm. Toast the rye bread slices, and butter evenly. Place two slices of toasted rye bread on each serving plate. Place the sliced flank steak evenly atop the toasted rye bread on each plate. Ladle ¼ cup of the marinade sauce evenly over the steak slices, and serve.

* For information about this base, see chapter 3.

STUFFED FLANK STEAK

Yield: 8 servings

2 POUNDS FLANK STEAK
SALT AND PEPPER TO TASTE
3 TABLESPOONS BUTTER
4 OUNCES ONIONS, DICED
2 GARLIC CLOVES, MINCED
4 OUNCES CARROTS, DICED
2 OUNCES CELERY, DICED
1 OUNCE ITALIAN PARSLEY, MINCED
4 OUNCES SMALL MUSHROOMS, THINLY
   SLICED

4 OUNCES COOKED HAM, DICED
THYME TO TASTE
2 EGGS, LIGHTLY BEATEN
4 OUNCES BREADCRUMBS
½ CUP RED WINE
2 CUPS BEEF STOCK
¾ CUP HEAVY CREAM

❖ Lay the flank steak flat on a cutting board. With a sharp knife, slice the flank "butterfly" style, being careful not to leave any holes. Pound the steak gently with a mallet until it is evenly flattened. Season the meat, and refrigerate.

Heat the butter in a sauté pan, add the onions, garlic, carrots, celery, parsley, mushrooms, and ham, and sauté until lightly cooked. Place the mixture in a bowl. Add salt, pepper, thyme, and eggs. Add the breadcrumbs a bit at a time, adding only enough to hold the mixture together. The stuffing should be smooth and moist.

Remove the steak from the refrigerator. Spread the stuffing evenly over the meat. Carefully roll the meat into a cylinder, and tie it gently with butcher's twine. Season with salt and pepper. Place in a roasting pan, and roast in a 350°F oven for about 1 hour, until the meat reaches an internal temperature of 140°F.

Remove the meat from the pan and keep warm. Deglaze the pan with the red wine. Add the beef stock, cream, and salt and pepper. Simmer until thickened to the desired consistency. Slice the roast thinly, and serve with the hot sauce.

BEEF TENDERLOIN POINTS MARINATED WITH LAUREL LEAVES

Yield: 4 servings

½ CUP OLIVE OIL
¼ CUP SALAD OIL
¼ CUP RED-WINE VINEGAR
1½ TEASPOONS KOSHER OR SEA SALT
1 TEASPOON FRESHLY GROUND BLACK
  PEPPER
¾ TEASPOON OREGANO
4 GARLIC CLOVES, FINELY CHOPPED

2 POUNDS BEEF TENDERLOIN TAILS, CUT
  INTO 1¼-INCH CUBES
2 BAY LEAVES
5 ONIONS, QUARTERED LENGTHWISE
½ CUP WHITE WINE
½ CUP BÉARNAISE SAUCE (SEE RECIPE
  IN CHAPTER 3)
CHOPPED PARSLEY TO GARNISH

❖ Combine the oils, vinegar, salt, pepper, oregano, and garlic in a shallow glass pan. Add the beef and 1 bay leaf. Refrigerate, covered, for 24 hours. When ready to assemble the brochettes, simmer the onions and remaining bay leaf in the white wine, covered, for 2 to 3 minutes. On four 10-inch skewers, string pieces of onion and marinated beef. Broil 3 to 4 inches from the heat to the desired degree of doneness, brushing with the marinade while cooking. To serve, top with béarnaise sauce or hot butter, and sprinkle with chopped parsley.

Note: For eye appeal and flavor, simmer chunks of red and green peppers with the onions, and add to the skewers.

GLAZED CORNED BEEF

Yield: 6 servings

3 POUNDS CORNED BEEF
1 CUP ORANGE MARMALADE

4 TABLESPOONS DIJON-STYLE MUSTARD
4 TABLESPOONS BROWN SUGAR

❖ Place the corned beef in a large pot, and cover with boiling water. Bring to a boil, reduce the heat, cover partially, and simmer as slowly as possible for about 3 hours, until very tender when tested with a fork. Remove the meat from the pot, and drain.

Preheat the oven to 350°F. Mix marmalade, mustard, and sugar together in a small bowl. Place the corned beef in a baking dish, and pour the marmalade mixture over it, coating it thoroughly. Bake the corned beef for 30 minutes, until the glaze is crisp and brown. Serve hot or at room temperature.

BRAISED STEAK

Yield: 8 servings

8 SWISS STEAKS, 5 OUNCES EACH
SALT AND PEPPER, TO TASTE
1 CUP FLOUR
½ CUP VEGETABLE OIL
1 LARGE ONION, DICED
1 CELERY STALK, SLICED
1 LARGE CARROT, PEELED AND SLICED
¾ CUP DRY WHITE WINE (CHABLIS OR
    SIMILAR)

2 CUPS BEEF STOCK OR CANNED BEEF
    CONSOMMÉ
PINCH OF MARJORAM
PINCH OF THYME
1 BAY LEAF
1 GARLIC CLOVE, FINELY CHOPPED
1 CUP SOUR CREAM
½ CUP CHOPPED FRESH PARSLEY

❖ Season the steaks with salt and pepper. Dredge the seasoned steaks in the flour, shaking off any excess flour. Heat the vegetable oil in a large skillet over medium heat. Add the steaks, and brown on both sides. Transfer the steaks to an ovenproof baking dish.

Add the onions, celery, and carrots to the same skillet; sauté for a few minutes. Deglaze the skillet with the white wine, scratching the bottom of the skillet. Pour the wine and sautéed vegetables over the meat in the baking dish. Add the beef stock, marjoram, thyme, bay leaf, and garlic. Cover the dish tightly, and braise the meat in a 325°F oven for about 2 hours, until tender. Remove from the oven, place the meat on a serving platter, and keep hot.

Strain the braising liquid into a saucepan, add the sour cream, and adjust the seasonings. Bring to a boil, and remove from the heat immediately. Pour the sauce over the steaks. Sprinkle with the parsley, and serve at once.

BRAISED BEEF, PIEMONTESE STYLE

Yield: 10 servings

4½ POUNDS BEEF SIRLOIN
3½ TABLESPOONS OIL
⅓ CUP DICED ONIONS
⅓ CUP DICED CELERY
⅓ CUP DICED CARROTS
¼ CUP DICED BACON
3½ TABLESPOONS TOMATO PUREE

2 TEASPOONS SALT
½ TEASPOON PEPPER
1 CUP RED WINE
1 QUART BEEF STOCK
1 TABLESPOON CORNSTARCH (OPTIONAL)
¼ CUP MADEIRA WINE

(continued)

❖ Heat the oil in a large sauté pan, add the sirloin, and brown it. Remove and set aside. Add the onions, celery, carrots, and bacon, and brown. Add the tomato puree, salt, and pepper. Deglaze the pan with the red wine. Reduce the liquid until syrupy. Add the beef stock and browned sirloin. Cover the pan, and braise the meat for 45 minutes to 1 hour until tender, turning occasionally. Remove the meat from the pan. Reduce the sauce to the desired consistency, or if desired, bind with cornstarch. Strain, and skim the fat. Add the Madeira wine. Cover the meat, and pour a small quantity of the sauce over the meat before serving; serve the remaining sauce separately.

SHORT RIBS OF BEEF

Yield: 4 servings

4 SHORT RIBS, ¾ POUND EACH	3 CUPS WATER
½ CUP BUTTER	2 CUPS RED WINE
2 ONIONS, DICED	2 BAY LEAVES
2 CARROTS, CHOPPED	2 CUPS TOMATO PUREE
1 CELERY STALK, CHOPPED	2 FRESH TOMATOES, CHOPPED
2 GARLIC CLOVES, MINCED	SALT AND PEPPER TO TASTE
½ CUP FLOUR	

❖ In a 400°F oven, roast the short ribs for about 15 minutes, until well browned.

In a separate pan, heat the butter, and add the onions, carrots, celery, and garlic, and sauté until brown. Add the flour, and cook for 2 minutes. Add the water, wine, bay leaves, tomato puree, and tomatoes. Bring to a boil, stirring constantly. Skim off any scum that rises to the top. Add the short ribs, cover, and cook slowly on top of the stove for about 2 hours. (When a fork is plunged into the meat and comes out clean, the meat is fully cooked.)

Remove the meat, and set aside, keeping warm. Skim the fat from the sauce, and strain. Rectify the seasonings; if necessary, strengthen the flavor by reducing until the desired taste is achieved. Serve with a garniture of cooked carrots, onions, mushrooms, and green peas.

HUNGARIAN BEEF GOULASH

Yield: 8 to 10 servings

5 TABLESPOONS SHORTENING
5 POUNDS LEAN TOP ROUND BEEF, CUT
   INTO 1½-INCH CUBES
4 MEDIUM ONIONS, FINELY CHOPPED
3 GARLIC CLOVES, FINELY CHOPPED
4 TABLESPOONS HUNGARIAN PAPRIKA
¼ CUP FLOUR
1½ QUARTS BEEF STOCK OR WATER
   (PREFERABLY HOT)

2 TABLESPOONS SALT
1 BAY LEAF
16 OUNCES CANNED TOMATO SAUCE
1 BOUQUET GARNI: 6–8 CARROT STICKS,
   3 SMALL RIBS OF CELERY, AND
   PARSLEY STEMS, ALL TIED TOGETHER
   WITH STRING

❖ Melt the shortening in saucepan, add the cubed meat, and brown slightly. Add the finely chopped onions, and stew for about 10 minutes. Add the garlic and paprika, and cook, stirring, for 2 minutes. Add the flour, mixing well. Add half (3 cups) the stock or water, stir well to incorporate, and add the remaining liquid. Bring to a boil, add the salt, bay leaf, tomato sauce, and bouquet garni. Cook slowly for about 2½ hours, until the meat is well done. Stir occasionally while cooking, and skim off any grease or foam that accumulates on top. Correct the seasoning. Remove and discard the bay leaf and bouquet garni. Serve with noodles, boiled potatoes, potato pancakes, or spaetzle.

BEEF STROGANOFF, COUNTRY STYLE

Yield: 8 servings

1 GARLIC CLOVE, MINCED
1 CUP CHOPPED ONIONS
6 TABLESPOONS BUTTER
½ CUP FLOUR
1 PINT HOT BEEF STOCK
2½ POUNDS TOP ROUND OR
   TENDERLOIN OF BEEF, CUT IN ¼"- BY
   ½- BY 2-INCH STRIPS

8 OUNCES MUSHROOMS, SLICED (ABOUT
   2⅓ CUPS)
10 OUNCES RIPE BLACK OLIVES, SLICED
⅔ CUP TOMATO PASTE
1 TABLESPOON DILL WEED
1¼ CUPS SOUR CREAM
2 TABLESPOONS BRANDY

(continued)

❖ Sauté the garlic and onions in the butter until translucent. Add the flour, and cook for 5 minutes. Add the hot beef stock. In a separate pan, brown the beef. Add the browned beef, mushrooms, olives, and tomato paste to the beef stock mixture. Cook for 15 minutes. Add the dill weed, sour cream, and brandy. Cook for 10 minutes. Serve with buttered noodles.

BEEF ROULADES BOURGUIGNONNE

Yield: 6 servings

6 ROUND STEAK SLICES, 6 OUNCES
   EACH
2 TABLESPOONS MUSTARD
6 SLICES SMOKED BACON
3 DILL PICKLES
1 ONION
6 TABLESPOONS OIL OR MARGARINE

8 OUNCES CANNED TOMATO PUREE
1 CUP RED WINE
1½ TEASPOONS SALT
¼ TEASPOON PEPPER
1 TEASPOON SUGAR
2 CUPS BEEF STOCK
3 TEASPOONS FLOUR

❖ Lay out the meat slices, and pound to ¼-inch thickness. Spread 1 teaspoon of mustard on each slice. Dice the bacon, pickles, and onion finely, and mix. Spoon this mixture along the length of each meat slice, roll, and secure with toothpicks or twine.

Heat the oil or margarine in a deep skillet. Add the roulades, and brown on all sides. Remove the meat from the skillet and set aside; keep warm. Add the tomato puree, salt, pepper, and sugar to the skillet. Sauté for 2 minutes. Add the wine; bring to a simmer. Place the roulades in the sauce. Add the stock, and simmer for 1 hour, until the meat is tender.

Remove the meat from the sauce; set aside and keep warm. Thicken the sauce with the flour; cook for 3 minutes. Taste and adjust the seasoning. Serve the meat and sauce on pasta.

SAUERBRATEN

Yield: 10 servings

1 ONION, SLICED
1 CARROT, COARSELY CHOPPED
1 CUP COARSELY CHOPPED CELERY
2 CUPS BURGUNDY WINE
1 TEASPOON SALT
1 BAY LEAF
½ TEASPOON CRUSHED PEPPERCORNS
7 CUPS WARM WATER

5 POUNDS TOP ROUND BEEF
¼ CUP OIL
6 OUNCES BROWN SAUCE PREP*
1 SLICE PUMPERNICKEL BREAD, TORN
  INTO PIECES
1 OUNCE GINGERSNAPS, CRUSHED
2 OUNCES TOMATO PASTE

❖ Combine the onions, carrots, celery, wine, salt, bay leaf, peppercorns, and 1 cup of water to make a marinade. Add the beef, and marinate for three days in the refrigerator, turning once every day.

Remove the meat from the marinade. Heat the oil, and brown the meat. Add the marinade, including the vegetables. Cook for 2 hours, covered, until the meat is tender. Remove the meat, and let rest for 15 minutes, then slice thinly and keep hot.

Blend the remaining 6 cups of water with the brown sauce prep, mixing well. Add to the marinade, stirring well. Add the bread, gingersnaps, and tomato paste, and bring to a boil. Reduce the heat, and simmer for 30 minutes. Strain the sauce, taste, and adjust the seasonings. Serve hot over the sliced beef.

* For information about this preparation, see chapter 3.

BEEF BRISKET WITH HERB MUSTARD SAUCE

Yield: 8 servings

¼ CUP VEGETABLE OIL
3 TO 4 POUNDS BEEF BRISKET, TRIMMED
2 CUPS BEEF STOCK OR CANNED BEEF
  BROTH
½ CUP TOMATO PASTE
¼ TEASPOON DRY TARRAGON
PINCH OF GROUND THYME

1 BAY LEAF
SALT AND PEPPER TO TASTE
2 TABLESPOONS FLOUR
2 TABLESPOONS CORNSTARCH
½ CUP DRY WHITE WINE
2 TABLESPOONS PREPARED MUSTARD
2 TABLESPOONS BUTTER

(continued)

❖ In a large skillet, heat 2 tablespoons of the oil, add the brisket, and brown on all sides. Remove the meat to a heavy saucepan. Add the beef stock, tomato paste, tarragon, thyme, bay leaf, salt, and pepper to the skillet; mix well. Pour the mixture over the meat. Cover and cook over low heat for 2½ hours, until the meat is tender. Remove the meat, and keep warm.

Combine the flour and cornstarch. Combine the white wine and mustard, and dissolve the flour/cornstarch mixture in it. Slowly add the starch mixture to the cooking liquid, stirring constantly. Simmer for 10 minutes. (If the sauce is too thick, add a little beef stock.) Swirl in the butter, and adjust the seasonings.

Slice the meat across the grain. Place on a serving platter, and pour the sauce over.

CHILI CON CARNE

Yield: 4 quarts

3 POUNDS GROUND CHUCK OR LEAN
   BEEF
1½ CUPS CHOPPED ONIONS
½ CUP ALL-PURPOSE FLOUR
2 TABLESPOONS CHILI POWDER
½ TEASPOON CHILI PEPPER
28 OUNCES CANNED CRUSHED
   TOMATOES IN PUREE (SEE NOTE
   BELOW)

3½ CUPS HOT WATER
60 OUNCES CANNED KIDNEY BEANS,
   DRAINED
1 TABLESPOON SUGAR
4 TABLESPOONS BEEF BASE*
SALT TO TASTE

❖ In a heavy 8-quart stockpot over medium heat, cook and stir the ground beef and onions until the beef is browned, about 10 to 15 minutes. Stir in the flour, chili powder, and chili pepper. Remove from the heat. Add the crushed tomatoes, hot water, drained kidney beans, sugar, and beef base, mixing well. Add salt if desired. Bring to a boil, reduce the heat, and gently simmer for 25 to 30 minutes. Serve hot in individual casseroles.

Note: The crushed tomatoes in puree may be replaced with 29 ounces of canned tomato puree.

* For information about this base, see chapter 3.

ALL-PURPOSE MEATBALLS

Yield: 6 servings

1 TABLESPOON BEEF BASE*
½ CUP HOT MILK
¾ CUP DRY BREADCRUMBS
1 EGG, SLIGHTLY BEATEN
3 TABLESPOONS FINELY CHOPPED
  ONIONS

1 TABLESPOON DRIED PARSLEY FLAKES
1 TEASPOON WORCESTERSHIRE SAUCE
1½ POUNDS GROUND LEAN BEEF OR
  CHUCK
1 QUART HOT BROWN GRAVY OR SAUCE
BUTTERED RICE, OR PASTA

❖ In a large mixing bowl, combine the beef base with the hot milk, stirring well. Let stand for 5 to 10 minutes; then stir until the beef base is completely dissolved. Mix in the dry breadcrumbs, slightly beaten egg, onions, parsley flakes, and Worcestershire sauce. Add the ground beef, and mix only enough to combine thoroughly.

Using a tablespoon, form 30 to 32 meatballs and arrange in a 9-by-13 baking pan. Bake uncovered in a 400°F oven for 25 to 30 minutes, until lightly browned. Remove from the oven, and pour off any excess fat.

Pour the hot gravy or sauce evely over the meatballs. Cover the pan tightly, and continue baking in a 400°F oven for 25 to 30 minutes, until the meatballs are done. Serve hot over buttered noodles, rice, or spaghetti.

* For information about this base, see chapter 3.

BEEF AND MACARONI WITH TOMATOES

Yield: 6 servings

¼ CUP OIL
⅔ CUP FINELY DICED ONIONS
1 POUND GROUND CHUCK
29 OUNCES CANNED CRUSHED
  TOMATOES IN PUREE (SEE NOTE
  BELOW)

3 CUPS HOT WATER
2 TABLESPOONS SUGAR
2 TABLESPOONS BEEF BASE*
1 POUND ELBOW MACARONI, COOKED
GRATED ROMANO OR PARMESAN
  CHEESE

(continued)

✤ Heat the oil in a skillet, add the onions, and sauté until brown. Add the ground beef, and sauté for 10 minutes. Add the tomatoes, and cook for 5 minutes. Add the water, sugar, and beef base, reduce the heat, and simmer for 25 minutes. When the meat is tender, add the cooked macaroni, and simmer for 5 more minutes. Serve hot with grated Romano or Parmesan cheese.

Note: The crushed tomatoes in puree may be replaced with 29 ounces of canned tomato puree.

* For information about this base, see chapter 3.

MEAT LOAF

Yield: 6 servings

1½ TABLESPOONS BEEF BASE*
⅓ CUP DEHYDRATED MINCED ONION
⅔ CUP BOILING WATER
1½ CUPS SOFT BREADCRUMBS (ABOUT 3
    SLICES)

2 EGGS, SLIGHTLY BEATEN
2 POUNDS LEAN GROUND BEEF OR
    CHUCK

✤ In a large bowl, combine the beef base, dehydrated onion, and boiling water; stir well. Let the mixture stand for 5 to 10 minutes; then stir until the beef base is well dissolved. Mix in the breadcrumbs and slightly beaten eggs. Add the ground beef, and mix thoroughly. Place in a lightly greased (5-by-9) loaf pan, spreading evenly. Bake in a 375°F oven for 45 to 50 minutes. Pour off the fat. Slice the meat loaf, and serve with brown gravy, whipped potatoes, and buttered mixed vegetables.

* For information about this base, see chapter 3.

CHAPTER FIVE

Veal, Pork, Lamb, and Game

Most of the cooking principles described in the previous chapter on beef also apply to veal, pork, lamb, and game. Veal and pork are almost always cooked well done, whereas lamb and game may be cooked from rare to well done.

Veal has very little fat because it is from an extremely young animal. The small amount of fat can result in a lack of moisture, and so veal is often cooked in or served with sauces. Many of the recipes in this chapter reflect this practice. Sometimes veal is also covered during roasting to prevent moisture loss.

Although the parasite trichina is rarely found in today's pork, it is recommended that pork be cooked until well-done to ensure that the parasite is destroyed if present. For most cuts of pork, slow cooking is recommended. Allow thirty-five to forty minutes per pound of meat for roasting pork. A meat thermometer can be used to determine doneness. In addition, if the large portion of muscle is pierced with a fork and red juices run out, you will know the pork is not done; if clear juices appear, the meat is done. Care should be taken as there is a fine line between the pork being done to perfection and being overcooked.

Lamb is far more available today in supermarkets throughout the country than it was just a few years ago. Lamb is prepared in much the same manner as beef, with many recipes being interchangeable. Because lamb fat tends to burn at a lower temperature than that of other meats, however, it is even more important to avoid high temperatures when preparing lamb, to prevent off flavors and odors.

Large game animals, such as venison and elk, tend to be very lean and often require moist-heat methods of preparation, such as stewing. Choice cuts from very young deer, however, can be roasted or broiled. Some game, such as rabbit, can be prepared using recipes for chicken.

In most cases, age determines how wild birds should be cooked. Leaner than domestic birds, they are generally cooked for less time. The interior of the bird may be salted or rinsed with brandy or sherry; to reduce further any possible "gamy" flavor, an apple, onion, carrot, or parsley may be placed in the bird's cavity.

Veal, Pork, Lamb, and Game

VEAL AND LOBSTER ROULADEN

VEAL AND SHRIMP

VEAL CUTLET MARTIAL

SLICED SWISS VEAL

CITRONEN SCHNITZEL (VIENNESE)

VEAL MILANESE

VEAL RICCA DONNA

VEAL CUTLETS PARMIGIANA

VEAL SCALLOPINI JASON

VEAL CHOPS WITH TARRAGON

ROAST RACK OF VEAL

ROAST SHOULDER OF VEAL

VEAL AND HAM PIE

VEAL BIRDS

BRAISED VEAL SHANK (OSSO BUCO)

CALF'S LIVER WITH YOGURT

LIVER, VENICE STYLE

SWEET-AND-SOUR BROCHETTES

ROAST PORK WITH CABBAGE

PORK CUTLETS PAPAGALLO

PORK WILHELM TELL

BAKED PORK CHOPS VERMONT STYLE

STUFFED PORK CHOPS

SAUSAGE AND PEPPERS

SADDLE OF LAMB IN PASTRY WITH GARLIC

SHISH KEBAB

SPRING-STYLE NAVARIN

LAMB RAGOUT

RABBIT STEW CIOCIARA

VENISON STEW

VEAL AND LOBSTER ROULADEN

Yield: 6 servings

2½ CUPS BUTTER

2 MEDIUM EGGPLANTS, PEELED, CUT IN
⅛-INCH SLICES

2 POUNDS FRESH LEAF SPINACH,
SAUTÉED

6 VEAL MEDALLIONS, 3 OUNCES EACH,
POUNDED THIN

SALT AND PEPPER TO TASTE

12 THIN SLICES PROSCIUTTO

6 LOBSTER TAILS, 2 OUNCES EACH,
REMOVED FROM THE SHELL

1 CUP FLOUR

4 EGGS, BEATEN

2 CUPS FRESH BREADCRUMBS

2 CUPS FENNEL SAUCE (SEE RECIPE IN
CHAPTER 3)

❖ Heat 1 cup of the butter in a skillet, add the eggplant slices, and sauté for 2 to 3 minutes. Remove the eggplant and set aside. Discard the butter in the pan. Heat ½ cup of butter and in the same pan, add the cleaned spinach leaves, and sauté for 3 to 5 minutes; remove and keep warm.

Lay out the veal medallions, and season with salt and pepper. Place 2 thin slices of prosciutto on each medallion, and cover the ham with the sautéed eggplant slices. Top each with the lobster tail meat, lightly season with salt and pepper. Roll tightly, into rouladen, tucking in the loose ends. Lightly season with salt and pepper. Dredge the rouladen in the flour, dip them in the beaten eggs, and coat with the breadcrumbs.

Heat the remaining 1 cup of butter in a skillet and sauté the rouladen until golden brown. Finish in an oven at 375°F, baking for approximately 15 minutes. Slice and serve on a bed of the sautéed spinach, covered with fennel sauce. Fresh pasta makes an excellent accompaniment.

VEAL AND SHRIMP

Yield: 6 servings

½ CUP BUTTER
1½ POUNDS VEAL SCALLOPS (CUTLETS)
SALT AND PEPPER TO TASTE
½ CUP MINCED SHALLOTS
OREGANO TO TASTE

2 CUPS HEAVY CREAM
2 TABLESPOONS OLIVE OIL
12 SHRIMP, 26- TO 30-PER-POUND SIZE
2 TABLESPOONS BRANDY

✦ Heat the butter in a skillet, and brown the veal. Season with salt and pepper, and set the veal aside, keeping warm. Sauté the shallots in the same butter for 2 minutes. Add the oregano and cream, and reduce by half. In a separate skillet, heat the olive oil, add the shrimp, and sauté until the shrimp begin to curl. Add the brandy, and flame. Add the sauce, and bring to short boil. Place the veal on serving plates, and top with the shrimp and sauce.

VEAL CUTLET MARTIAL

Yield: 4 servings

4 VEAL CUTLETS, 4 OUNCES EACH
4 SLICES COOKED HAM, 1 OUNCE EACH
4 SLICES SWISS CHEESE, 1 OUNCE EACH
4 LARGE MUSHROOM SLICES
SALT AND PEPPER TO TASTE
FLOUR TO DREDGE AND COAT
2 EGGS, BEATEN

3 TABLESPOONS OIL
¼ CUP BUTTER
¼ CUP SHERRY WINE
JUICE OF ½ LEMON
1 CUP BROWN SAUCE (SEE RECIPE IN
   CHAPTER 3)

✦ Place the veal between 2 sheets of waxed paper, and pound until about ⅛-inch thick. Place a slice of ham, Swiss cheese, and mushroom atop each cutlet, and fold into a square. Season. Secure the rolls with toothpicks. Dredge the veal in the flour, dip in the beaten egg, and then coat with flour. Heat the oil and 2 tablespoons of butter in a skillet, add the veal, and sauté until brown on both sides, about 12 to 15 minutes. Remove the veal, and keep warm. Deglaze the pan with the sherry wine and lemon juice. Add the brown sauce, and swirl in remaining 2 tablespoons of butter; do not boil. Nap the veal with the sauce to serve.

SLICED SWISS VEAL

Yield: 4 servings

½ CUP BUTTER
1 POUND VEAL, THINLY SLICED
½ CUP DEMI-GLACE (SEE RECIPE IN
　CHAPTER 3)
2 TABLESPOONS DRY SAUTERNE

½ TEASPOON LEMON JUICE
1 TABLESPOON PAPRIKA
SALT AND WHITE PEPPER TO TASTE
½ CUP HEAVY CREAM
8 OUNCES FRESH MUSHROOMS, SLICED

❖ Heat ¼ cup of the butter in a skillet, add the veal, and sauté quickly, about 1 minute per side. Place the veal on a warm serving plate. Reduce the pan drippings by half, and deglaze the pan with the demi-glace and wine. Reduce the sauce half. Add the lemon juice, paprika, salt, pepper, and cream. Bring to a simmer, then remove from the heat.

In a separate skillet, heat the remaining ¼ cup of butter, add the mushrooms, and sauté until tender. Add the mushrooms to the sauce. Pour the sauce over the veal. Serve with spaetzle, noodles, or hash browns.

CITRONEN SCHNITZEL (VIENNESE)

Yield: 6 servings

6 VEAL CUTLETS, 6 OUNCES EACH
½ CUP FLOUR, SEASONED
¼ CUP BUTTER
2 OUNCES SHALLOTS, CHOPPED
1 CUP SOUR CREAM

2 TABLESPOONS LEMON JUICE
3 TABLESPOONS FLOUR
¼ CUP WATER
1 LEMON, SLICED
⅓ CUP CHOPPED PARSLEY

❖ Dredge the veal cutlets lightly in the seasoned flour. Heat the butter in a skillet, add the veal, and sauté each side for 1 minute. Remove the veal. Add the chopped shallots to the pan, and sauté lightly. Return the veal to the pan, and simmer for a few minutes. Combine the sour cream, lemon juice, flour, and water, and pour into the pan; simmer for 3 to 4 minutes. Remove the meat, place on serving plates, and strain the sauce over it. Place a slice of lemon on each slice of veal, and sprinkle with the chopped parsley.

VEAL MILANESE

Yield: 6 servings

6 VEAL LOIN PIECES, 5 OUNCES EACH
1 CUP BREADCRUMBS
¼ CUP GRATED PARMESAN CHEESE
SALT AND PEPPER TO TASTE
3 TABLESPOONS FLOUR, SEASONED (SEE
    NOTE BELOW)

3 EGGS, BEATEN
¼ CUP BUTTER
¼ CUP VEGETABLE OIL
2 TEASPOONS LEMON JUICE
2 TABLESPOONS CHOPPED PARSLEY
6 LEMON SLICES

✛ Pound the veal between two pieces of plastic wrap until very thin. Combine the breadcrumbs and cheese. Season the veal with salt and pepper, and dredge in the flour, shaking off any excess. Dip the veal in the beaten eggs, then in the breadcrumb and cheese mixture. Heat the butter and oil in a skillet, add the veal, and sauté until evenly browned on both sides. Sprinkle with the lemon juice, and remove from the pan. Serve garnished with the parsley and lemon slices.

Note: The flour may be seasoned with paprika.

VEAL RICCA DONNA

Yield: 6 servings

2 POUNDS VEAL ROUND, CUT IN
    JULIENNE
½ CUP FLOUR, SEASONED WITH SALT,
    PEPPER, AND PAPRIKA
1 CUP BUTTER

1 BUNCH SCALLIONS, CHOPPED
⅓ TEASPOON OREGANO
DASH OF SALT
1½ CUPS DRY VERMOUTH

✛ Dredge the veal in the seasoned flour. Heat the butter in a skillet, add the veal, and sauté until slightly brown. Remove the veal. Add the chopped scallions to the pan, sauté lightly. Add the oregano, salt, and dry vermouth, and stir gently to deglaze the pan. Return the meat to the sauce, and cook gently for a few minutes, until the sauce thickens. Add more vermouth if a thinner sauce is desired. Taste and adjust the seasonings. Serve over your favorite pasta or rice.

VEAL CUTLETS PARMIGIANA

Yield: 6 servings

6 VEAL CUTLETS, 4 OUNCES EACH
SALT AND PEPPER TO TASTE
2 EGGS, BEATEN
¾ CUP MILK
2 CUPS FRESH WHITE BREADCRUMBS
½ CUP FRESHLY GRATED PARMESAN
  CHEESE

1 TEASPOON CHOPPED PARSLEY
FLOUR TO DREDGE
¼ CUP OLIVE OIL
2 CUPS TOMATO SAUCE
6 SLICES MOZZARELLA CHEESE

❖ Season the veal cutlets with salt and pepper. Combine the beaten eggs with
the milk. Combine the breadcrumbs, Parmesan cheese, and parsley. Dredge each
cutlet in the flour, dip in the eggwash, and coat with the breadcrumb mixture.
Fry the veal cutlets in the olive oil until golden brown. Divide the tomato sauce
among 6 individual casseroles; add a veal cutlet to each, and top with a slice of
mozzarella cheese. Bake until the cheese is melted.

VEAL SCALLOPINI JASON

Yield: 6 servings

½ CUP VEGETABLE OIL
3 GREEN PEPPERS, SEEDED AND CUT IN
  ½-INCH SLICES
1 POUND MUSHROOMS, SLICED
1 LARGE FRESH TOMATO, PEELED,
  SEEDED, AND DICED
1 POUND SHRIMP, CLEANED, SHELLED,
  COOKED, AND SLICED CROSSWISE

SALT AND PEPPER TO TASTE
2 POUNDS VEAL CUTLETS, POUNDED
  VERY THIN (ABOUT 18 PIECES)
½ CUP FLOUR
½ CUP SHERRY

❖ Heat ¼ cup of the oil in a large skillet, add the sliced peppers, and sauté 5 or
6 minutes. Add the sliced mushrooms and diced tomatoes, and cook for 5
minutes longer. Add the cooked shrimp, season with salt and pepper to taste,
and simmer for 2 minutes. Remove the mixture from the skillet, place in a
casserole, and keep warm.

Dredge the veal cutlets in the flour. Add the remaining ¼ cup of oil to the

(continued)

same skillet, and sauté the cutlets for 2 minutes on each side. Remove the veal from the skillet, and place on 6 preheated serving plates. Divide the shrimp mixture on top of the veal.

Return the skillet to the stove, pour in the sherry, scraping all sides with a spatula, and reduce by half. Strain this sauce, and pour over the veal.

VEAL CHOPS WITH TARRAGON

Yield: 4 servings

4 VEAL CHOPS, ABOUT 8 OUNCES EACH
SALT AND FRESHLY GROUND BLACK
   PEPPER TO TASTE
½ CUP FLOUR
2 TABLESPOONS OLIVE OIL
2 TABLESPOONS BUTTER
3 SHALLOTS, FINELY MINCED

2 TABLESPOONS COGNAC
⅔ CUP DRY WHITE WINE
½ CUP HEAVY CREAM
1½ TABLESPOONS DIJON MUSTARD
1 TABLESPOON CHOPPED FRESH
   TARRAGON

❖ Season the veal chops with salt and pepper, and dredge them lightly in the flour. Heat the oil in butter in a sauté pan. Add the veal chops, and brown for 4 to 5 minutes on each side. Remove the chops from the pan; keep warm.

Add the shallots to the sauté pan. Deglaze the pan with the Cognac and white wine. Return the chops to the sauté pan. Reduce the liquid by half. Remove the chops to a heated serving platter.

Add the cream to the pan, stirring constantly. Add the mustard, and adjust the seasonings. Add the chopped tarragon. Cook until the cream is heated through. Pour the sauce over the chops, and serve at once.

ROAST RACK OF VEAL

Yield: 8+ servings

5 POUNDS RACK OF VEAL
SALT AND BLACK PEPPER TO TASTE
2 TABLESPOONS VEGETABLE OIL
2 TABLESPOONS BUTTER
½ CUP CHOPPED CARROTS
½ CUP CHOPPED CELERY
½ CUP CHOPPED ONIONS
1 SMALL GARLIC CLOVE, MINCED

1 CUP CHOPPED TOMATOES, FRESH OR
   CANNED
½ TEASPOON DRIED THYME
1 BAY LEAF
4 TO 5 FRESH PARSLEY SPRIGS
1 CUP WHITE WINE
½ CUP DEMI-GLACE (SEE RECIPE IN
   CHAPTER 3) OR BROWN GRAVY

❖ Season the veal with salt and pepper. Heat the oil and butter in a large skillet, add the veal, and brown all around to a light brown color. Remove the meat from the skillet. Add the carrots, celery, onions, and garlic to the skillet; sauté briefly. Transfer the vegetables to a roasting pan. Add the tomatoes, thyme, bay leaf, and parsley to the pan. Place the roast on top.

Deglaze the skillet with the white wine. Add the demi-glace or brown gravy, and baste the meat with this sauce. Cover the roasting pan, and bake in a 350°F oven for approximately 45 minutes. Remove the cover, and continue cooking until the meat is tender, about 45 minutes. Remove the meat, and let it set in a warm place for 15 minutes before slicing. Skim the fat from the cooking liquid and strain, pressing the vegetables to extract all the juices. Slice and arrange the veal on a serving platter. Pour some of the sauce over the meat, and serve the remaining sauce on the side.

ROAST SHOULDER OF VEAL

Yield: 8 servings

4½ POUNDS VEAL SHOULDER, BONED
    AND TIED
1 SMALL GARLIC CLOVE, THINLY
    SLIVERED
¼ CUP PREPARED DIJON-STYLE
    MUSTARD
1 TEASPOON DRIED THYME

SALT AND FRESHLY GROUND PEPPER TO
    TASTE
8 BACON STRIPS
½ CUP SWEET BUTTER, AT ROOM
    TEMPERATURE
¾ CUP DRY WHITE WINE

❖ Preheat oven to 350°F. Cut tiny slits in the veal with the tip of a sharp knife, and insert the garlic slivers. Set the veal on a rack in a shallow baking pan that is just large enough to hold it comfortably. Rub mustard over the veal, and sprinkle with the thyme, salt, and pepper. Wrap the bacon around the meat to cover it completely, tucking the bacon ends under the meat. Spread the butter generously over the bacon and meat; pour the white wine into the pan. Roast for 2 hours and 15 minutes (about 30 minutes per pound) basting frequently, until the juices run clear when pricked with a skewer. Let the roast stand for 20 minutes before carving. Serve the pan juices in a gravy boat alongside the veal.

VEAL AND HAM PIE

Yield: 6 servings

¼ CUP BRANDY
¼ CUP MADEIRA
½ TEASPOON SALT
¼ TEASPOON PEPPER
1 POUND VEAL CUTLETS

1 POUND SMOKED HAM, SLICED
½ CUP SLICED SHALLOTS SAUTÉED
2½ OUNCES PASTRY DOUGH
1 EGG YOLK, BEATEN

❖ Combine the brandy, Madeira, salt, and pepper to make a marinade. Add the veal cutlets, and marinate for 2 hours. In a 9- by 13-inch baking dish, layer the ham slices and veal, placing a few sautéed shallots between each layer. Add the marinade. Roll out the pastry dough, and cover the pie. Decorate as desired. Brush the dough with the egg yolk. Place in a 350°F oven. As soon as the dough cover puffs up a little and slightly splits, pierce a hole in center to allow steam to escape. Bake for about 40 minutes.

VEAL BIRDS

Yield: 6 servings

½ CUP CHOPPED SHALLOTS
¼ CUP BUTTER
2 TABLESPOONS SHERRY
2 EGGS
12 OUNCES GROUND VEAL
¾ CUP COARSELY CHOPPED SPINACH,
   COOKED

2 TABLESPOONS CREAM
1 CUP FRESH WHITE BREADCRUMBS
SALT AND PEPPER TO TASTE
6 VEAL CUTLETS, 6 OUNCES EACH
2 CUPS THIN BROWN GRAVY

❖ Sauté the chopped shallots in the butter until tender. Mix the shallots with the wine, eggs, ground veal, spinach, cream, breadcrumbs, salt, and pepper. Divide into 6 equal portions, and place on the 6 cutlets. Roll the cutlet around the stuffing, and secure with toothpicks. Arrange the veal in a roasting pan, and place in a 400°F oven, and brown. Add the gravy, reduce the oven to 350°F, and cook, covered, for 45 minutes; remove the cover, and cook for 15 minutes more. Remove the toothpicks, pour the gravy over the veal, and serve.

BRAISED VEAL SHANK (OSSO BUCO)

Yield: 6 servings

6 VEAL SHANKS, CUT CROSS, 6 TO
  9 OUNCES EACH
2 TABLESPOONS SALT
⅛ TEASPOON PEPPER
FLOUR TO DREDGE
½ CUP OIL
1 TABLESPOON BUTTER
⅔ CUP FINELY CHOPPED ONIONS
2 GARLIC CLOVES, MINCED
10 TO 14 OUNCES CARROTS, CELERY,
  AND LEEKS, FINELY DICED

¼ CUP TOMATO PUREE
¾ CUP TOMATO CONCASSÉ (PEELED,
  SEEDED, AND CRUSHED TOMATOES)
1½ CUPS RED WINE
2 CUPS BROWN GRAVY
1 TABLESPOON FINELY CHOPPED
  PARSLEY
2 GARLIC CLOVES, FINELY CHOPPED
1 TEASPOON GRATED LEMON ZEST

❖ Season the veal shanks with the salt and pepper, and dredge in the flour. Heat the oil in a skillet, add the veal, and brown on all sides. Place the veal in a braising pan. In a separate pan, heat the butter and slightly sauté the onions, garlic, carrots, celery, and leeks. Add the tomato puree, tomato concassé, wine, and gravy. Reduce by half. Add the sauce to the meat in the pan, cover tightly, place in a 350°F oven, and braise until tender, about 2 hours. When serving, spoon the liquid over the shanks, and sprinkle the finely chopped parsley, garlic, and grated lemon zest (a mixture called *gremolada*).

CALF'S LIVER WITH YOGURT

Yield: 4 servings

1 ONION, MINCED
1 TABLESPOON CLARIFIED BUTTER
1 TABLESPOON OLIVE OIL
1 GARLIC CLOVE, MINCED
1 TEASPOON TURMERIC
½ TEASPOON GROUND CUMIN
½ TEASPOON GROUND CORIANDER

¼ TEASPOON GROUND GINGER
PINCH OF THYME
1 POUND CALF'S LIVER, CUT IN
  1-INCH STRIPS
½ CUP PLAIN YOGURT
SALT AND WHITE PEPPER TO TASTE

❖ Sauté the onions in the butter and oil until soft. Add the garlic, turmeric, cumin, coriander, ginger, and thyme, and sauté for 2 minutes. Add the liver, and cook until browned. Stir in the yogurt, and heat through. Season; serve with steamed rice.

LIVER, VENICE STYLE

Yield: 6 servings

¼ CUP BUTTER
¼ CUP OIL
6 PORTIONS SLICED CALF'S LIVER,
  4 OUNCES EACH
6 MEDIUM ONIONS, THINLY SLICED

¼ CUP CHOPPED PARSLEY
¼ TEASPOON SAGE
1 TEASPOON SALT
1 TEASPOON BLACK PEPPER
½ CUP BEEF STOCK OR BOUILLON

❖ In a skillet, heat the butter and oil, add the liver, and sauté until slightly browned. Remove the liver from the pan, and set side, keeping warm. Sauté the onions in the same butter and oil. Add the parsley, sage, salt, pepper, and stock. Bring to a very short boil, and serve atop the liver.

SWEET-AND-SOUR BROCHETTES

Yield: 12 to 16 brochettes

15¼ OUNCES CANNED PINEAPPLE
  CHUNKS PLUS LIQUID
⅔ CUP LUKEWARM WATER
1½ TEASPOONS CHICKEN BASE*
3 TABLESPOONS WHITE DISTILLED
  VINEGAR
¼ CUP BROWN SUGAR
1 TABLESPOON SOY SAUCE
2 TEASPOONS WORCESTERSHIRE SAUCE

1 POUND BONELESS LOIN PORK,
  TRIMMED AND CUT INTO 1½-INCH
  CUBES
2 TABLESPOONS CORNSTARCH
1 GREEN PEPPER, CUT INTO 2-INCH
  SQUARES
1 RED BELL PEPPER, CUT INTO 2-INCH
  SQUARES
1 MEDIUM ONION, CUT INTO WEDGES

❖ Drain the pineapple liquid into a large glass mixing bowl; set the pineapple aside. Add the water, chicken base, vinegar, brown sugar, soy sauce, and Worcester sauce to the liquid. Mix well with a wire whisk until the base is dissolved. Add the pork, cover, and refrigerate for 2 hours.

Remove the pork from the marinade; set aside. Pour the marinade into a heavy 1-quart saucepan. Add the cornstarch to the marinade, mixing with a wire whisk until well blended. Bring to a boil over medium heat. Boil and stir for 1 minute. Reduce the heat, and simmer for 5 minutes, stirring constantly. Set aside.

Arrange the pork, green peppers, red peppers, onions, and pineapple chunks on 4-inch skewers (two pieces of each per skewer). Place in a shallow baking pan, and brush with the marinade (about 2 tablespoons per skewer). Bake at 425°F for 30 to 40 minutes, turning and basting several times, until the pork is done. Place 3 brochettes on each serving plate; rice can first be mounded beneath if desired. (These brochettes can also be served as appetizers.)

* For information about this base, see chapter 3.

ROAST PORK WITH CABBAGE

Yield: 6 servings

1 PORK LOIN, RIB END,
   ABOUT 4 POUNDS
SALT TO TASTE
1 TEASPOON DRY MUSTARD
1 TEASPOON THYME
GROUND BLACK PEPPER TO TASTE
3 HEADS RED CABBAGE, SHREDDED
1 CUP WINE VINEGAR

HOT WATER, AS NEEDED
1 ONION
¼ CUP BACON FAT
3 TABLESPOONS RED-CURRANT JELLY
2 GREEN APPLES, CORED, PEELED AND
   SLICED
¼ CUP BEEF CONSOMMÉ, AS NEEDED

❖ Rub the pork with the salt, mustard, thyme, and black pepper; let stand for 2 to 3 hours. Place the red cabbage in a pot, and pour over the vinegar and enough hot water to cover; let stand.

Place the pork in a roasting pan, and roast in a 400°F oven for 30 minutes. Meanwhile, sauté the onions in the bacon fat until translucent. Add the currant jelly, drained cabbage, and apples. Add the consommé (or water), and season with salt and pepper. Pour the cabbage mixture over the roast, and continue cooking 1 to 1½ hours, until the pork reaches an internal temperature of 170°F. Remove and slice the pork, place the cabbage on a platter, and top with pork. Serve with boiled potatoes.

PORK CUTLETS PAPAGALLO

Yield: 6 servings

12 PORK CUTLETS FROM THE CENTER
 LOIN, 3 OUNCES EACH
1 CUP FLOUR, SEASONED
½ CUP VEGETABLE OIL
1 ONION, FINELY CHOPPED
2 GARLIC CLOVES, FINELY CHOPPED
29 OUNCES CANNED PEELED TOMATOES,
 DRAINED, SEEDED, AND CHOPPED

1 CUP DRY WHITE WINE
6 OUNCES MUSHROOMS, SLICED
1 CUP HEAVY CREAM
SALT AND WHITE PEPPER TO TASTE
2 TABLESPOONS CHOPPED PARSLEY
12 SLICES MONTEREY JACK CHEESE

❖ Pound cutlets until very thin. Dredge them in the seasoned flour. Heat ¼ cup of the oil in a skillet, add the pork, and fry until golden brown; remove and set aside. In a separate pan, heat the remaining ¼ cup of oil, add the onions, and sauté until translucent. Add the garlic and chopped tomatoes, and sauté for 2 minutes. Stir in the wine, bring to a simmer, add the mushrooms, and cook for 2 minutes. Add the cream, and cook until the mixture thickens. Season with salt, pepper, and chopped parsley.

Place the browned cutlets in a nonreactive baking dish, cover with tomato mixture, and top with a slice of cheese. Bake in a 400°F oven until the cheese melts and is golden brown. Serve with roasted parsley and spring vegetables.

PORK WILHELM TELL

Yield: 4 servings

8 SLICES PORK TENDERLOIN, 2 TO
 3 OUNCES EACH
SALT AND PEPPER TO TASTE
6 TABLESPOONS BUTTER
¼ CUP KIRSCHWASSER
3 APPLES, PEELED, CORED, AND DICED
4 OUNCES HAM, DICED (ABOUT ¾ CUP)

6 TABLESPOONS WHITE WINE
¾ CUP DEMI-GLACE (SEE RECIPE IN
 CHAPTER 3)
3 OUNCES SWISS CHEESE, DICED (ABOUT
 ¾ CUP)
¼ CUP HEAVY CREAM, WHIPPED

❖ Season the pork with salt and pepper. Heat the butter in a skillet, add the pork, and sauté until brown. Flame the meat with the Kirschwasser, remove, and keep warm. Sauté the apples and ham in the same butter for 10 minutes, until the apples are soft but not mushy. Add the Swiss cheese, and fold in the whipped cream. Adjust the seasonings. Bring to a simmer, and cook until the cheese melts. Arrange the pork on serving plates, and cover with the sauce. Serve with roasted potatoes or spaetzle and braised romaine lettuce.

BAKED PORK CHOPS VERMONT STYLE

Yield: 6 servings

1 CUP PORK STOCK (SEE NOTE BELOW)
1 CUP MAPLE SYRUP
¼ CUP COLD WATER

1½ TABLESPOONS CORNSTARCH
6 PORK CHOPS, 6 OUNCES EACH

❖ Combine the pork stock and maple syrup in a saucepan, and bring to a boil. Blend the water and cornstarch, and pour into the stock mixture to thicken slightly. Remove from the heat. Place the pork chops in a baking pan. Pour half the sauce over chops; reserve the remaining sauce and keep warm. Bake the chops in a 325°F oven for about 30 minutes. (Do not overcook, or the chops will be tough and stringy.) Place the chops on serving plates, cover with the reserved sauce, and serve.

Note: To prepare pork stock, place 2 pounds of pork neck bones, 3 large onions, coarsely chopped, and 3 large celery ribs in a stockpot. Cover with 3 to 4 inches of water, and simmer for 3 hours, skimming any fat that accumulates on top. Strain, and keep refrigerated until needed.

STUFFED PORK CHOPS

Yield: 6 servings

⅓ CUP CHOPPED CELERY
⅓ CUP CHOPPED ONIONS
¼ CUP BUTTER OR MARGARINE
6 OUNCES SAUSAGE MEAT
¾ CUP PEELED AND DICED APPLES
6 SLICES WHITE BREAD, 2 TO 3 DAYS
   OLD, SOAKED IN MILK AND
   SQUEEZED DRY

1 EGG
2 TABLESPOONS CHOPPED PARSLEY
SALT AND PEPPER TO TASTE
6 CENTER-CUT PORK CHOPS, 6 OUNCES
   EACH, WITH POCKETS FOR STUFFING
¼ CUP FLOUR, SEASONED
COOKING OIL, AS NEEDED
THIN BROWN GRAVY, AS NEEDED

✤ Sauté the celery and onions in the butter or margarine until very light brown. Add the sausage meat, and cook for 10 minutes. Cool. In a bowl, combine the vegetable-sausage mixture, apples, bread, egg, parsley, salt, and pepper. Stuff the chops with the mixture; dredge in flour. Brown chops in the oil; then transfer them to a baking dish. Cover with the gravy, and bake at 350°F for 1½ hours. Serve with good spiced fruit.

SAUSAGE AND PEPPERS

Yield: 8 servings

2 POUNDS ITALIAN SAUSAGE
2 OUNCES BUTTER
3 GREEN PEPPERS, CHOPPED
1 LARGE ONION, CHOPPED
4 OUNCES CANNED MUSHROOMS

16 OUNCES CANNED CRUSHED
   TOMATOES WITH PUREE
½ TEASPOON BASIL
1 TEASPOON GARLIC SALT
SALT AND PEPPER TO TASTE

✤ Bake the sausage in a 375°F oven for about 1 hour; drain and save the grease. Heat the butter in a skillet, add the green peppers and onions, and sauté for 5 to 10 minutes, adding the mushrooms after a few minutes (do not overcook: the onions should be translucent but not brown). Heat the tomatoes in a pot; add the basil, garlic salt, salt, and pepper. Cover, and simmer for 30 minutes. Add some of the reserved sausage grease, to taste. Add the sausage and pepper mixture to the tomatoes, and cook, covered, for 15 more minutes.

SADDLE OF LAMB IN PASTRY WITH GARLIC

Yield: 8 servings

1 SADDLE OF LAMB, 7 TO 8 POUNDS
2 GARLIC HEADS
VEGETABLE OIL AS NEEDED
9 OUNCES BUTTER
SALT AND PEPPER TO TASTE
¼ TEASPOON DRIED THYME
¼ TEASPOON DRIED PARSLEY
¼ TEASPOON DRIED SAGE

¼ TEASPOON DRIED ROSEMARY
⅛ TEASPOON CRUSHED PEPPERCORNS
2 POUNDS FRESH SPINACH, WASHED, DRIED, AND STEMMED
6 POUNDS FROZEN PUFF PASTRY DOUGH SHEETS, THAWED AND ROLLED TO ¹⁄₁₆-INCH THICK
1 EGG, BEATEN

❖ Bone the saddle of lamb, trimming off all fat and inedible tissue. Keep about 2 inches of bib. Separate the garlic cloves, peel, and blanch; remove and pat dry. Tie both the boned saddle parts with kitchen twine, and sear them in hot oil. Cool the roasts, and remove the twine.

Prepare rolled roasts of lamb, putting 1 cup of butter, the garlic cloves, salt, pepper, thyme, parsley, sage, rosemary, and peppercorns along their centers.

Chop the fresh spinach and sauté it quickly in the remaining 2 tablespoons of butter. Drain. Spread the spinach on top of the lamb, and wrap each roast completely in the puff pastry. Seal the seams with the beaten egg. Roast in a 425°F oven for about 30 minutes. Let the meat rest on top of the oven for 20 minutes before carving.

SHISH KEBAB

Yield: 12 skewers

1 CUP DRY RED WINE
1 CUP OIL
1 ONION, SLICED
1 BAY LEAF
3 GARLIC CLOVES, CRUSHED
½ TEASPOON PEPPERCORNS, CRUSHED
1 TEASPOON SALT
½ TEASPOON OREGANO

1 TEASPOON WORCESTERSHIRE SAUCE
2½ POUNDS LEG OF LAMB, CUT INTO 1-OUNCE CUBES (48 CUBES)
24 SMALL MUSHROOMS
24 CHERRY TOMATOES
24 PEARL ONIONS
2 GREEN PEPPERS, CUT INTO 24 SQUARES

(continued)

❖ Combine the red wine, oil, onions, bay leaf, garlic, peppercorns, salt, oregano, and Worcestershire sauce. Place the cubed lamb in this marinade; mix well. Cover, and refrigerate overnight.

Drain the lamb cubes, and dry on absorbent paper. Skewer, in order: a mushroom, a tomato, a lamb cube, an onion, a lamb cube, a pepper square, a lamb cube, an onion, a lamb cube, a pepper square, a tomato, and a mushroom. Repeat, to make 12 skewers. Broil under moderate heat until the meat reaches the desired degree of doneness. Serve on a bed of rice.

SPRING-STYLE NAVARIN

Yield: 8 servings

1 TABLESPOON VEGETABLE OIL
1 TABLESPOON BUTTER
3 POUNDS LEAN LAMB, CUBED
SALT AND FRESHLY GROUND PEPPER TO
  TASTE
8 OUNCES PEARL ONIONS
1 TEASPOON GRANULATED SUGAR
2 GARLIC CLOVES, MINCED
1 CUP DRY WHITE WINE
3 CUPS BEEF STOCK OR WATER

1 LARGE TOMATO, PEELED, SEEDED, AND
  DICED
PINCH OF THYME
8–10 ROSEMARY LEAVES
1 BAY LEAF
2 CUPS DICED TURNIPS
1¾ CUPS SLICED CARROTS
2 CUPS DICED POTATOES
1⅔ CUPS SHELLED PEAS
¼ CUP CORNSTARCH

❖ Heat the oil and butter in a sauté pan. Add the lamb cubes, season with salt and pepper, and sauté over high heat until nicely browned. Transfer the lamb cubes to a heavy-bottomed saucepan.

Reduce the heat, and add the onions to the sauté pan. Sprinkle the onions with the sugar, and glaze heavily. Remove the onions, and set aside.

Add the garlic to the sauté pan; sauté briefly. Deglaze the pan with the white wine. Add the beef stock. Pour this mixture over the lamb cubes in the saucepan. Add the diced tomato, thyme, rosemary, and bay leaf. Cover the pan; simmer for 1 hour. Add the turnips, carrots, and potatoes, and simmer for another 15 minutes. Add the reserved glazed onions and the peas.

Remove ½ cup of cooking liquid, and cool it. Stir the cornstarch into the cooled liquid and add this mixture slowly to the stew, stirring constantly until thickened. Simmer until the meat is tender and all the vegetables are cooked. Skim off the fat, remove the bay leaf, and adjust seasonings. Serve at once.

LAMB RAGOUT

Yield: 6 servings

½ CUP BUTTER OR OIL
2 POUNDS LAMB SHOULDER, CUT INTO
   1-INCH CUBES
SALT, PEPPER AND THYME TO TASTE
4–5 TABLESPOONS FLOUR
4–5 GARLIC CLOVES, FINELY CHOPPED
2 CUPS FINELY DICED ONIONS
1 QUART HOT WATER OR BEEF OR LAMB
   STOCK

½ CUP TOMATO PUREE
2 OUNCES PEARL ONIONS (ABOUT
   ⅓ CUP)
2¾ CUPS SLICED CARROTS, COOKED
12 OUNCES SMALL ROUND POTATOES,
   COOKED
1¼ CUPS GREEN PEAS, BLANCHED

❖ Heat the butter or oil in a heavy pot. Add the lamb, season with the salt, pepper, and thyme, and sauté until brown. Add the flour, and cook for 2 to 3 minutes. Sprinkle with the garlic and onions. Cook for a few more minutes, then add the hot water or stock. Bring to boil, stirring to avoid lumps. Add the tomato puree. Cover, and simmer slowly for 1 hour. Add the pearl onions, cooked carrot slices, cooked potatoes, and peas, and cook for 5 minutes more. Serve immediately.

RABBIT STEW CIOCIARA

Yield: 6 servings

2 RABBITS, 3 POUNDS EACH, CLEANED
   AND CUT FOR FRYING
SALT AND FRESHLY GROUND PEPPER TO
   TASTE
6 TABLESPOONS OLIVE OIL
2 GARLIC CLOVES, FINELY CRUSHED
1 CUP DICED SMOKED HAM (½-INCH
   CUBES)

1 CUP DRY WHITE WINE
2 POUNDS TOMATOES, PEELED, SEEDED,
   AND CHOPPED
3 TABLESPOONS CHOPPED FRESH
   PARSLEY

(continued)

✤ Dry the pieces of rabbit, and season with salt and pepper. Heat the oil in a large, heavy braising pan. Brown the pieces of rabbit on all sides. Add the garlic and diced ham. Cook until the garlic begins to color. Add the wine, and cook until it has evaporated. Add the tomatoes, adjust seasonings, and cook, covered, over low heat for about 1 hour, until the rabbit is tender. Transfer to a casserole or serving dish. Sprinkle with the chopped parsley. Serve with polenta or risotto.

VENISON STEW

Yield: 6 servings

8 OUNCES MIREPOIX (DICED, PARED
   CARROTS, ONIONS, AND CELERY)
1 QUART BURGUNDY
½ CUP WINE VINEGAR
½ TEASPOON JUNIPER BERRIES
4 PEPPERCORNS
1 BAY LEAF
2 CLOVES
2-POUND VENISON BREAST, BONED, AND
   CUT INTO ½-INCH CUBES

¼ CUP VEGETABLE OIL
⅔ CUP FLOUR
2 CUPS BEEF STOCK
SALT TO TASTE
3 OUNCES BACON STRIPS, FRIED
2 CUPS SLICED FRESH MUSHROOMS,
   SAUTÉED

✤ Combine the mirepoix, Burgundy, wine vinegar, juniper berries, peppercorns, bay leaf, and cloves. Marinate the venison in this mixture for 24 hours, stirring occasionally.

Drain the meat, reserving the marinade liquid and mirepoix; separate meat and mirepoix. Heat the oil in a large pan; add the venison cubes, and brown. Add the mirepoix, and continue sautéing for 2 minutes. Sprinkle the flour over the meat, and sauté until brown. Add the reserved marinade and the beef stock, and bring to a boil; taste, and adjust the seasoning. Simmer for 2½ to 3 hours, until the meat is tender. Remove the meat to serving plates; strain the sauce and pour it over meat. Arrange the bacon and mushrooms over the stew. Serve with noodles, spaetzle, or whipped potatoes.

CHAPTER SIX

Poultry

Poultry has become a more popular item on American tables in recent years, not only because of favorable prices, but also because of the improved quality of poultry products. Quick maturity for market, a high ratio of weight gain to feed consumed, and mass raising and processing techniques have helped to make poultry one of the lowest-cost, highest-quality protein foods on the market. While duck, goose, turkey, and a few other poultry species are still somewhat seasonal in production, chicken is in plentiful supply year-round. A chicken can be sold as a 3½-pound broiler in twelve weeks. In addition to fresh products, high-quality frozen poultry is easily found.

The variety of poultry products on the market has also increased. Imitation ham made from turkey, turkey or chicken sausage or bacon, chicken nuggets, and a host of other products are available, requiring short preparation times. And, perhaps most important to today's health-conscious consumers, lean poultry meat—with the skin and fat removed—is low in calories, cholesterol, and saturated fat.

Most poultry is quite tender because the birds are marketed at a very young age. Very few mature birds reach the consumer market; most are used for processed items. Thus, moist-heat cooking methods are not needed to tenderize poultry meat. No matter what cooking method is used, a tender product will usually result, unless the product is cooked at too high a heat or is improperly handled in some other way.

To reduce calories and fat intake, some recommend that the skin be removed from poultry *before* cooking, as most of the fat in a bird will be found under the skin, attached to the meat. Such a procedure does reduce calorie and fat intake. However, it also removes fat that could otherwise act as a moistening agent in cooking, basting the meat as it cooks. For this reason, other chefs recommend that the skin be removed *after* cooking. However, this procedure does leave some fat, which melts and drips off during cooking. It is often possible to buy skinless poultry portions; these products are, however, usually more expensive.

Often a chicken or turkey is roasted in a roasting pan breast-side down for a good portion of the roasting time. Toward the end of the cooking time, the bird is turned to allow the breast to brown. This may be important if the bird is carved at the table, but if carved in the kitchen and served, it is unnecessary and the bird can be roasted completely breast-side down. Chickens and turkeys are roasted in this way because the breast is lean, whereas the back contains much more fat. Having the back up allows this fat to melt and run down, thus basting the breast and helping to conserve moisture. This eliminates the need for basting by hand or other treatments that reduce the drying of the breast portion. This method is not needed for commercially grown goose or duck, since they have enough fat on the breast side to require no extra fat in basting.

Poultry should be cooked to a fairly high internal temperature, around 160°F or more. Only duck is usually cooked rare. Some recommend the final temperature to be as high as 180°F, which may be desirable for those who like the meat quite well done. Others may prefer a slightly lower temperature to ensure a moist product. To test doneness, pierce the flesh in a thick muscle, such as the thigh, and observe the color of the juices that run out. If the juices are reddish, the bird is not done; if the juices run clear, the bird is done.

POULTRY

BREAST OF CHICKEN WITH ORANGE SAUCE
AND PINEAPPLE

BREAST OF CHICKEN ALL' ALAMEDA

BREAST OF CHICKEN WITH ARTICHOKES
AND MUSHROOMS

BREAST OF CHICKEN EUGÉNIE

SAUTÉED CHICKEN IN CREAM SAUCE

RASPBERRY CHICKEN

CHICKEN FRANÇAISE

ORIENTAL FRIED CHICKEN

CHICKEN CURRY

CHICKEN PAPRIKASH

BREAST OF CHICKEN TONNATO

BAVARIAN CHICKEN BREASTS EN CASSEROLE

BAKED CHICKEN WITH ORANGES

BAKED CHICKEN BREASTS WITH
HERBED CHEESE

STUFFED CHICKEN BREASTS ATHENIAN

STUFFED BREAST OF CHICKEN POJARSKI

SWEET-AND-SOUR CHICKEN WINGS

RANCH-STYLE BARBECUED CHICKEN

GRILLED MARINATED CHICKEN ON SKEWERS

CHICKEN CHARDONNAY

SUPRÊMES OF CHICKEN WITH
ASPARAGUS BUTTER

CHICKEN PANCAKES ROMANIAN STYLE

ROAST CORNISH HEN WITH
ALMOND STUFFING

ROCK CORNISH HEN VERONIQUE

ROAST DUCKLING WITH CALVADOS,
CHEF'S STYLE

ROAST GOOSE WITH SAUERKRAUT
AND FRUIT

TURKEY CUTLETS ON GREEN RICE
WITH OLIVE SAUCE

SAUTÉED TURKEY CUTLETS WITH
ALE CREAM SAUCE

BREAST OF CHICKEN WITH ORANGE SAUCE AND PINEAPPLE

Yield: 6 servings

6 CHICKEN BREASTS, 5 TO 6 OUNCES
   EACH, BONED, WITH ONLY THE FIRST
   WING JOINT LEFT INTACT, SKIN ON
¼ CUP LIME JUICE
3½ TEASPOONS SALT
FRESHLY GROUND BLACK PEPPER TO
   TASTE
3 TABLESPOONS VEGETABLE OIL
¼ CUP DRY COCKTAIL SHERRY
1 CUP ORANGE JUICE

¼ CUP SEEDLESS RAISINS
2 TABLESPOONS GRATED LEMON ZEST
2 TABLESPOONS CATSUP
¼ TEASPOON DRIED OREGANO
½ CUP CHICKEN STOCK
¾ CUP CUBED FRESH PINEAPPLE (¾-INCH
   CUBES)
1 TABLESPOON CORNSTARCH
2 TABLESPOONS WATER
¼ CUP RUM

✤ Pat the chicken dry with paper towels. Rub it with the lime juice, and sprinkle it with 1 tablespoon of salt and the pepper. Let the chicken stand for 20 minutes.

Heat the oil in a large skillet until a faint haze forms above; place the breasts, skin side down, side by side, in the hot oil; brown and turn. When well browned on both sides, remove the breasts from the skillet, and place on a platter. (Should the skillet be too small to accommodate all the breasts at one time, brown in two steps, using half of the oil each time.)

Discard the oil, and add the sherry to the skillet. Scrape all the drippings from the surface of the pan, and simmer until all the drippings are dissolved. Then add the orange juice, raisins, lemon zest, catsup, ½ teaspoon of salt, oregano, and chicken stock. Simmer for 5 minutes, well covered.

Return the chicken to the sauce, skin side up, and simmer for another 10 minutes, well covered. Do not turn the chicken. Add the pineapple, and continue to simmer for another 5 minutes, or until the chicken is done. Remove the chicken from the sauce onto a serving platter.

Dilute the cornstarch in the water, and slowly stir the mixture into the simmering sauce until it thickens. Pour the sauce over the chicken. In a ladle or small skillet, warm the rum; ignite it carefully, and pour the burning rum over the chicken at the table before serving. Serve with white rice.

BREAST OF CHICKEN ALL' ALAMEDA

Yield: 6 servings

1 WHOLE BREAST OF CHICKEN,
   APPROXIMATELY 22 OUNCES
4 OUNCES CREAM CHEESE
2 OUNCES BLUE CHEESE
¼ CUP COARSELY GROUND WALNUTS
8 SLICES HARD SALAMI
4 FRESH SPINACH LEAVES
1 CUP PLUS 5 TABLESPOONS FLOUR
2 EGGS

1 CUP MILK
2 CUPS BREADCRUMBS
3 TABLESPOONS GRATED PARMESAN
   CHEESE
1 TEASPOON HERB SEASONING
1 CUP VEGETABLE OIL
¼ CUP BUTTER
2 CUPS STRONG CHICKEN BROTH
¼ CUP HEAVY CREAM

❖ Split the chicken breast lengthwise; skin and debone completely, leaving only the first (wing) joint. Remove the chicken tender; flatten the split breasts with a mallet. Make a pocket inside each of the breasts.

Combine the cream cheese and blue cheese, add the walnuts, and roll into two cylinders. Wrap the salami and spinach leaves around the cylinders. Place inside the pockets in the chicken, and cover with tenderloin.

Dredge the breasts in 1 cup of the flour. Beat together the eggs and milk, and dip the chicken breasts in this eggwash. Combine the breadcrumbs, Parmesan cheese, and herb seasoning, and bread the chicken breasts. Heat the oil in a skillet, and fry the coated breasts until golden brown. Remove and keep warm.

Melt the butter in a saucepan. Add the remaining 5 tablespoons of butter, and stir until smooth and bubbly. Add the chicken broth, and cook for about 5 minutes, stirring constantly. Add the heavy cream, and reduce to the desired consistency. Serve with the fried chicken breast.

BREAST OF CHICKEN WITH ARTICHOKES AND MUSHROOMS

Yield: 6 servings

4 WHOLE CHICKEN BREASTS, BONED
  AND SKINNED
SALT AND PEPPER TO TASTE
FLOUR FOR DREDGING
OLIVE OIL FOR SAUTÉING
1 ONION, CHOPPED
1 CUP QUARTERED MUSHROOMS

1 CUP QUARTERED ARTICHOKE HEARTS
1 CUP PEELED AND DICED TOMATOES
1 TABLESPOON CHOPPED PARSLEY
6 TABLESPOONS WHITE WINE
¾ CUP DEMI-GLACE (SEE RECIPE IN
  CHAPTER 3)

✤ Sprinkle the chicken breasts with salt and pepper, and dredge in the flour. Heat the olive oil in a skillet, add the chicken, and sauté until brown. Remove and keep warm. Add the onions, mushrooms, artichoke hearts, and tomatoes to the same oil, and simmer for several minutes. Add the white wine and demi-glace, and cook for 3 minutes. Season the sauce with salt and pepper. Place the chicken breasts on serving plates, nap with the sauce, and serve.

BREAST OF CHICKEN EUGÉNIE

Yield: 4 servings

½ CUP BUTTER
4 BONELESS CHICKEN BREASTS
4 LARGE FRESH MUSHROOMS, SLICED
4 SLICES COUNTRY HAM

4 SLICES TOAST
½ CUP PLUS A DASH OF SHERRY WINE
2 CUPS HEAVY CREAM
SALT AND PEPPER TO TASTE

✤ Heat the butter in a skillet, add the chicken breasts, and sauté until light brown on both sides. Add the mushrooms, cover, and cook slowly for 10 minutes. Place the ham on the top of the breasts, and cook 4 to 5 minutes. Remove the ham, chicken breasts, and mushrooms from the pan; place on the toast. To the same pan, add ½ cup of sherry. Reduce by one-half. Add the cream, and simmer for 10 to 12 minutes. Season to taste. Pour this sauce over the chicken breasts. Sprinkle with a dash of sherry.

SAUTÉED CHICKEN IN CREAM SAUCE

Yield: 4 servings

5 POUNDS BONELESS CHICKEN BREASTS
1 CUP FLOUR, SEASONED
2 TABLESPOONS BUTTER
2 TABLESPOONS VEGETABLE OIL
3 TABLESPOONS CHOPPED SHALLOTS

½ CUP WHITE WINE
1 CUP HEAVY CREAM
1 TEASPOON CORNSTARCH
2 TABLESPOONS WATER
SALT AND WHITE PEPPER TO TASTE

❖ Dredge the chicken breasts in the flour. Heat the butter and oil in an oven-proof skillet, add the chicken, and sauté until lightly browned. Cover the skillet, and braise the chicken in a 400°F oven for 15 minutes, until tender. Remove and keep warm. Sauté the shallots in the same skillet until light brown. Add the wine, and deglaze the pan. Add the cream, and simmer for 2 minutes. Dissolve the cornstarch in the water, add to the sauce, and cook for 2 more minutes. Strain the sauce over the chicken. Serve with steamed rice or pasta.

RASPBERRY CHICKEN

Yield: 4 servings

2 WHOLE BONELESS, SKINLESS CHICKEN
  BREASTS, ABOUT 2 POUNDS
2 TABLESPOONS BUTTER
¼ CUP FINELY CHOPPED ONIONS
4 OUNCES FRESH MUSHROOMS, SLICED
¼ CUP RASPBERRY VINEGAR
¼ CUP CHICKEN STOCK OR CANNED
  CHICKEN BROTH

¼ CUP HEAVY CREAM
1 TABLESPOON CANNED CRUSHED
  TOMATOES
16 FRESH RASPBERRIES
SALT AND WHITE PEPPER TO TASTE

❖ Cut each chicken breast in half along the breastbone line. Remove the filet mignon, the finger-size muscle on the back of each half, and reserve for another use. Flatten each breast half by pressing it gently with the palm of the hand. Heat the butter in a large skillet, add the chicken breasts, and cook for about 3 minutes per side, or until lightly colored. Remove from the skillet, and reserve.

Add the onions to the pan and cook, covered, over low heat until tender; add

(continued)

the mushrooms. Add the vinegar, raise the heat, and cook, uncovered, stirring occasionally, until the vinegar is reduced to a syrupy spoonful. Whisk in the chicken stock, heavy cream, and crushed tomatoes, and simmer for 1 minute.

Return the chicken breasts to the skillet, and simmer them gently in the sauce, basting often until they are just done and the sauce has been reduced and thickened slightly, about 5 minutes. Do not overcook. Remove the chicken breasts with a slotted spoon, and arrange on a heated serving platter. Add the raspberries to the sauce in the skillet, and cook over low heat for 1 minute (do *not* stir the berries with a spoon; merely swirl them in the sauce by shaking the skillet). Season to taste. Pour the sauce over chicken breasts, and serve immediately.

Variation: Strawberry Chicken: Follow the same procedure, substituting ¼ cup of strawberry vinegar for the raspberry vinegar, and 8 medium strawberries for the raspberries.

CHICKEN FRANÇAISE

Yield: 6 servings

15 SLICES WHITE BREAD, CRUSTS
   TRIMMED
4 OUNCES GRATED GRUYÈRE CHEESE
6 SPLIT BONELESS CHICKEN BREASTS
2 EGGS

¾ CUP MILK
SALT AND PEPPER TO TASTE
6 TABLESPOONS OIL OR CLARIFIED
   BUTTER

✤ In a food processor or blender, make breadcrumbs with the bread. Mix the cheese and breadcrumbs. Remove the skin from the chicken breasts, and flatten the breasts, not too thinly. Beat the eggs, and stir in the milk. Season the chicken with salt and pepper, and dip in the eggwash; then coat with the breadcrumbs and cheese. In a seasoned skillet or nonstick pan, heat oil or butter until hot but not smoking. Carefully, add the chicken, one breast at a time. Do not crowd the skillet. Do not allow the chicken to stick: shake pan a little or use a spatula to prevent sticking. Brown the breasts on one side to a nice color, then brown on the other side for a few minutes. Remove from the skillet, and bake for 15 to 20 minutes in a 300°F to 325°F oven, until done.

Variation: Chicken Modenese: Proceed as for chicken française, but before placing in the oven, slice ham, mushrooms, and mozzarella cheese, and place in this order on top of the chicken. Bake as for chicken française.

ORIENTAL FRIED CHICKEN

Yield: 6 servings

½ CUP SOY SAUCE
1 CUP RED WINE
3 TABLESPOONS LEMON JUICE
1 TABLESPOON WORCESTERSHIRE SAUCE
1 TEASPOON CRUSHED PEPPERCORNS

3 CUPS PEANUT OIL
3 POUNDS CHICKEN THIGHS AND
    DRUMSTICKS, SEPARATED, WASHED
    THOROUGHLY, DRAINED WELL

❖ Combine the soy sauce, red wine, lemon juice, Worcestershire sauce, crushed peppercorns, and peanut oil in a nonreactive shallow pan. Add the chicken, cover, and refrigerate overnight.

Place the chicken and its marinade in a pot. Bring to a boil, reduce the heat, and simmer for 20 minutes. Remove the pan from the heat. Remove the chicken; reserve the marinade. Heat ¼ inch of vegetable oil in a pan, add the chicken, and pan-fry until golden brown, skin side first.

Strain the marinade. Return it to a shallow pan, and reduce until thickened to the desired consistency.

CHICKEN CURRY

Yield: 6 servings

3 CHICKENS, 2 POUNDS EACH, BONED,
    QUARTERED, AND SKINNED
1 CUP FLOUR, SEASONED
¾ CUP OIL
1 CUP CHOPPED CELERY
1 CUP CHOPPED ONIONS
4 APPLES, PARED AND CHOPPED
3 TABLESPOONS CURRY POWDER

1/16 TEASPOON CAYENNE PEPPER
1 OUNCE CHICKEN BASE*
2 TABLESPOONS CHUTNEY
SALT AND FRESHLY GROUND BLACK
    PEPPER TO TASTE
3 CUPS BOILING WATER
½ CUP HEAVY CREAM

❖ Dredge the chicken in the flour. Heat the oil in a skillet, add the chicken, and sauté for 5 minutes, until brown. Remove and keep hot. Add the celery, onions, and apples to the skillet, and sauté for 5 to 10 minutes. Stir in the curry powder, cayenne, chicken base, chutney, salt, and pepper; add the chicken and

(continued)

boiling water. Cover, and cook for 15 minutes. Remove the chicken. Strain the sauce and finish it by swirling in the cream. Pour the sauce over the chicken, and serve with rice and curry condiments, such as grated coconut, chutney, chopped peanuts, diced bananas, and diced cucumbers.

* For information about this base, see chapter 3.

CHICKEN PAPRIKASH

Yield: 4 servings

½ CUP OIL
2½ POUNDS FRYING CHICKEN, CUT INTO
   EIGHTHS
¾ CUP FLOUR
1¼ POUNDS ONIONS, SLICED

1½ QUARTS WATER
4 OUNCES CHICKEN BASE*
4 OUNCES TOMATO PASTE
1 OUNCE PAPRIKA
1 CUP SOUR CREAM

❖ Heat the oil in large skillet. Dredge the chicken in the flour, and brown well in the hot oil. Remove the chicken. Add the onions, and sauté until tender. Add the water, chicken base, tomato paste, paprika, and browned chicken. Cover, and simmer for 45 minutes. Remove the chicken, and strain the sauce. Add a bit of the sauce to the sour cream to temper it, and add it to the finished sauce.

* For information about this base, see chapter 3.

BREAST OF CHICKEN TONNATO

Yield: 6 servings

MARINADE
1 CUP DRY WHITE WINE
6 JUNIPER BERRIES, CRUSHED
2 GARLIC CLOVES, CRUSHED
1 CELERY RIB, DICED
½ CUP DICED ONION

½ TEASPOON THYME
2 BAY LEAVES, CRUMBLED
½ CUP WATER
1 CARROT, DICED
SALT AND WHITE PEPPER TO TASTE

CHICKEN
3 BONELESS SKINLESS CHICKEN
   BREASTS, HALVED

6 ANCHOVIES

TUNA SAUCE

6½ OUNCES CANNED TUNA IN OIL
2 GARLIC CLOVES
6 ANCHOVIES
1 TEASPOON CAPERS

1 CUP WHIPPING CREAM
SALT TO TASTE
½ TEASPOON WHITE PEPPER

GARNISH

6 LEMON SLICES
18 BLACK OLIVES, PITTED

½ CUP CHOPPED PARSLEY
1½ TABLESPOONS CAPERS, DRAINED

✣ Combine the marinade ingredients in a saucepan, bring to a simmer, and cook for 10 minutes. Remove from the heat, and allow to cool.

Make a slit in the underside of each chicken breast half, and insert an anchovy. Place the chicken in the cool marinade, and refrigerate for 2 hours. Remove the breasts. Heat the marinade to a simmer, add the chicken, and poach gently until firm, about 8 to 10 minutes. Cool, and refrigerate in the marinade until cold.

Remove the chicken from the marinade, and set aside. Strain the marinade, reserving the vegetables (discard the liquid). In a food processor, process the tuna, garlic, reserved marinade, vegetables, anchovies, and capers until smooth. Slowly add the cream. Season with salt and pepper.

To serve, cut the chicken breasts into ¼-inch slices on the bias. Coat with the tuna sauce, and garnish with the lemon slices, black olives, parsley, and capers.

BAVARIAN CHICKEN BREASTS EN CASSEROLE

Yield: 8 servings

8 WHOLE CHICKEN BREASTS, WITH RIB
    BONES
⅓ CUP FLOUR
½ TEASPOON THYME
½ TEASPOON SALT
½ TEASPOON WHITE PEPPER
½ CUP CORN OIL

⅓ CUP CHOPPED SCALLIONS
½ CUP CHICKEN BROTH
⅔ CUP DRY WHITE WINE
16 SLICES CANADIAN BACON
⅔ CUP HALF-AND-HALF CREAM
1 TABLESPOON CHOPPED PARSLEY

(continued)

✣ Dredge the chicken breasts in the flour seasoned with the salt, pepper, and thyme. Heat the corn oil in a skillet, add the chicken breasts, and sauté until brown. Add the chopped scallions, chicken broth, and wine; cover, and cook over low heat for about 30 minutes. Remove the chicken. Make incisions on each side of each breast, and insert 1 slice of Canadian bacon into each incision. Set aside. Stir the cream into the cooking liquid, and add the chopped parsley. Place the chicken breasts in individual casseroles. Pour the cream sauce over the chicken breasts, and bake at 350°F for 10 to 15 minutes.

Note: To lower the fat in this recipe, roast the chicken with the skin, rather than sautéing and poaching, and then remove the skin and cut the incisions; use 2-percent or skim milk in place of half and half.

BAKED CHICKEN WITH ORANGES

Yield: 8 servings

2 FRYER CHICKENS, 2½ TO 3 POUNDS
  EACH, CUT INTO 8 PIECES EACH, SKIN
  REMOVED
4 TABLESPOONS FLOUR
⅓ CUP CORN OIL

2 JUICE ORANGES
½ CUP WATER
1 TEASPOON GROUND MACE
3 TABLESPOONS HONEY

✣ Lightly dust the chicken pieces with the flour. Heat the oil in a skillet over medium heat, add the chicken, and lightly brown all sides. Remove the chicken from the skillet, and place in a baking dish. Peel the oranges; grate the orange zest, and separate the orange sections. Deglaze the skillet with the water, and add the grated orange rind, mace, and honey. Pour this mixture over chicken; add the orange sections. Bake, covered, in a 325°F oven for 45 minutes.

Variation: Add ½ cup of chopped scallions and ½ cup of dry white wine.

BAKED CHICKEN BREASTS WITH HERBED CHEESE

Yield: 6 servings

6 BONELESS CHICKEN BREASTS,
   8 OUNCES EACH
12 OUNCES CREAM CHEESE
2½ TEASPOONS GARLIC POWDER
1½ TABLESPOONS CHOPPED CHIVES
½ TEASPOON DILL WEED
½ TEASPOON SWEET BASIL
½ TEASPOON SALT

⅛ TEASPOON WHITE PEPPER
1½ TEASPOONS CORNSTARCH
1½ CUPS MILK
3 OUNCES FLOUR (½ CUP)
3 CUPS DRY BREADCRUMBS
6 TABLESPOONS MELTED BUTTER
6 ORANGE SLICES
6 STRAWBERRIES, CUT INTO FANS

❖ Remove the skin from the chicken breasts, and discard. Gently flatten the chicken breasts with the palm of the hand.

In a small mixing bowl, combine the cream cheese, garlic powder, chives, dill weed, basil, salt, white pepper, and cornstarch. Blend together well. Place ⅙ of the cheese mixture in the center of each chicken breast. Roll the chicken breast around the cream cheese mixture, tucking in the ends; secure with toothpicks.

Mix the milk and flour to form a batter. Dip the rolled chicken breasts in the milk batter. Drain; then roll in the dry breadcrumbs to coat. Deep fry in a 350°F deep-fat fryer until light brown (approximately 2½ to 3 minutes). Remove, and place in a buttered baking pan. Bake in 375°F oven for 10 minutes, until the chicken breast is cooked. Remove from the oven. Garnish each with an orange wheel and a strawberry fan, and serve.

STUFFED CHICKEN BREASTS ATHENIAN

Yield: 4 servings

4 BONELESS, SKINLESS CHICKEN
  BREASTS, 8 OUNCES EACH
2 TABLESPOONS CRUMBLED BLUE OR
  FETA CHEESE
8 OUNCES FROZEN BROCCOLI, THAWED
1 TABLESPOON CHOPPED WALNUTS OR
  PECANS
3 MEDIUM EGGS

¾ CUP FLOUR
¼ TEASPOON PEPPER
¼ TEASPOON SALT
2 TABLESPOONS MILK
¼ CUP VEGETABLE OR OLIVE OIL
1 TABLESPOON GRATED PARMESAN
  CHEESE

S A U C E

1 TABLESPOON FLOUR
1 TABLESPOON BUTTER

1½ CUPS HOT CHICKEN STOCK OR MILK

✛ Lay the chicken breasts on a solid chopping board, cover with wax paper, and flatten by pounding; do not tear the meat. Set aside.

Mix the crumbled cheese, broccoli, walnuts or pecans, and 1 egg until well blended. Spoon this filling in the center of each chicken breast, and roll up, tucking in the ends. Combine the flour, salt, and pepper. Dredge the chicken rolls in the flour. Beat the remaining 2 eggs and the milk together, and coat the floured breast in this eggwash. Place the breasts on a slotted drainboard to allow the excess eggwash to drip off.

Heat the oil in a skillet until medium hot (do not overheat or the batter will brown). Put two stuffed breasts in the oil, and roll until light brown. Remove from the pan, and repeat for the other two breasts. Set the chicken in a greased pie plate, and bake in a 350°F oven for 15 minutes, until the cheese starts to ooze out.

To make the sauce, mix the flour with the butter. Heat, but do not color. Add the hot milk or stock, and cook for 3 to 5 minutes. Season as desired. Top the chicken with this white sauce, and sprinkle with the grated cheese.

STUFFED BREAST OF CHICKEN POJARSKI

Yield: 6 servings

1½ POUNDS FINELY GROUND LEAN MILK-
   FED WHITE VEAL
SALT AND PEPPER TO TASTE
DASH OF NUTMEG

½ CUP WHIPPING CREAM
3 EGG WHITES
6 BONELESS BREASTS OF CHICKEN,
   7 OUNCES EACH

HUNGARIAN SAUCE

½ TEASPOON PAPRIKA
½ CUP SHERRY
3 CUPS CHICKEN BROTH
3 TABLESPOONS BUTTER

3 TABLESPOONS FLOUR
SALT AND WHITE PEPPER TO TASTE
2 TABLESPOONS SOUR CREAM

✤ Place the ground veal, salt, pepper, and nutmeg in a mixing bowl. Beat at medium speed, gradually adding the whipping cream and the egg white alternately, until smooth. Divide this forcemeat into 6 equal portions. Stuff the breasts of chicken with this forcemeat, wrapping the chicken well around the stuffing. Seal with a band of wax paper. Bake in a 375°F to 400°F oven for approximately 45 minutes. Do not let the tops of the breasts get too brown. Remove the chicken from the pan, and keep warm.

To make the sauce, sprinkle the paprika over the chicken drippings in the pan. Add the sherry, and deglaze the pan. Add the broth, and bring to a boil. Prepare a white roux with the butter and flour, and add to the broth. Cook for 3 to 5 minutes, stirring constantly. Strain, season, and add the sour cream. Arrange the breasts of chicken on a platter, cover with the sauce, and serve.

SWEET-AND-SOUR CHICKEN WINGS

Yield: 4 servings

20 CHICKEN WINGS
2 CUPS WATER
SALT TO TASTE
3 EGGS, BEATEN
1 CUP CORNSTARCH
½ CUP COOKING OIL

2 TABLESPOONS VERY FINELY CHOPPED
GARLIC
½ CUP CATSUP
1 TABLESPOON SOY SAUCE
1 CUP SUGAR
½ CUP CIDER VINEGAR

(continued)

❖ Cut the tips from the wings, reserving the wings. Place the tips in the water, bring to a boil, reduce the heat, season with salt, and simmer for 20 minutes. Strain the broth; reserve 1 cup for the sweet-and-sour sauce; use any remaining for another recipe.

Dip the reserved wings in the beaten eggs, then in the cornstarch. Heat the oil in a sauté pan. Add the garlic, and cook until garlic begins to color. Fry the wings in the garlic and oil until brown. Remove to a large baking dish.

Mix the cup of chicken broth, catsup, soy sauce, sugar, and vinegar. Pour this sauce over the chicken wings. Bake in a 350°F oven until tender, about 45 minutes.

RANCH-STYLE BARBECUED CHICKEN

Yield: 6 servings

½ CUP WHITE VINEGAR
½ CUP SALAD OIL
1½ TEASPOONS WORCESTERSHIRE
   SAUCE
½ TEASPOON MINCED ONION
1 GARLIC CLOVE, MINCED
1 TABLESPOON SALT
1 TEASPOON PAPRIKA

1½ TEASPOONS TOMATO PUREE
6–8 DROPS HOT PEPPER SAUCE
   (TABASCO)
½ TEASPOON DRY MUSTARD
3 FRYING CHICKENS, 2–3 POUNDS EACH,
   CUT INTO PIECES
½ CUP BUTTER OR MARGARINE, MELTED

❖ Combine the vinegar, oil, Worcestershire sauce, onion, garlic, salt, paprika, tomato puree, hot pepper sauce, and dry mustard. Brush the chicken pieces with the melted butter. Prepare a grill with charcoals. Sear the chicken over the charcoal for 5 minutes; turn. Brush with the sauce, cook for 5 minutes, and turn; continue this procedure until the chicken is done, about 45 to 60 minutes.

Note: For best results, prepare the basting sauce 24 hours in advance.

GRILLED MARINATED CHICKEN ON SKEWERS

Yield: 12 skewers

12 CHICKEN NUGGETS OR 3 SINGLE
  BREASTS CUT INTO 4 STRIPS
SALT AND WHITE PEPPER TO TASTE
½ CUP OLIVE OIL
1 CUP RASPBERRY OR TARRAGON
  VINEGAR
4 GARLIC CLOVES, CHOPPED

4 SHALLOTS, CHOPPED
1 BUNCH FRESH ROSEMARY, CHOPPED
  (LEAVES ONLY)
¼ CUP POMMEROY MEAUX MUSTARD
  (WHOLE-GRAIN PREPARED MUSTARD)
¼ CUP CRACKED BLACK PEPPER OR
  FRESH, COARSELY GROUND PEPPER

❖ Season the chicken with the salt and white pepper. Thread each chicken strip onto a 4- to 6-inch skewer lengthwise. Combine the olive oil, flavored vinegar, garlic, shallots, rosemary, mustard, and black pepper in a jar; cover, and shake well to blend. Pour this marinade over the chicken; cover, and refrigerate overnight or up to 2 days.

Remove the chicken from the marinade, and grill over moderate heat for 3 to 5 minutes on each side. Serve over steamed rice.

Note: This dish can also be served as an appetizer.

CHICKEN CHARDONNAY

Yield: 4 servings

10 OUNCES BUTTER (1¼ CUPS)
2 BONELESS CHICKEN BREASTS, CUT
  INTO 1-INCH STRIPS
8 MUSHROOMS, SLICED
⅓ CUP CHOPPED SHALLOTS
½ OUNCE CHOPPED GARLIC
  (2 TABLESPOONS)

¾ CUP CHARDONNAY
2 CUPS HEAVY CREAM (SEE NOTE
  BELOW)
10 PEPERONCINI (RED CHILI PEPPERS)—
  MILD
SALT AND WHITE PEPPER TO TASTE

(continued)

❖ Heat ¼ cup of the butter in a skillet, add the chicken strips, and sauté; when half-cooked, add the mushrooms, shallots, and garlic. Cook until glazed. Pour the Chardonnay into the pan with the chicken; reduce by one-half. Add the heavy cream, and reduce by one-half again. Add the peperoncini. Remove from the heat, and swirl in the remaining 1 cup of butter. Taste and season.

Note: If you prefer not to use cream, add 1 cup of chicken stock or bouillon instead. Proceed as if using cream.

SUPRÊMES OF CHICKEN WITH ASPARAGUS BUTTER

Yield: 6 servings

6 SUPRÊMES OF CHICKEN (BONELESS, SKINLESS BREASTS OF YOUNG CHICKENS)
SALT AND WHITE PEPPER TO TASTE
½ CUP FLOUR
8 OUNCES BUTTER (1 CUP)
1 POUND GREEN ASPARAGUS TIPS

1 CUP MADEIRA WINE
¼ CUP COGNAC
¼ CUP CHICKEN STOCK
½ CUP HALF-AND-HALF CREAM
12 ASPARAGUS SPEARS
2 LEEK LEAVES

❖ Season the chicken breasts with salt and pepper. Dust with the flour, carefully shaking off any excess. Heat ½ cup (4 ounces) of the butter in an ovenproof skillet just large enough to hold the breasts. Lightly brown both sides of the chicken over medium heat. Baste the breasts with the butter. Cover tightly, and glaze in preheated 400°F oven for 6 to 8 minutes.

Meanwhile, cook the asparagus tips in a little salted water until very tender; drain and cool.

Remove the chicken to platter; keep warm. Pour excess fat from the skillet. Deglaze the pan with the Madeira; reduce to ½ cup. Add the Cognac, chicken stock, and cream, and simmer for a few minutes. Puree this sauce in a food processor until smooth. Return the sauce to low heat.

Cream 6 tablespoons of butter and the cooked asparagus tips in a mixer. Force the mixture through a fine sieve. Remove the sauce from the heat, and finish it by whisking in this asparagus butter. Adjust the seasonings.

Blanch the asparagus spears in salted water; blanch the leek leaves in salted water. Cut six ¼-inch-wide strips from leek leaves. Tie two asparagus stalks with each leek strip. Melt the remaining 2 tablespoons of butter, and baste the asparagus bundles with it.

To serve, pour a small amount of the sauce on preheated serving plates. Place the suprêmes over the sauce. Ladle a small cordon of sauce over the suprêmes. Garnish each plate with an asparagus bundle.

CHICKEN PANCAKES ROMANIAN STYLE

Yield: 6 servings

4 BONELESS, SKINLESS CHICKEN
  BREASTS
1½ CUPS CHICKEN BROTH
1 MEDIUM ONION, CHOPPED
¼ TEASPOON WHITE PEPPER
¼ TEASPOON THYME

4 FRESH MEDIUM BARTLETT PEARS (NOT
  TOO RIPE), PEELED, CORED, AND
  CUBED
3 TABLESPOONS FLOUR
5 EGGS, BEATEN UNTIL LEMON-COLORED

❖ In a saucepan, place the chicken breasts, chicken broth, onions, pepper, and thyme. Cover and bring to a boil; skim off the froth. Reduce the heat, and simmer, covered, for about 20 minutes. Add the cubed pears, and continue cooking until they are very tender. Remove the chicken, onion, and pears from the broth, and cool; discard the broth. Place the chicken mixture in a food processor, and chop finely. Place in a mixing bowl, sprinkle the flour over the top, and the beaten eggs, and mix well. Ladle spoonfuls of the batter onto a griddle, and fry the pancakes to a golden brown on each side. Serve at once. Hot orange marmalade is a good accompaniment.

ROAST CORNISH HEN WITH ALMOND STUFFING

Yield: 2 to 4 servings

2 ROCK CORNISH HENS
SALT AND PEPPER TO TASTE
2 BAY LEAVES
3½ SLICES WHITE BREAD
3½ TABLESPOONS MILK
2 HEAPING TABLESPOONS SOFT BUTTER
2 EGG YOLKS

PINCH OF NUTMEG
1 TEASPOON CHOPPED CHIVES
6 TABLESPOONS SLICED ALMONDS
2 EGG WHITES
¼ CUP MELTED BUTTER
½ CUP ORANGE JUICE
½ CUP CHICKEN STOCK

❖ Preheat the oven to 350°F. Remove the giblets from the hens; season the insides with salt, pepper, and a bay leaf in each. Loosen the skin and flesh of each, from the neck opening toward the end of the breastbone, down to the wings.

To prepare the stuffing, trim the crusts from the bread and discard; dice the bread into 1-inch cubes. Sprinkle the bread cubes with the milk, and set aside. In a bowl, cream the butter with the egg yolks; add a pinch of salt, the nutmeg, chives, and almonds; stir in the bread, without mashing it too much. In another clean bowl, using a very clean whisk, whip the egg whites until the peaks hold. Fold the egg whites into the bread mixture; do not overmix.

Using a spoon, stuff the cavity of each bird. Fold the neck skin flap down over the opening, and truss the hens with string. Place the giblets in a roasting pan, with the hens on top. Sprinkle with a little salt, and brush with the melted butter.

Place in the preheated 350°F oven, and roast for approximately 1½ hours, until golden brown and tender. Lift the birds from the pan, and set aside. Add the orange juice and stock to the pan drippings, and reduce to the desired consistency and flavor; strain. Split the hens lengthwise for four servings; serve whole for two. Pour the sauce over the chicken, and accompany with stewed fruit or vegetables.

ROCK CORNISH HEN VERONIQUE

Yield: 6 servings

½ CUP BUTTER

½ CUP CHOPPED SHALLOTS

8 OUNCES MUSHROOMS, SLICED

1 CUP THICK CREAM SAUCE (SEE RECIPE IN CHAPTER 3)

2 EGGS, WELL BEATEN

12 OUNCES COOKED WILD RICE

1 CUP FRESH WHITE BREADCRUMBS

½ CUP SLIVERED ALMONDS, TOASTED

6 TABLESPOONS SHERRY

SALT AND PEPPER TO TASTE

6 ROCK CORNISH HENS, ABOUT 1 POUND EACH

¼ CUP FLOUR

2 CUPS CHICKEN STOCK (SEE NOTE BELOW)

1 CUP WHITE SEEDLESS GRAPES

❖ Heat ¼ cup of the butter in a skillet, add the shallots and mushrooms, and sauté until tender. Stir in the cream sauce, eggs, wild rice, breadcrumbs, almonds, sherry, salt, and pepper. Cover, and refrigerate overnight.

Stuff each Cornish hen with the dressing; tuck the wings under, with the legs upward. Cut strips of brown butcher paper about 2 inches wide and long enough to wrap around each hen leg twice. Oil the paper on both sides so it will stick to the hen; wrap the paper around each hen leg front to back; do not cover the breasts. Melt the remaining ¼ cup of butter, and brush each hen's breast with it. Arrange in a roasting pan, and roast for 45 minutes to 1 hour at 350°F. Remove the hens from the pan; keep warm.

To make gravy, strain the juices from the Cornish hens. Pour off and reserve the fat. Heat ¼ cup of the reserved fat in a saucepan. Add the flour, and stir until blended. Combine the pan drippings and enough chicken stock to make 2 cups. Stir slowly into the fat/flour mixture until smooth; simmer for 5 minutes. Season with salt and pepper. Serve the gravy alongside the hens. Garnish the hens with the grapes.

Note: The chicken stock for the gravy may be homemade, canned, or prepared from powdered base or bouillon.

ROAST DUCKLING WITH CALVADOS, CHEF'S STYLE

Yield: 4 servings

1 DUCKLING, 4 TO 5 POUNDS
1 CUP ONION-AND-GARLIC PASTE
3 TABLESPOONS LIQUID SMOKE
1½ CUPS CALVADOS
SALT AND PEPPER, TO TASTE
1 LARGE ONION, DICED
5 GARLIC CLOVES, MINCED
3 CELERY STALKS, CHOPPED

2 CARROTS, DICED
½ TEASPOON ROSEMARY
3 BAY LEAVES
½ CUP FLOUR
1 CUP CHICKEN STOCK
2 TABLESPOONS CURRANT JELLY
¼ CUP HONEY

✤ Firmly pierce the skin of the duckling all over with a fork, so that the marinade will adhere and subsequently self-baste the duckling as it roasts. Combine the onion-and-garlic paste, liquid smoke, 1 cup of Calvados, and salt and pepper to make a marinade. Pour the marinade over the duck, and refrigerate for 2 to 3 days, turning occasionally.

In a roasting pan, place the onions, garlic, celery, carrots, rosemary, and bay leaves. Place the duck, breast side up, on the vegetables; add the marinade. Roast the duck in a 350°F oven for 30 to 40 minutes per pound, until golden brown and crisp. Pour off the fat, reserving 3 tablespoons. Add the flour to these drippings, and brown briefly. Add the chicken stock, and boil for 5 minutes. Strain. Add the remaining ½ cup of Calvados and the currant jelly; taste, and adjust seasonings. Glaze the duck with the honey, and pour on the sauce. Serve with boiled parsley potatoes, braised cabbage, stewed apples, and prune compote.

ROAST GOOSE WITH SAUERKRAUT AND FRUIT

Yield: 6 to 8 servings

1 GOOSE, 12 TO 16 POUNDS
2 POUNDS SAUERKRAUT, DRAINED (USE SAUERKRAUT PACKED IN BAGS, NOT CANNED)
1 MEDIUM POTATO, PEELED AND GRATED

1 LARGE RED DELICIOUS APPLE, PEELED, CORED, AND SLICED
8 DRIED APRICOTS, CHOPPED
1 TEASPOON BLACK PEPPER

✤ Wash the goose, and make sure the cavity is clean. Mix the sauerkraut, grated potato, apple, apricots, and black pepper together. Stuff the sauerkraut mixture into goose's cavity. Place the goose on a rack in a roasting pan, cover, and roast at 325°F for about 2½ to 3 hours, until the goose is tender, basting occasionally with the pan drippings. (Remove the cover for the last 30 minutes of roasting if more browning is required.) Serve with boiled potatoes with their jackets or homemade buttered noodles tossed lightly with buttered breadcrumbs.

TURKEY CUTLETS ON GREEN RICE WITH OLIVE SAUCE

Yield: 8 servings

GREEN RICE

¼ CUP BUTTER
2 SMALL ONIONS, FINELY CHOPPED
2 CUPS RICE
4½ CUPS BOILING WATER
SALT AND WHITE PEPPER TO TASTE

1 BAY LEAF
½ CUP CHOPPED SCALLIONS AND
   PARSLEY, PASSED THROUGH A MEAT
   GRINDER OR VERY FINELY CHOPPED IN
   A BLENDER

TURKEY CUTLETS

8 TURKEY CUTLETS (WHITE MEAT),
   4 OUNCES EACH
SALT AND PEPPER, TO TASTE
½ CUP FLOUR

2 EGGS, BEATEN WITH A LITTLE MILK
1½ CUPS BREADCRUMBS
½ CUP BUTTER OR MARGARINE

OLIVE SAUCE

2 CUPS CHICKEN BROTH
4 TABLESPOONS BUTTER
3 TABLESPOONS FLOUR
½ CUP WHIPPING CREAM
1 EGG YOLK

1 DOZEN STUFFED GREEN OLIVES,
   SLICED
RIPE GREEN OLIVES OR PIMENTOS FOR
   GARNISH

✤ To prepare green rice, heat 3 tablespoons of butter in a skillet, add the onions, and sauté until the onions become translucent (not brown). Add the rice, mixing thoroughly so each grain is well coated with butter. Add the boiling water, salt, pepper, and bay leaf; reduce the heat. Cover tightly, and cook at a slow boil for 20 minutes, or until all the moisture is absorbed and the rice

(continued)

separates easily. Sauté the scallion and parsley mixture in the remaining butter; add to the rice, and mix well.

Season the turkey cutlets with salt and pepper; dredge in the flour. Dip the cutlets in the eggwash, then coat with the breadcrumbs. Heat the butter in a skillet, add the breaded cutlets, and sauté until golden brown on both sides; do not cook the cutlets too quickly: the turkey must have a chance to cook.

Start the olive sauce by preparing a chicken velouté: bring the chicken broth to a boil; in another pan, melt 3 tablespoons of butter, add the flour, and stir together until bubbly and smooth; add the boiling chicken stock to this roux, and cook and stir until the velouté has the consistency of boiled custard. Remove from the heat. Heat the whipping cream, and whisk in the remaining tablespoon of butter and the egg yolk. Add this liaison to the velouté. Rinse the sliced olives under hot water to reduce their acidity, drain, and add them to the sauce.

To serve, make a bed of the rice, top with the turkey cutlets, and pour the olive sauce over the turkey. Garnish with more sliced olives and strips of ripe olives or pimentos.

SAUTÉED TURKEY CUTLETS WITH ALE CREAM SAUCE

Yield: 4 servings

4 TURKEY CUTLETS, 6 OUNCES EACH
6 TABLESPOONS BUTTER
2 TABLESPOONS BRANDY
4 SHALLOTS, FINELY DICED
3 TABLESPOONS CATSUP
1 TABLESPOON CORNSTARCH

¾ CUP DARK ALE
SALT AND PEPPER TO TASTE
1 TABLESPOON WORCESTERSHIRE SAUCE
2 TABLESPOONS WHIPPING CREAM
1 TEASPOON CHOPPED CHERVIL

❖ Pound the turkey cutlets until thin. Heat half of the butter in a skillet; add the turkey, and sauté for 5 minutes. Flame with the brandy; remove the turkey, keeping it warm. Add the remaining butter to the pan and sauté the shallots until translucent. Add the catsup, and brown. Dust with the cornstarch, and brown. Add the ale, and simmer for 5 to 10 minutes. Season with salt and pepper, and add the Worcestershire sauce. Return the turkey cutlets to the pan, and simmer for 3 minutes; remove the turkey, and arrange on a serving dish.

Whip the cream to soft peaks, and fold in the chervil, add salt and pepper. Fold the whipped cream into the pan sauce; pour sauce over the turkey, and serve.

CHAPTER SEVEN

Fish and Shellfish

THE consumption of fish and shellfish has grown significantly in recent years because many items in this food category are thought to be low in cholesterol and fat. They are also often lower in calories than other protein sources because they contain less fat. Although this is true for most seafood, there are some exceptions. Although low in fat, some shellfish are high in cholesterol. And, salmon, trout, and other fatty fish are fairly high in calories.

Nutritionally, saltwater seafood is a good source of iodine, a mineral not generally found in other flesh foods. Fish and shellfish contain good amounts of B vitamins, protein, and some minerals but are not as good a source of iron as meat or poultry is.

Fish and shellfish are generally easy to cook, but many people unfortunately overcook them. Too much heat tends to toughen seafood, making it very rubbery. Fish and shellfish have very little connective tissue; they are therefore tender, and do not require the tenderizing cooking methods used for mature poultry or tougher meat cuts.

Fish should be cooked *just* until it flakes; no longer. Be careful never to overcook shellfish, including lobster, crab, shrimp, clams, and oysters. In preparing an oyster stew, bring the oysters just to the boiling point and then blend them with the hot rich milk and serve. Steamed clams should be cooked only until the shells open, no more. Overboiling a lobster toughens it.

Fish and shellfish are highly perishable and should be used as soon as possible after purchasing. They tend to become stronger in flavor as they stand. If they must be stored—and it is best to limit storage to twenty-four hours—place in a cold, but not freezing, space in the refrigerator. Sometimes putting the fish between sealed bags of ice in a refrigerator is desirable. Oysters, clams, lobsters, crab, and other shellfish should be alive when purchased, or already cooked.

Fish are often divided into two categories for cooking: fatty fish and lean fish (shellfish are all low in fat). Fish with plenty of fat may be baked, broiled, or prepared using other dry-heat methods. They also can be cooked using moist-heat methods, such as poaching, boiling, or steaming. Low-fat fish are best cooked with the moist-heat methods (it is difficult to broil a lean sole), but they are often sautéed or deep-fried to add fat in the cooking process. When fat is added in this manner, the item is, of course, no longer considered a low-fat food, because the seafood (and any breading) absorbs the cooking fat.

Serving fish and shellfish fairly frequently can add variety and interest to a menu, in addition to contributing nutritionally. It is often wise to purchase seasonally. Fish and shellfish are available in plentiful supply during certain seasons and are at their best at these times, as well as being at the most favorable prices. Much frozen fish on the market is also of good quality; the practice of processing it just after it is caught on the fishing boats while at sea has done much to improve the product. Aquacultured fish is also now in good supply. For example, salmon from the Northwest and Canada are now raised in huge ponds, removing the seasonal nature of this fish. Catfish is another fish being farm-raised using aquaculture. Many canned fish products can also be successfully used in certain kinds of dishes.

In purchasing fish, be aware that some of the items may seem inexpensive, but waste makes them high-cost items. For example, uncooked shrimp in the shell lose 50 percent of their weight when cooked and shelled. The edible portion of an uncleaned fish, with a large head, a lot of scales, and internal organs, is often only one-third the weight of the whole fish. Thus, when considering fillets or steaks versus a whole fish, allow for the waste in the whole fish as well as the work involved in cleaning it when evaluating cost.

Fish and Shellfish

BROILED BASS WITH ONION CONFIT

FRESH COD LIVORNESE

POACHED HALIBUT STEAK WITH
CAPER SAUCE

MONKFISH WITH LOBSTER BRANDY SAUCE

FILLETS OF FLORIDA POMPANO,
MARYLAND STYLE

BLACKENED RED SNAPPER FILLETS

SALMON WITH POACHED EGGS
SALMON COULIBIAC
SALMON FILLETS WITH
FRESH HERB CRUMBS
SALMON AND BASS WITH SORREL SAUCE
DUBLIN-STYLE DOVER SOLE
BAKED FILLETS OF LEMON SOLE DUQUESNE
SWORDFISH WITH MACADAMIA NUTS
TROUT MOUSSE WITH LOBSTER SAUCE
QUENELLES WITH LOBSTER SAUCE
FISH PIE
CIOPPINO
CRABMEAT CHAUMIÈRE
DEVILED CRAB IMPERIAL
KING CRABMEAT, NEW ORLEANS STYLE
KING CRABMEAT CRÊPES
MUSSELS WITH CREAM SAUCE
OYSTER SOUFFLÉ
SCALLOPS WITH APPLES AND SNOW PEAS
SCALLOPS WITH VEGETABLES JULIENNE
SCALLOPS WITH WATERCRESS COULIS
SHRIMP TEMPURA
SHRIMP HAR KOW
SHRIMP FRIED RICE
SHRIMP CANTONESE
PRAWNS AND ARTICHOKES CHARDONNAY
SHRIMP CALYPSO
FLAMED SHRIMP BOMBAY
SEAFOOD THERMIDOR

BROILED BASS WITH ONION CONFIT

Yield: 4 servings

4 MEDIUM RED ONIONS, MINCED
1¼ CUPS RED WINE
¼ CUP SHERRY WINE VINEGAR
¾ CUP WATER
1 TEASPOON HONEY
4 TEASPOONS BUTTER

SALT AND PEPPER TO TASTE
10 MEDIUM TOMATOES, PEELED, SEEDED, AND CRUSHED
2 POUNDS SUNSHINE BASS FILLETS
¼ CUP OLIVE OIL

✤ Place the onions, red wine, sherry vinegar, and water in a heavy skillet, and cook until the onions are tender. Add the honey and 1 teaspoon of the butter; adjust the seasonings. In a separate pan, heat the remaining 3 teaspoons of butter, add the tomatoes, and cook to a fine puree. Brush the fish with the olive oil, season, and broil for 5 to 6 minutes per side, until the fish flakes easily. Ladle the onion confit onto a heated serving plate. Place the tomato puree around the confit, and place the fish on the confit. Serve with fried or oven-baked potatoes.

Variations: John Dory, Alaskan red snapper, or red snapper can be used in place of the bass in this recipe. The fish may also be fried in a skillet, rather than broiled.

FRESH COD LIVORNESE

Yield: 6 servings

3 TABLESPOONS BUTTER
1 TABLESPOON FINELY CHOPPED ONIONS
1 FINELY CRUSHED GARLIC CLOVE
8 PLUM TOMATOES, PEELED, SEEDED, AND CHOPPED
¼ TEASPOON DRIED CRUSHED THYME

1 SMALL BAY LEAF, CRUMBLED
SALT AND PEPPER TO TASTE
8 OUNCES FRESH COD FILLETS
FLOUR TO DREDGE
½ CUP VEGETABLE OIL
2 TABLESPOONS CHOPPED PARSLEY

❖ Melt the butter in a saucepan over medium heat. Add the onions and garlic; cook until golden and tender. Add the tomatoes, thyme, and bay leaf, and cook for 15 minutes. Season with salt and pepper and remove from the heat.

Season the fish with salt and pepper, and dredge in the flour. Heat the oil in a frying pan, add the fish, and sauté until golden brown on both sides, approximately 5 minutes per side. Transfer the fillets to a hot serving platter. Pour the sauce over, and sprinkle with the chopped parsley.

POACHED HALIBUT STEAK WITH CAPER SAUCE

Yield: 6 servings

2-POUND CENTER-CUT HALIBUT
3 BAY LEAVES
1 TEASPOON SALT
½ CUP DRY WHITE WINE
½ CUP WATER
1 CUP THINLY SLICED ONIONS
1 CUP THINLY SLICED CELERY

2 TABLESPOONS BUTTER
2 EGG YOLKS
2 TABLESPOONS MELTED BUTTER
JUICE OF 1 LEMON
PINCH OF CAYENNE PEPPER
½ TEASPOON SALT
3 TABLESPOONS CAPERS, WELL DRAINED

❖ Cut the halibut into six 5-ounce steaks. Place the steaks in a poaching pan; add the bay leaves, salt, wine, water, onions, and celery. Bring to a boil; reduce the heat so that the fish barely simmers; poach for 15 minutes. Lift the steaks onto a preheated platter, dot each steak with the butter; cover and keep hot. Strain the poaching liquid and reserve ⅔ cup, which should be kept hot. In the top section of a double-boiler, beat the egg yolks slightly. Combine 1 tablespoon of the melted butter with the lemon juice, and add to the egg yolks. Cook over boiling water, stirring briskly, for 1 minute. Add the remaining 1 tablespoon of melted butter, and continue stirring until the mixture begins to thicken, about 3 minutes. Gradually stir in the reserved poaching liquid, cayenne, and salt, until the sauce is creamy smooth. Add the capers. Pour the sauce over the halibut, and serve immediately.

MONKFISH WITH LOBSTER BRANDY SAUCE

Yield: 6 servings

¼ CUP OLIVE OIL
1 TABLESPOON FINELY CHOPPED
   SHALLOTS
1 TEASPOON CHOPPED GARLIC
1½-POUND MONKFISH, CUT INTO
   CHUNKS
¼ CUP BRANDY
½ CUP DICED RED PEPPERS

½ CUP DICED GREEN PEPPERS
1 CUP SLICED MUSHROOMS
2 CUPS HEAVY CREAM
¼ CUP WATER
1½ TEASPOONS LOBSTER BASE*
2 MEDIUM TOMATOES, PEELED, SEEDED,
   AND CHOPPED

✤ Heat 2 tablespoons of the olive oil in a skillet, add the shallots, garlic, and monkfish, and sauté for 5 minutes. Flame with the brandy, remove the fish, and keep warm. In a separate pan, sauté the peppers and mushrooms in the remaining 2 tablespoons of olive oil for 2 to 3 minutes; add to the skillet in which the fish was cooked. Add the cream, water, lobster base, and tomatoes, and reduce to 1½ cups of liquid. Add the monkfish, warm briefly, and serve over rice or puff-pastry fleurons.

* For more information about this base, see chapter 3.

FILLETS OF FLORIDA POMPANO MARYLAND STYLE

Yield: 4 servings

4 FLORIDA POMPANO FILLETS,
   6–7 OUNCES EACH
½ CUP MILK
½ CUP FLOUR
½ CUP CLARIFIED BUTTER
¼ CUP OLIVE OIL
½ CUP BUTTER

4 TEASPOONS CHOPPED SHALLOTS
8 OUNCES LUMP CRABMEAT (½ CUP)
⅓ CUP TOASTED ALMOND SLIVERS
½ CUP DRY WHITE WINE
SALT AND PEPPER TO TASTE
2 TABLESPOONS CHOPPED PARSLEY

COLD APPETIZERS: BRANDIED BLUE CHEESE MOLD (TOP LEFT); SALMON AND TROUT MOUSSE WITH CAVIAR AND GREEN ASPARAGUS SAUCE (CENTER); HICKORY-SMOKED HAM DIP (BOTTOM RIGHT)

HOT APPETIZERS: QUICHE LORRAINE (TOP); SPINACH AND SAUSAGE PINWHEELS AND SPINACH-CHEESE PUFF TRIANGLES (BOTTOM LEFT); CLAMS CASINO (BOTTOM RIGHT)

CUCUMBER, TOMATO, AND SHRIMP SALAD WITH HONEY-MUSTARD DRESSING

MINESTRONE SOUP

BRAISED STEAK

ROAST RACK OF VEAL WITH BREADED DUCHESS POTATOES

SADDLE OF LAMB IN PASTRY WITH
GARLIC CLOVES

SWEET 'N SOUR PORK BROCHETTES

ROAST DUCKLING WITH CALVADOS

FLAMED SHRIMP BOMBAY (SHOWN IN OMELET)

BAY SCALLOPS WITH JULIENNE OF VEGETABLES

SALMON AND BASS WITH SORREL SAUCE

PASTA A LA GIARDINIERE

MUFFINS; CROISSANTS; FRENCH, WHEAT, ITALIAN, RYE, AND PUMPERNICKEL BREADS; SOFT ROLLS; AND DANISH PASTRY

ALSACE LORRAINE GUGELHUPF COFFEE CAKE

HAWAIIAN ICE CREAM BOMBE (SHAPED LIKE A PINEAPPLE); ALMOND STAR COOKIES (FOR OUT-
SIDE OF PINEAPPLE)

FRUIT TARTE

CHARLOTTE ROYAL WITH BAVARIAN CREAM AND SPONGE FOR JELLY ROLL (TOP LEFT); CREPES
NORMANDY WITH VANILLA SAUCE (MIDDLE LEFT); CRANBERRY NUT SOUFFLÉ (BOTTOM LEFT);
CARAMEL CUSTARD (CRÈME CARAMEL, CRÈME BRÛLÉE) (CENTER TOP); LINZER TORTE (CENTER);
STRAWBERRIES 'N CREAM (TOP RIGHT); LEMON CHIFFON PIE (BOTTOM RIGHT).

✤ Place the fillets in a bowl, cover with the milk, and let steep for 10 minutes. Remove the fish from the milk, and dredge in the flour, coating very well. Heat the clarified butter and olive oil in a skillet, add the fillets, and sauté for about 10 to 12 minutes, until golden brown. Remove to a platter, and keep warm. Discard the clarified butter and oil, and heat ½ cup of butter in the same skillet. Add the shallots, and cook for a few minutes; add the crabmeat and toasted almonds, and stir-fry gently. Add the wine, adjust the seasonings, and heat. When the sauce is hot, pour it over the pompano fillets, sprinkle with the chopped parsley, and serve.

BLACKENED RED SNAPPER FILLETS

Yield: 6 servings

1 TABLESPOON PAPRIKA
1 TEASPOON ONION POWDER
½ TEASPOON GARLIC POWDER
½ TEASPOON CAYENNE PEPPER
½ TEASPOON BLACK PEPPER
½ TEASPOON WHITE PEPPER
½ TEASPOON THYME

½ TEASPOON OREGANO
1 TABLESPOON SALT
¼ CUP LEMON JUICE
6 RED SNAPPER FILLETS
½ CUP MELTED BUTTER
3 OUNCES BUTTER

✤ Combine the paprika, onion powder, garlic powder, cayenne, black pepper, white pepper, thyme, oregano, and salt; keep dry. Sprinkle 2 tablespoons of lemon juice on the fish fillets, dip in the melted butter, and then dredge in the spice mixture. Fry the fish in the remaining melted butter in a very hot skillet for 2 minutes on each side, until lightly burned. Finish by baking in a 450°F oven for 3 to 5 minutes.

Brown the 3 ounces of butter, add the remaining 2 tablespoons of lemon juice, and serve with the fish. Boiled Russet potatoes and buttered green beans are good accompaniments.

SALMON WITH POACHED EGGS

Yield: 6 servings

2 CUPS WATER
6 SALMON SLICES, 3 OUNCES EACH
¼ CUP WHITE WINE
1 TEASPOON CHOPPED SHALLOTS
1 CUP WHIPPING CREAM
1 TABLESPOON CHOPPED FRESH DILL

1 TEASPOON SALT
¼ TEASPOON WHITE PEPPER
2 TEASPOONS BUTTER
6 POACHED EGGS
3 TEASPOONS RED SALMON CAVIAR

❖ Heat the water to just simmering, add the salmon, and poach for 5 minutes; remove and keep warm. Add the wine and shallots to the poaching liquid, and reduce by half. Add the whipping cream, and again reduce by half. Add the dill, salt, pepper, and butter. Place fish on serving plates, nap with the sauce, and decorate with the poached eggs and red salmon caviar. Baked parsleyed potatoes go well with this dish.

SALMON COULIBIAC

Yield: 8 servings

4 OUNCES SEMOLINA
1½ CUPS WELL-SEASONED CHICKEN
   BROTH
½ CUP BUTTER
2 TABLESPOONS CHOPPED ONIONS
8 OUNCES FRESH SPINACH, BLANCHED
   AND COARSELY CHOPPED
1 TEASPOON CHOPPED FRESH DILL
½ TEASPOON FINELY CHOPPED FENNEL
   SEEDS

SALT AND WHITE PEPPER TO TASTE
NUTMEG TO TASTE
14 OUNCES PUFF-PASTRY DOUGH
1½ POUNDS RAW SALMON FILLET,
   SKINNED AND BONED
3 HARD-BOILED EGGS, SLICED
1 EGG
2 TABLESPOONS WATER

❖ Cook the semolina in the chicken broth according to package directions. Melt the butter in a casserole, add the chopped onions, spinach, dill, and fennel. Season with the salt, white pepper, and nutmeg, and sauté until well heated. Let cool. Roll out the puff-pastry dough into a fairly thick oblong shape. In the middle of the dough sheet, spread half the semolina in a layer. On top of this, place the salmon fillets, a layer of the spinach mixture and the slices of hard-boiled eggs. Cover with another layer of semolina. Fold the dough, moisten the ends with water, close together, and place upside down on a buttered baking sheet. Decorate with trimmings of dough. Make a hole in the top to allow steam to escape. Beat the egg and water together, and brush the dough with this eggwash. Bake in a 375°F oven for approximately 45 minutes. Serve with sour cream sauce or melted butter.

SALMON FILLETS WITH FRESH HERB CRUMBS

Yield: 4 portions

4 SALMON FILLETS, BONELESS AND
   SKINLESS, 6 OUNCES EACH
SALT AND WHITE PEPPER TO TASTE
½ BUNCH FRESH DILL, CHOPPED (LEAVES
   ONLY)
1 BUNCH FRESH PARSLEY, CHOPPED
   (LEAVES ONLY)

2 LEMONS
1¼ CUPS OLIVE OIL
10 WHITE BREAD SLICES
2 BUNCHES FRESH TARRAGON (LEAVES
   AND THIN STEMS ONLY)
2 BUNCHES FRESH BASIL (LEAVES ONLY)
2 CUPS GRATED PARMESAN CHEESE

❖ Spread the salmon fillets in the bottom of a glass pan. Sprinkle with the salt, white pepper, dill, and half of the chopped parsley. Squeeze the lemons over the fish, and cover with olive oil. Refrigerate, covered, at least overnight, but not more than 2 days.

Place the bread in a food processor with a metal blade, and process to make crumbs. With the motor running, add the tarragon, basil, remaining parsley, cheese, salt, and pepper. Combine thoroughly.

Dredge the salmon fillets in the herb crumbs, and place on a lightly greased baking sheet. Bake at 350°F for approximately 20 minutes, depending on the thickness of the fillets. Test for doneness by pressing the fillets with the fingertips: if done, the fish will give slightly under pressure. Increase the oven temperature to 450°F to brown the herb crumbs if desired.

SALMON AND BASS WITH SORREL SAUCE

Yield: 6 servings

3 SALMON FILLETS, 6 TO 8 OUNCES
   EACH
3 BASS FILLETS, 6 TO 8 OUNCES EACH
4½ TABLESPOONS BUTTER
¼ CUP FINELY CHOPPED SHALLOTS
1 CUP DRY WHITE WINE

1 CUP FRENCH VERMOUTH (DRY WHITE)
SALT AND WHITE PEPPER TO TASTE
2 TABLESPOONS LEMON JUICE
1 CUP MEDIUM CREAM
1½ TABLESPOONS FLOUR
8 OUNCES SORREL LEAVES, CHOPPED

❖ Cut the salmon fillets into 6 medallions, repeat with the bass fillets; set aside.

Melt 2 tablespoons of the butter in a saucepan over medium heat, add the shallots, and sauté for a few minutes; do not brown. Add the white wine and vermouth, and simmer for 2 to 3 minutes. Pour into a baking dish just big enough to accommodate the salmon and bass medallions. Arrange the fish medallions in the baking dish, season with salt and white pepper, and sprinkle with the lemon juice. Cover, and bake in a preheated 350°F oven, for approximately 10 minutes, until the fish flakes when tested with a fork. Remove the fish to another dish; cover and keep warm.

Strain the cooking liquid through a fine sieve. Add the cream, and simmer for 5 minutes. Knead together the flour and 1½ tablespoons of butter to make a beurre manié; add to the sauce, and cook, stirring, until thickened to the desired consistency. Heat the remaining tablespoon of butter in a skillet. Add the chopped sorrel; reduce the sorrel to a puree by turning constantly with a spoon until almost dry. Add the sorrel to the sauce. Adjust the seasonings.

Pour a small amount of the sauce on each warmed serving plate. Arrange 1 medallion of salmon and 1 medallion of bass over the sauce. (Sprinkle with blanched lemon zest and julienne of truffle, if desired.) Parsleyed boiled potatoes are a good accompaniment.

DUBLIN-STYLE DOVER SOLE

Yield: 6 servings

2 POUNDS FILLETS OF DOVER SOLE
(18 FILLETS)
¾ CUP MELTED BUTTER
½ CUP FLOUR, SEASONED WITH SALT
AND WHITE PEPPER
18 SHRIMP, 16-TO-20-PER-POUND SIZE,
SHELLED

2 CUPS DRY WHITE WINE
2 CUPS HEAVY CREAM
SALT AND PEPPER TO TASTE
3 HARD-BOILED EGGS, CHOPPED
½ CUP CHOPPED PARSLEY
6 LEMON SLICES

❖ Dip the fillets in the melted butter, and dredge in the seasoned flour, shaking off any excess. Lay out the fillets, place one shrimp on the tail of each, and roll into roulades. Place roulades in an ovenproof dish, pour the melted butter on top, and bake for 25 minutes at 375°F; cover during the last 10 minutes. Place the wine in a small casserole, and reduce by half. Add the heavy cream, and again reduce by half. Season the sauce. To serve, pour the sauce over the fish roulades, sprinkle with the chopped eggs and parsley, and decorate with lemon slices.

BAKED FILLETS OF
LEMON SOLE DUQUESNE

Yield: 6 servings

3 OUNCES BUTTER, MELTED
3 MEDIUM TOMATOES, PEELED AND
SLICED
12 LEMON SOLE FILLETS, 3 OUNCES
EACH
SALT TO TASTE
JUICE OF 3 LIMES

¾ CUP WHITE WINE
3 TABLESPOONS BREADCRUMBS
3 TEASPOONS GRATED PARMESAN
CHEESE
1½ TEASPOONS CRUSHED PEPPERCORNS
2 TABLESPOONS BUTTER

❖ Butter six shirred-egg dishes (cocottes) with the melted butter. On the bottom of each dish, place 2 slices of tomato. Sprinkle the fillets of sole with the salt and lime juice, and place 2 fillets atop the tomatoes in each dish. Add 2 tablespoons of the wine, sprinkle with the breadcrumbs, cheese, and peppercorns; dot each with 1 teaspoon of butter. Bake in a 450°F oven for 15 to 18 minutes.

SWORDFISH WITH MACADAMIA NUTS

Yield: 4 servings

4 SWORDFISH STEAKS, 6 OUNCES EACH
SALT AND PEPPER TO TASTE
3 TABLESPOONS OIL
¼ CUP WHITE WINE

6 TABLESPOONS BUTTER
¼ CUP MACADAMIA NUTS
JUICE FROM 1 LEMON OR LIME
2 TABLESPOONS CHOPPED PARSLEY

✣ Preheat the oven to 350°F. Season the fish with salt and pepper. Heat the oil in an ovenproof skillet, add the swordfish, and sauté over medium heat for 2 minutes on each side. Add the white wine, and bake in the preheated oven for 3 to 4 minutes. Remove the fish to a serving platter. In a separate pan, sauté the nuts in the butter for 2 to 3 minutes; add the lemon or lime juice, and spoon over the fish. Sprinkle with the chopped parsley. Serve with boiled potatoes.

TROUT MOUSSE WITH LOBSTER SAUCE

Yield: 6 servings

¼ CUP BUTTER
¾ CUP SOFT BREADCRUMBS
SALT TO TASTE
⅛ TEASPOON DILL WEED
1 CUP HALF-AND-HALF CREAM
10 OUNCES POACHED TROUT, SKINNED,
    BONED, AND FLAKED

2 EGGS, WELL BEATEN
¼ CUP WHITE WINE
2 CUPS LOBSTER SAUCE (RECIPE
    FOLLOWS)

✣ Preheat the oven to 350°F. Melt butter in a double-boiler, and stir in the crumbs, salt, and dill weed. Add the half-and-half, and cook for 5 to 10 minutes, stirring often. Mix the flaked trout, eggs, and wine, and add to the cream mixture. Pour into a food processor or blender, and puree until smooth. Pour the mixture into buttered glass custard cups, place in a warm water bath, and bake for 50 minutes, until firm. To serve, insert a knife between the mousse and the edge of the mold to loosen mousse. Invert onto a serving plate, and tap gently. Remove the mold. Pour the lobster sauce over the top, and serve.

LOBSTER SAUCE

Yield: 2 cups

2 TABLESPOONS MARGARINE OR BUTTER
¼ CUP ALL-PURPOSE FLOUR
1½ CUPS HOT WATER
1 TABLESPOON LOBSTER BASE*

½ CUP HOT HALF-AND-HALF CREAM
1 TABLESPOON PALE DRY COCKTAIL
   SHERRY

❖ Melt the margarine or butter over low heat. Whisk in the flour, and stir over medium heat until well blended, smooth, and bubbly, about 2 to 3 minutes. Remove from the heat. Add the hot water gradually, mixing well. Stir in the lobster base. Heat to boiling, stirring constantly. Boil and stir for 1 minute. Add the hot cream and dry sherry, mixing well. Simmer for 1 minute.

* For information about this base, see chapter 3.

QUENELLES WITH LOBSTER SAUCE

Yield: 6 servings

1½ POUNDS WHITE FISH FILLETS (SUCH
   AS SNAPPER, COD, PIKE, SOLE)
3 EGG WHITES
1 TABLESPOON FRESHLY CHOPPED
   PARSLEY
¼ TEASPOON WHITE PEPPER
½ TEASPOON SALT

¾ TABLESPOON LOBSTER BASE*
3 TABLESPOONS BRANDY
1 CUP HEAVY CREAM
½ OUNCE FISH BASE*
2 CUPS HOT WATER
2 CUPS LOBSTER SAUCE (RECIPE
   FOLLOWS)

❖ Place the fish in food processor, and chop to a paste. Add the egg whites, parsley, pepper, salt, lobster base, and brandy, and process for 3 minutes. Place the mixture in stainless-steel bowl over ice. Using a wooden spoon, mix in the heavy cream until very well blended. Refrigerate for 30 minutes.

Add the fish base to the hot water, and mix well. Bring to a very slow simmer. Form quenelles (dumplings) with the fish mixture, using two large soup spoons dipped in hot water. Poach the quenelles in the simmering fish stock for 5 to 6 minutes, until firm; do not overcook. Serve with the lobster sauce.

(continued)

LOBSTER SAUCE

Yield: 2 cups

2 TABLESPOONS BUTTER OR MARGARINE
¼ CUP FLOUR
1½ CUPS HOT WATER

1 TABLESPOON LOBSTER BASE *
½ CUP HOT HALF-AND-HALF CREAM

✤ Heat the butter over low heat in a saucepan. Whisk in the flour, and cook, stirring constantly, until smooth and bubbly, about 2 to 3 minutes. Remove from the heat. Gradually add the hot water; mix well. Stir in the lobster base. Bring to a boil; boil for 1 minute. Lower the heat, add the hot half-and-half, and simmer for 1 minute.

* For information about these bases, see chapter 3.

FISH PIE

Yield: 6 servings

1½ POUNDS FISH FILLETS (COD,
   HADDOCK, SNAPPER, OR HALIBUT)
1 QUART WATER
LEMON JUICE TO TASTE
6–8 OYSTERS
6–8 LARGE SHRIMP
1 TABLESPOON CAPERS
6–8 BLACK OLIVES

1 TABLESPOON FINELY CHOPPED
   SHALLOTS OR ONIONS
½ CUP BUTTER
1 CUP FLOUR
1 CUP HALF-AND-HALF CREAM
SALT AND PEPPER TO TASTE
1 POUND PIECRUST DOUGH
1 EGG, BEATEN

✤ Lightly poach the fish in the water and lemon juice until almost done. Remove the fish, reserving 1 cup of the poaching liquid; discard the remaining poaching liquid. Cut the fish into pieces, and place in a casserole with the oysters, shrimp, capers, and olives; set aside. Heat the butter in a saucepan, add the shallots or onions, and sauté until translucent. Add the flour, and stir until smooth, about 3 minutes. Slowly stir in the half-and-half. Add the reserved poaching liquid. Simmer for 5 minutes; adjust the seasonings. Cover the fish casserole with the sauce. Top with the piecrust pastry, and cut slits in the pastry to allow steam to escape. Brush with the beaten egg, and bake in a 350°F oven for 20 to 25 minutes.

CIOPPINO

Yield: 12 servings

¼ CUP OLIVE OIL
½ CUP CHOPPED ONIONS
2 GARLIC CLOVES, CRUSHED
½ CUP DICED GREEN PEPPERS
½ CUP DICED CELERY
6 TOMATOES, PEELED, SEEDED, AND
  CHOPPED
½ CUP TOMATO PUREE
SALT TO TASTE (SEE NOTE BELOW)
1 TEASPOON CRACKED BLACK PEPPER
2 CRABS, CRACKED

10–12 SEA SCALLOPS, QUARTERED
10–12 JUMBO SHRIMP, WITH SHELLS
10–12 CLAMS
3 CUPS DRY WHITE WINE
1 POUND RED SNAPPER (OR ANY COD-
  FAMILY FISH, SUCH AS HADDOCK,
  HAKE, OR POLLOCK), CUT IN 1-INCH
  CUBES
3 TABLESPOONS CHOPPED FRESH
  PARSLEY

✢ Heat the oil in a pan, add the onions, garlic, green peppers, and celery, and sauté for 5 to 6 minutes. Add the tomatoes and tomato puree, salt, pepper, cracked crabs, scallops, shrimp, clams, and wine. Cook for about 5 minutes. Add the fish, and cook for 5 additional minutes. Sprinkle with the parsley. Serve with garlic bread.

Note: The salt may be replaced by 1 teaspoon of clam base. (For information about this base, see chapter 3.)

CRABMEAT CHAUMIÈRE

Yield: 6 servings

6 ICEBERG LETTUCE LEAVES
1 POUND FRESH LUMP CRABMEAT
2 WHOLE RIPE AVOCADOS, SLICED
12 PIMENTO STRIPS

12 ANCHOVY FILLETS
1 PINT OIL AND VINEGAR DRESSING (SEE
  RECIPE BELOW)
FRESHLY CHOPPED CHIVES

✢ Place the lettuce leaves in a small salad bowl. Divide the crabmeat evenly into 6 portions on the lettuce leaves. Place the avocado slices around the crabmeat; top with the pimento strips and anchovies. Pour or ladle the dressing over the salad, sprinkle with the chopped chives, and serve cold.

(continued)

OIL AND VINEGAR DRESSING

Yield: 1 pint

1⅓ CUPS GOOD-QUALITY OLIVE OIL
⅔ CUP TARRAGON VINEGAR

SALT AND FRESHLY GROUND BLACK
  PEPPER

✤ Combine the oil, vinegar, salt, and pepper; stir or shake vigorously.

DEVILED CRAB IMPERIAL

Yield: 6 servings

¾ CUP HALF-AND-HALF CREAM
1 CUP BREADCRUMBS
3 TABLESPOONS BUTTER
2 TABLESPOONS FINELY CHOPPED GREEN
  PEPPERS
1 TEASPOON CHOPPED CHIVES
1 TEASPOON PREPARED MUSTARD

1 TEASPOON WORCESTERSHIRE SAUCE
1 TEASPOON SALT
HOT PEPPER SAUCE (TABASCO) TO
  TASTE
2 POUNDS LUMP CRABMEAT
BUTTERED BREADCRUMBS TO GARNISH

✤ Combine the cream and breadcrumbs, and let set for 30 minutes. Add the butter, chopped peppers, chives, prepared mustard, Worcestershire sauce, salt, and hot pepper sauce. Mix until the ingredients are well blended and the mixture is soft and creamy. Very gently fold in the lump crabmeat. Fill 6 ramekins or crabshells with the mixture, and top with buttered breadcrumbs. Bake for 20 minutes in a 350°F oven.

KING CRABMEAT, NEW ORLEANS STYLE

Yield: 4 servings

½ CUP BUTTER
2 SHALLOTS, CHOPPED
1 POUND KING CRABMEAT, CHOPPED
¾ CUP FLOUR
1 CUP SCALDED MILK
½ CUP SAUTERNES
2 HARD-BOILED EGGS, CHOPPED
1 TEASPOON WORCESTERSHIRE SAUCE

½ CUP CHOPPED PARSLEY
HOT PEPPER SAUCE (TABASCO) TO
  TASTE
1 TEASPOON DRY MUSTARD
4 THREADS SAFFRON, CRUSHED
20 OUNCES DUCHESS POTATOES (SEE
  RECIPE IN CHAPTER 9)
¼ CUP GRATED PARMESAN CHEESE

❖ Heat the butter in a pan, add the shallots, and sauté until golden brown. Add the crabmeat, and simmer for 3 minutes. Stir in the flour and milk, and cook, stirring, until thickened. Remove from the heat. Fold in the Sauternes, eggs, Worcestershire sauce, parsley, hot pepper sauce, dry mustard, and saffron. Mound this crab mixture in centers of four scallop shells. Pipe the duchess potatoes around the crab mixture, and sprinkle with the Parmesan cheese. Bake in a 350°F oven for 25 minutes, until golden brown.

KING CRABMEAT CRÊPES

Yield: 6 servings

1 POUND KING CRABMEAT
2 TABLESPOONS BUTTER
1⅓ CUPS SLICED MUSHROOMS
½ CUP DRY SHERRY
SALT AND PEPPER TO TASTE
½ TEASPOON PAPRIKA
1 CUP HEAVY WHITE SAUCE (SEE RECIPE
   BELOW)

4 EGGS
1½ CUPS MILK
½ CUP FLOUR
SALT, TO TASTE
BUTTER FOR FRYING
3 CUPS MOCK HOLLANDAISE SAUCE (SEE
   RECIPE IN CHAPTER 3)
6 PARSLEY SPRIGS

❖ Heat the crabmeat in the butter. Add the mushrooms, sherry, salt, pepper, and paprika. Cook until the liquid is reduced by half. Stir in the heavy white sauce, and set aside, keeping warm.

Whisk together the eggs and milk. Add the flour and salt, and beat until smooth. Let set for 30 minutes. Heat the butter in an 8-inch omelet pan. Add ¼ cup of the batter to the pan, tilting the pan to coat evenly. Fry for about 2 minutes, until the underside is brown. Carefully flip, and cook the other side until brown, about 30 seconds. Repeat until all the batter has been used; there will be about 12 crepes.

Spread a heaping tablespoon of the crab filling in the center of each crêpe, and roll up. Place 2 crepes on each serving plate. Top each serving with ½ cup of the mock hollandaise sauce. Brown quickly under the broiler, decorate with a parsley sprig, and serve.

HEAVY WHITE SAUCE

Yield: 1 cup

3 TABLESPOONS BUTTER
3 TABLESPOONS FLOUR

1 CUP MILK

(continued)

❖ Melt the butter in a saucepan over low heat. Add the flour, and cook, stirring constantly, over low heat for 3 to 5 minutes. Slowly stir in the milk. Cook, stirring constantly, until thickened.

MUSSELS WITH CREAM SAUCE

Yield: 4 servings

4 DOZEN MUSSELS, WELL SCRUBBED
2 CUPS DRY WHITE WINE
1 TABLESPOON CHOPPED CHIVES
1 TEASPOON FRESHLY GROUND WHITE
  PEPPER
1 PARSLEY SPRIG, CHOPPED
1 TABLESPOON CHOPPED FRESH THYME
1 BAY LEAF

SHALLOTS OR SCALLIONS, TO TASTE,
  MINCED
1 CUP HEAVY CREAM
4 EGG YOLKS
FRESH PARSLEY, CHOPPED, TO GARNISH
FRESH CHIVES, CHOPPED, TO GARNISH
12 SLICES GARLIC TOAST

❖ Combine the mussels, wine, tablespoon of chopped chives, pepper, chopped sprig of parsley, thyme, bay leaf, and shallots in a shallow casserole. Steam, covered, until the mussels open (discard any that do not open). Strain the cooking liquid through cheesecloth into a saucepan, and reduce by two-thirds. Combine the heavy cream and egg yolks. Add a little of the cooking liquid to this liaison, then return to the cooking liquid. Remove and discard half the shell from each mussel. Cover each mussel with sauce, and arrange the mussels on a platter, with the remaining sauce in the center. Garnish with the parsley and chives, and serve with the garlic toast.

OYSTER SOUFFLÉ

Yield: 6 servings

3 TABLESPOONS BUTTER
1 TABLESPOON FINELY MINCED
  SHALLOTS
3 TABLESPOONS SIFTED FLOUR
1 CUP WARMED MILK
3 EGG YOLKS, BEATEN
½ TEASPOON GRATED LEMON ZEST

½ TEASPOON FINELY CHOPPED PARSLEY
½ TEASPOON FINELY CHOPPED
  SCALLIONS
SALT AND PEPPER TO TASTE
18 OYSTERS, SHELLED AND CHOPPED
3 EGG WHITES, BEATEN UNTIL STIFF

❖ Heat the butter in a saucepan, add the shallots, and sauté until translucent, about 3 to 5 minutes. Stir in the flour and cook until smooth and bubbly. Add the milk and cook, stirring constantly, until thickened. Blend in carefully the beaten egg yolks, stirring constantly. Add the lemon zest, parsley, scallions, herbs, and salt and pepper to taste. Add the chopped oysters, and simmer for 5 to 7 minutes. Fold the beaten egg whites into the oyster mixture. Pour into a well buttered casserole or soufflé pan. Bake in a 350°F oven for 30 minutes, until golden brown. Serve immediately.

SCALLOPS WITH APPLES AND SNOW PEAS

Yield: 6 to 8 servings

1 POUND SNOW PEAS, TRIMMED
   AND STRINGED
6 TABLESPOONS SWEET BUTTER
2 LARGE, FIRM, TART APPLES, PEELED
   AND THICKLY SLICED
2 TABLESPOONS GRANULATED SUGAR

½ CUP FINELY MINCED ONIONS
2 POUNDS SMALL SCALLOPS
¾ CUP DRY WHITE WINE OR VERMOUTH
⅔ CUP PREPARED DIJON-STYLE
   MUSTARD (SEE NOTE BELOW)
¾ CUP HEAVY CREAM

❖ Bring a large pot of salted water to a boil, and drop in the snow peas. When tender but still crunchy, after about 3 minutes, drain and plunge the peapods immediately into ice water. Reserve. In a large skillet, melt 2 tablespoons of the butter, and sauté the apple slices over medium heat until tender but not mushy, about 5 minutes. Sprinkle the slices with the sugar and raise the heat, rapidly turning the apple slices until they are brown and lightly caramelized. Using a spatula, remove the slices from the skillet, and reserve.

In the same skillet, melt the remaining 4 tablespoons of butter, and gently cook the minced onions, covered, over medium heat, until tender and lightly colored, about 25 minutes. Raise the heat, add the scallops, and stir and toss them rapidly in the butter until they are firm, about 3 minutes (do *not* overcook). Remove the scallops from the skillet, and reserve.

Pour the wine or vermouth into the skillet, and over high heat, reduce by two-thirds. Turn down the heat, and stir in the mustard with a wire whisk. Pour in the cream, and simmer, uncovered, stirring occasionally, for 15 minutes or

(continued)

until sauce is reduced slightly. Drain the snow peas thoroughly, and pat dry with paper towels. Add them, along with the reserved apples and scallops, to the mustard-cream sauce, and simmer together for 1 minute. Serve immediately.

Note: Instead of Dijon-style mustard, try experimenting with flavored mustard, such as tarragon, orange, green-peppercorn, or sherry mustard.

SCALLOPS WITH VEGETABLES JULIENNE

Yield: 8 servings

1 LARGE LEEK, WHITE PORTION ONLY
1 CARROT
1 CELERY HEART
6 SHALLOTS
6 TABLESPOONS WHITE WINE

2 TABLESPOONS FISH FUMET
1 QUART HEAVY CREAM
2 QUARTS SMALL SCALLOPS
32 PINK PEPPERCORNS

❖ Cut the leek white, carrot, and celery heart into a thin julienne. Peel and chop the shallots, place in a pan, add the white wine and fish fumet and reduce until syrupy. Add the cream, and reduce to the desired consistency.

Poach the scallops in a large pot of boiling water for no more than 1 minute. Drain the scallops and serve with a julienne of vegetables on hot plates; cover with the sauce. Decorate each plate with 4 peppercorns.

SCALLOPS WITH WATERCRESS COULIS

Yield: 4 servings

3 TABLESPOONS BUTTER
1 TABLESPOON MINCED SHALLOTS
12 OUNCES FRESH MUSHROOMS,
  WASHED AND SLICED
½ TEASPOON LEMON JUICE
PINCH OF NUTMEG

SALT AND FRESHLY GROUND WHITE
  PEPPER TO TASTE
2 BUNCHES WATERCRESS, CLEANED,
  WASHED, AND CHOPPED
¾ CUP LIGHT CREAM
1½ POUNDS SMALL SCALLOPS

❖ Heat 2 tablespoons of the butter in a skillet, add shallots, mushrooms, lemon juice, and nutmeg, and cook over high heat until dry. Season with salt and pepper, and puree in a blender. Keep warm.

Heat the remaining tablespoon of butter in a saucepan, add the chopped watercress, and sauté briefly over high heat. Add the cream, salt, and pepper, reduce the heat, and simmer for 1 to 2 minutes.

Cook the scallops briefly in lightly salted boiling water. Drain, and keep warm.

Divide the mushroom puree among four cleaned scallop shells or four small casseroles. Place the scallops atop the puree. Spoon the watercress coulis over the scallops. Serve at once.

SHRIMP TEMPURA

Yield: 4 servings

1 CUP ALL-PURPOSE FLOUR
½ CUP CORNSTARCH
1 TEASPOON BAKING POWDER
¼ TEASPOON SALT

1 EGG
2½ CUPS COLD WATER
16 SHRIMP, 16- TO 20-PER-POUND SIZE
VEGETABLE OIL FOR FRYING

❖ Combine ½ cup of the flour, the cornstarch, baking powder, and salt in a bowl. In another bowl, beat the egg and 2 cups of water together with a fork; stir into dry mixture. Let the batter stand for 30 minutes or longer before using (this gives an extra-crisp coating to tempura). Add the additional ½ cup of water if a thinner batter is desired. To prepare the shrimp, remove the shells, leaving the tail shells intact. Slit the shrimp to devein. With a very sharp knife, butterfly the shrimp. Cover all the shrimp with sheet of wax paper, and refrigerate until ready to fry. Dip each shrimp in the remaining ½ cup of flour and then in the batter, touching the sides of the bowl to remove excess batter. Heat 1 inch of vegetable oil to 350°F, add the shrimp, and fry for 2 to 3 minutes, until golden brown.

SHRIMP HAR KOW

Yield: 6 servings

1½ CUPS OIL
30 SHRIMP, 16- TO 20-PER-POUND SIZE,
    PEELED, DEVEINED, AND BUTTERFLIED
6 GARLIC CLOVES, FINELY CHOPPED
6 SCALLIONS, CUT IN 1-INCH PIECES

¾ CUP CHILI SAUCE
6 TABLESPOONS SOY SAUCE
DASH OF HOT PEPPER SAUCE (TABASCO)
PINCH OF SALT
6 TABLESPOONS SHERRY

❖ Heat the oil in a skillet, add the shrimp, and fry for about 4 minutes (the shrimp will curl up when placed in hot oil). Remove the shrimp, and set aside. Pour off most of the oil, leaving a few tablespoons. Add the garlic and scallions, and sauté until translucent. Add the chili sauce, soy sauce, hot pepper sauce, and shrimp, and sauté together for 3 to 4 minutes. Add the sherry, and bring to short boil. Serve on steamed rice.

SHRIMP FRIED RICE

Yield: 4 servings

1⅓ CUPS HOT WATER
1½ TEASPOONS LOBSTER BASE*
½ CUP LONG-GRAIN WHITE RICE
1 TABLESPOON MARGARINE OR BUTTER
½ CUP FINELY CHOPPED FRESH
    MUSHROOMS

¼ CUP FINELY CHOPPED CELERY
¼ CUP FINELY CHOPPED SCALLIONS
4 OUNCES SHRIMP, PEELED, DEVEINED,
    AND DICED MEDIUM
2 EGGS
½ TEASPOON SOY SAUCE

❖ In a heavy 1-quart saucepan, bring the water and 1 teaspoon of the lobster base to a boil. Stir in the rice; cover, and simmer for 20 minutes. Remove from the heat, and set aside. In a large heavy skillet, heat margarine or butter, add the mushrooms, celery, scallions, and shrimp, and stir-fry for 3 minutes. In a small mixing bowl, beat the eggs and the remaining ½ teaspoon of lobster base with a wire whisk until well blended. Add to the skillet, cooking until the eggs are done, about 3 minutes. Add the rice and soy sauce, mixing well. Serve hot, with sautéed snow peas and grilled chicken.

* For information about this base, see chapter 3.

SHRIMP CANTONESE

Yield: 2 servings

12 SHRIMP, 16- TO 20-PER-POUND SIZE
1 CUP PLUS 2 TEASPOONS CORNSTARCH
2 CUPS OIL
1 TEASPOON FRESHLY CHOPPED GINGER
1 TEASPOON FRESHLY CHOPPED GARLIC
1 TEASPOON FRESHLY CHOPPED
  SCALLIONS
3 TABLESPOONS PEANUT OIL
8 OUNCES CANNED WATER CHESTNUTS,
  CHOPPED
1 TABLESPOON RINSED AND CHOPPED
  FERMENTED BLACK BEANS

2 TABLESPOONS SOY SAUCE
6 TABLESPOONS WATER
¾ TEASPOON LOBSTER BASE*
1 TABLESPOON SESAME OIL
2 TABLESPOONS DRY SHERRY
1 TEASPOON SUGAR
DASH OF BLACK PEPPER
COOKED WHITE RICE
CHOPPED SCALLIONS TO GARNISH

❖ Shell the shrimp, devein, cut in half lengthwise, and set aside. Heat the oil in a wok or pot. Dust the shrimp with 1 cup of cornstarch, and deep-fry for 1 minute. Remove and drain. In a wok or large skillet, stir-fry the ginger, garlic, and scallions in the peanut oil. When the mixture becomes fragrant, add the chopped water chestnuts and the fermented black beans. Combine the remaining 2 teaspoons cornstarch, soy sauce, water, lobster base, sesame oil, sherry, sugar, and black pepper. Add, with the cooked shrimp, to the black-bean/water-chestnut mixture, cook until the sauce thickens, about 2 minutes. Spoon onto a serving plate, and garnish with the chopped scallions. Serve with cooked white rice.

* For information about this base, see chapter 3.

PRAWNS AND ARTICHOKES CHARDONNAY

Yield: 4 servings

4 FRESH MEDIUM ARTICHOKES (SEE NOTE BELOW)
1 TABLESPOON LEMON JUICE
1 TEASPOON SALT
1 TEASPOON PEPPER
¼ CUP OLIVE OIL
1 TABLESPOON FINELY CHOPPED GARLIC
2 TABLESPOONS FINELY CHOPPED SHALLOTS OR SCALLIONS

20 LARGE SHRIMP (16- TO 20-PER-POUND SIZE) PEELED AND DEVEINED
2 CUPS CHARDONNAY
2 TEASPOONS CORNSTARCH
1 TABLESPOON WATER
2 TABLESPOONS BUTTER
1 TEASPOON CHOPPED FRESH BASIL
1 TEASPOON CHOPPED FRESH PARSLEY

✤ Remove the tough outside leaves of the artichokes and discard. Place the artichokes in a pot with 1 inch of water, the lemon juice, salt, and pepper. Cover tightly, and cook until tender, approximately 30 minutes. Remove the leaves, and reserve. Scoop out and discard the hairy choke, and slice the artichoke bottom. (This procedure may be done a day ahead.)

In a large skillet, heat the oil, and briefly sauté the garlic and shallots over medium-high heat. Add the shrimp, and sauté for a few seconds on each side. Add the Chardonnay, and reduce by half. Remove the prawns. Mix the cornstarch, and tablespoon of water, and whisk into the sauce. Cook, stirring constantly, until the sauce thickens. Add the butter, sliced artichoke bottoms, basil, and parsley. Toss the prawns with this sauce, and serve immediately.

Note: When artichokes are out of season, use canned artichoke bottoms.

SHRIMP CALYPSO

Yield: 6 servings

¾ CUP BUTTER
24 SHRIMP, 16- TO 20-PER-POUND SIZE,
    PEELED AND DEVEINED
¾ TEASPOON FRESHLY CHOPPED GARLIC
½ TEASPOON WHOLE-LEAF OREGANO
3 TABLESPOONS BRANDY
4½ CUPS SLICED ONIONS
1¾ TO 2 CUPS JULIENNE OF RED AND
    GREEN BELL PEPPERS

6 OUNCES HARD SALAMI, CUT INTO
    STRIPS
3 CUPS HEAVY CREAM
1¼ CUPS PEELED, SEEDED, AND
    CHOPPED TOMATOES
WHITE PEPPER TO TASTE

✤ Heat the butter in a skillet, add the shrimp, and sauté over high heat for 2 to 3 minutes. Stir in the garlic and oregano. Add the brandy, and flame. When the alcohol has burned off, add the onions, peppers, and hard salami. Add the cream, and reduce for 2 to 3 minutes. Add the tomatoes and pepper. Cover, simmer for 10 to 15 minutes, and serve.

A rice ring with fresh blanched leaf spinach inside is a colorful accompaniment.

FLAMED SHRIMP BOMBAY

Yield: 4 servings

12 SHRIMP, HALVED LENGTHWISE
6 TABLESPOONS BUTTER
2 TABLESPOONS BRANDY
2 TABLESPOONS CHOPPED SHALLOTS
2 TABLESPOONS APPLESAUCE
2 TEASPOONS MADRAS CURRY

¼ CUP HEAVY CREAM
SALT AND PEPPER TO TASTE
4 OMELETS, MADE WITH 2 EGGS EACH
1–2 TEASPOONS CHOPPED PARSLEY
1–2 TEASPOONS GRATED ALMONDS

✤ Heat 3 tablespoons of the butter in a skillet, add the shrimp, and sauté until pink. Flame with the brandy, and remove from the heat; keep warm. In a separate pan, heat the remaining 3 tablespoons of butter, add the chopped shallots; and sauté until translucent. Add the applesauce, curry, and cream; mix well. Season with salt and pepper. Add the shrimp, and heat. Spoon the shrimp mixture into the hot omelets, sprinkle with the parsley and grated almonds, and serve with rice pilaf.

SEAFOOD THERMIDOR

Yield: 8 servings

5 OUNCES BUTTER (¼ CUP + 2
　TABLESPOONS)
3 TABLESPOONS FINELY CHOPPED
　ONIONS
3 CUPS SLICED MUSHROOMS
12 OUNCES SEA SCALLOPS
12 OUNCES RAW SHRIMP, PEELED
　AND CLEANED
12 OUNCES IMITATION CRABMEAT
1 TEASPOON PAPRIKA
½ CUP SHERRY

¼ CUP BRANDY
1 TEASPOON TARRAGON
1 TEASPOON DRY MUSTARD
1 TEASPOON CHOPPED PARSLEY
4 TEASPOONS CRAB BASE*
¼ CUP COLD WATER
2.5 OUNCES MINOR'S DRY ROUX*
1 QUART HALF-AND-HALF CREAM
8 OUNCES SHARP CHEDDAR CHEESE,
　DICED SMALL

❖ Heat the butter in a saucepan, add the onions and mushrooms, and sauté over medium heat for 3 to 4 minutes. Add the scallops, shrimp, and imitation crab-meat, and simmer for 3 to 4 minutes, stirring constantly. Add the paprika, sherry, brandy, tarragon, dry mustard, parsley, and crab base to mixture, mixing well; simmer over medium heat for 2 to 3 minutes. Blend the cold water and Minor's dry roux together with wire whisk, mixing very well. Slowly add to the shellfish mixture, stirring constantly. Add the cream, and simmer for 3 to 4 minutes. Add the cheese to the sauce, mixing well. Remove from the heat when the cheese has melted. Serve over linguini.

* For information about these ingredients, see chapter 3.

CHAPTER EIGHT

Pasta and Grain Dishes

M<small>ANY</small> chefs will tell you that all that appears to be pasta is not pasta, at least not the right kind to produce an acceptable product. Pasta should be made from the appropriate kind of flour, specially ground to produce a proper paste. Thus, in choosing a pasta, select one made only from the durum wheat called semolina. It is from the hard winter wheat grown in the northern states, which produces a grain with exceptionally high gluten. Pasta made of semolina produces a firm product that holds its shape after cooking.

In many cases you can tell a good pasta simply by its appearance. It should be a yellowish white, not white or gray; a product high in gluten will have a yellow color. A pasta such as spaghetti or macaroni that is made in long strands can also be tested for quality by holding a strand firmly at either end and bending it. It should bend into an arch and then shatter with a rough break. Pasta made from wheat low in semolina will not bend in this manner. Good chefs are very particular about beginning with the right pasta. They know that the quality of their final product depends on starting with quality ingredients. In quantity production, pasta must sometimes wait in a steam table until service, and unless the right pasta is used, it will become soft and mushy, unacceptable to eat because of its texture. The same holds true for home preparation.

Pasta must be cooked properly. Do *not* overcook pasta; it is preferable to undercook it. Pasta is generally cooked *al dente*, an Italian term that literally means "to the tooth"; but in cooking terms, it means the pasta still offers some feeling of resistance. Such pasta holds up well if waiting for service and has a good, solid texture when eaten.

To cook pasta, bring *lightly* salted water to a rolling boil, and add the pasta, stirring as it is added. Use plenty of water for cooking the pasta, being sure to follow the recipe. Move the pieces apart as soon as they are added to the water, so they do not stick together. Cover, and simmer until the pasta is al dente; test a strand to check. Remove immediately from the heat, and plunge into cold water, rinsing well to remove excess starch. The pasta can then be put into cold water and held until needed.

Recipes for rice and other high-starch products are often grouped with pasta. Rice can also be cooked by simmering. In addition, the Oriental method can be used. In this method, for every measure of rice, two measures of water are added, and the mixture is brought to a boil. It is then tightly covered and placed over *low* heat to finish the cooking and allow the rice to swell. The cover is not removed as the rice steams. After about fifteen minutes, it is uncovered and tested. As with pasta, it is important not to overcook rice. After lifting the cover, the rice can be fluffed up to allow the steam to escape, and then kept warm until served. It is best not to hold rice too long before service. It will be lighter and the grains will be less likely to stick together and thus have the right texture if it is served as soon as possible after cooking.

Some chefs mix a bit of oil with the rice before cooking in the Oriental way, to produce a rice that separates; others, however, do not follow this practice. Sometimes such oiled rice is lightly sautéed before being cooked to give the rice extra flavor. It is best to add any desired seasonings when the rice is combined with the water, *before* cooking, to produce a better distribution of flavor and color.

Pasta and Grain Dishes

RISOTTO MILAN STYLE

VERMICELLI ALLA CARBONARA

LINGUINE AL PESTO GENOVESE

PASTA ALLA GIARDINIERA

CAPELLINI AL POMODORO

BOW TIES WILLARD

STUFFED PIZZA, PALERMO STYLE

PASTA WITH SHRIMP

RAVIOLI

FETTUCINE AND SAUSAGE WITH TOMATOES

PASTA WITH PESTO

MEXICAN LASAGNA

LINGUINE WITH WHITE CLAM SAUCE

PENNE ALL' ARRABBIATA

VERMICELLI CON SARI

GNOCCHI ALLA ROMANA
POLENTA DUMPLINGS
GORGONZOLA POLENTA
YORKSHIRE PUDDING
BUTTERED NOODLES POLONAISE
RICE PILAF

RISOTTO MILAN STYLE

Yield: 6 servings

4 CUPS CHICKEN STOCK
¼ CUP FINELY CHOPPED YELLOW
 ONIONS
5 TABLESPOONS BUTTER
2 TABLESPOONS VEGETABLE OIL

2 CUPS ITALIAN ARBORIO RICE
2 WHOLE SAFFRON THREADS
SALT AND FRESHLY GROUND WHITE
 PEPPER TO TASTE
¼ CUP GRATED PARMESAN CHEESE

❖ Bring the stock to a simmer. In a large saucepan, sauté the onions in 2 tablespoons of the butter and the vegetable oil until translucent. Add the rice, and stir until well coated. Dissolve the saffron in 1 cup of the hot stock. Add the dissolved saffron in stock to the rice, and simmer until all the liquid is absorbed. Add the remaining stock, ½ cup at a time, stirring after each addition until it is absorbed. Season with salt and pepper. Add the grated Parmesan cheese and remaining butter, stirring well to blend. Keep warm until serving.

VERMICELLI ALLA CARBONARA

Yield: 6 servings

8 OUNCES BACON
SALT AND PEPPER TO TASTE
½ CUP HEAVY CREAM
¼ CUP BUTTER

4 EGG YOLKS
⅓ CUP GRATED PARMESAN CHEESE
1½ POUNDS VERMICELLI,
 COOKED AL DENTE

(continued)

❖ Cut the bacon into 1-inch-square pieces, and fry until most of the fat has been rendered. Add a dash of salt and pepper, drain off the rendered grease, and set aside. In a large, separate pan, heat the cream and butter gently until the butter melts. Add the egg yolks and cheese, and mix well. Stir the pasta into the egg-cheese mixture. Stir in the bacon, and serve.

LINGUINE AL PESTO GENOVESE

Yield: 6 servings

40 FRESH BASIL LEAVES
10 PARSLEY SPRIGS
½ CUP OLIVE OIL
4 GARLIC CLOVES
¼ CUP GRATED PARMESAN CHEESE

5–6 OUNCES CREAM CHEESE
SALT TO TASTE
1½ POUNDS LINGUINE, COOKED
    AL DENTE

❖ Wash the basil and parsley, and place in a blender with the oil and garlic. Blend until the ingredients are finely chopped. Add the Parmesan, and blend until well mixed. Just before serving, blend in the cream cheese. Add salt if necessary, and blend in a bit of the water in which pasta was cooked to produce the consistency of light cream. Spoon the sauce over the hot linguine, mixing until the pasta is evenly coated.

PASTA ALLA GIARDINIERA

Yield: 6 servings

7 TABLESPOONS BUTTER
½ CUP OLIVE OIL
1 MEDIUM ONION, HALVED AND CUT
    INTO THIN STRIPS
1 GARLIC CLOVE, CRUSHED
2 GREEN PEPPERS, HALVED, SEEDED,
    AND CUT INTO THIN STRIPS
1 MEDIUM CARROT, PEELED, SLICED
    CROSSWISE, AND CUT INTO THIN
    STRIPS
1 CELERY RIB, PEELED AND CUT INTO
    THIN STRIPS

8 OUNCES MUSHROOMS, SLICED
½ CUP DRY RED WINE
1 POUND RIPE TOMATOES, PEELED
    AND CHOPPED
8 OUNCES FROZEN LIMA BEANS
8 OUNCES FROZEN GREEN PEAS
SALT AND PEPPER TO TASTE
1 POUND SPAGHETTI
½ CUP GRATED PARMESAN CHEESE

❖ Heat the butter and olive oil in a saucepan, add the onions and garlic, and sauté until golden brown. Add the peppers, carrots, celery, and mushrooms, and cook until tender. Add the wine, and cook until it has evaporated. Add the tomatoes, and simmer for 5 to 10 minutes. Add the lima beans, peas, and salt and pepper to taste, and simmer until the vegetables are tender and the sauce has thickened. Cook the spaghetti in boiling salted water until al dente. Drain it, place it in a deep bowl, add the sauce and grated cheese, and serve.

CAPELLINI AL POMODORO

Yield: 4 servings

1 POUND CAPELLINI (ANGEL HAIR PASTA)
3–4 GARLIC CLOVES, CHOPPED
¼ CUP OLIVE OIL
6 TOMATOES, PEELED, SEEDED, AND CHOPPED
½ TABLESPOON CLAM BASE*

1 TABLESPOON FINELY CHOPPED FRESH BASIL
2 TABLESPOONS GRATED PARMESAN CHEESE
1 TABLESPOON BUTTER

❖ Cook the capellini in boiling salted water for 7 to 8 minutes; drain. Sauté the chopped garlic in olive oil until translucent. Add the tomatoes, clam base, and fresh basil, and cook until heated through. Add the cooked capellini. Mix, and sauté until hot. Finish the dish by stirring in the Parmesan cheese and butter. Do not overcook.

* For information about this base, see chapter 3.

BOW TIES WILLARD

Yield: 6 servings

6 TABLESPOONS BUTTER
3 OUNCES SHALLOTS, FINELY CHOPPED
18 OUNCES SMALL SCALLOPS
18 OUNCES SHRIMP, 26- TO 30-PER-POUND SIZE, PEELED AND DEVEINED
9 FLUID OUNCES PESTO (SEE RECIPE IN CHAPTER 3)

SALT AND PEPPER TO TASTE
6 CUPS COOKED BOW-TIE PASTA (FARFALLE)
1¼ CUPS DICED RED AND YELLOW PEPPERS, ROASTED
¾ CUP GRATED PARMESAN CHEESE

(continued)

✤ Heat the butter in a large skillet, add the shallots, and sauté briefly: do *not* color. Add the scallops and shrimp, and sauté until the shellfish are tender but not rubbery. Add the pesto, and cook until heated through. Add the cooked bow ties, and cook until the pasta is heated. Serve, topped with the diced roasted peppers and Parmesan cheese.

STUFFED PIZZA, PALERMO STYLE

Yield: 6 portions

DOUGH

½ CUP WARM WATER
1¼ TEASPOONS ACTIVE DRY YEAST
1 TEASPOON SALT

2 TEASPOONS OLIVE OIL
1½ CUPS UNSIFTED ALL-PURPOSE FLOUR

FILLING

½ CUP WATER
½ CUP DEHYDRATED MINCED ONION
¼ CUP OLIVE OIL
1½ CUPS CANNED ITALIAN PLUM
   TOMATOES, DRAINED AND
   COARSELY CHOPPED
½ TEASPOON CRUSHED OREGANO
   LEAVES

½ TEASPOON SALT
¼ TEASPOON FRESHLY GROUND
   BLACK PEPPER
5 ANCHOVY FILLETS, FINELY CHOPPED
6 TABLESPOONS TOASTED
   BREADCRUMBS

✤ To make the dough, pour the warm water into a large mixing bowl, sprinkle the yeast over, and let stand until the yeast dissolves, about 5 minutes. Add the salt, olive oil, and ¾ cup of the flour; beat until blended. Gradually add the remaining flour, beating until the mixture forms a dough that can be kneaded. Turn the dough onto a floured surface, and knead until smooth and elastic, about 5 minutes. Place the dough in an oiled bowl; turn to oil all sides. Cover with wax paper; and let rise in a warm, draftfree space until doubled in size, about 1½ hours.

In a cup, combine the water and dehydrated onion; set aside to soften, about 10 minutes. In a medium-size heavy skillet, heat 2 tablespoons of the olive oil. Add the softened onion, and cook until golden, about 4 minutes. Add the tomatoes, oregano, salt, and pepper, and cook, stirring, over moderate heat until the liquid evaporates and the mixture thickens, about 7 minutes. Stir in the anchovies, and cool. Preheat the oven to 400°F.

Punch the dough down, and divide in half. Roll each half into a 10-inch circle. Transfer one circle to a greased baking sheet. Sprinkle with 3 tablespoons of the breadcrumbs. Spread the tomato mixture over the top, leaving a 1-inch border at the edge. Sprinkle with the remaining 3 tablespoons of breadcrumbs. Drizzle the remaining 2 tablespoons of olive oil over the top. Place the second circle of dough on top of the filling; seal the edges. Using a pastry brush, brush the top lightly with water. Bake until lightly browned, about 30 minutes. Cut into wedges, and serve.

Note: Ten ounces of prepared pizza dough may be substituted for the dough.

PASTA WITH SHRIMP

Yield: 6 servings

¼ CUP OLIVE OIL
1 TABLESPOON CHOPPED SHALLOTS
½ TEASPOON CHOPPED GARLIC
14½ OUNCES CANNED WHOLE
   TOMATOES, DRAINED AND CHOPPED
½ POUND CLEANED SHRIMP, CHOPPED
1 CUP HEAVY CREAM
1 TABLESPOON SHRIMP BASE*

1 POUND FETTUCINE OR SPAGHETTI,
   COOKED AL DENTE
¼ CUP FRESHLY GRATED PARMESAN
   CHEESE
½ TABLESPOON BUTTER
2 TABLESPOONS CHOPPED PARSLEY
SALT AND FRESH GROUND BLACK
   PEPPER TO TASTE

❖ Heat the olive oil in a large pan, add the shallots and garlic, and sauté until translucent. Add the chopped shrimp, tomatoes, and cream, and cook for 2 to 3 minutes. Stir in the shrimp base, and then add the pasta. Cook for about 2 minutes. Toss with the Parmesan cheese and butter, sprinkle with chopped parsley and serve.

* For information about this base, see chapter 3.

RAVIOLI

Yield: 6 servings

8 OUNCES VEAL
8 OUNCES PORK
10 OUNCES FROZEN CHOPPED
   SPINACH, THAWED
1 CUP RICOTTA CHEESE

¼ CUP GRATED PARMESAN CHEESE
3 EGGS
PINCH OF BLACK PEPPER
SALT TO TASTE

RAVIOLI DOUGH

3½ CUPS SIFTED ALL-PURPOSE FLOUR
4 EGGS

4–5 TABLESPOONS WATER
1 TEASPOON SALT

❖ Grind the veal and pork (medium grind). Brown this meat. Add the spinach, ricotta, Parmesan, eggs, salt, and pepper, mix well, and simmer for 5 minutes. Let cool.

To make the ravioli dough, place the flour on a long pastry or baker's board. Make a well in the center, and break the eggs into it. Add the water, a bit at a time, then the salt. Blend together, and knead until smooth and elastic. Cover, and let stand for 30 minutes. Divide the dough into four parts. Roll out the dough, wrapping it around the rolling pin, as thin as you can. Spread the dough out on a flat surface.

Spoon small mounds of the meat mixture onto the ravioli dough, leaving 2 inches of space between the mounds. When half the sheet of dough is filled, fold over the other half, and press firmly between the mounds. Cut out the ravioli squares with a pastry wheel, and let rest for approximately 40 minutes. Cook in salted boiling water; fresh pasta cooks quickly, so watch carefully and be careful not to overcook. Remove to a preheated serving dish, and cover with your favorite tomato sauce.

FETTUCINE AND SAUSAGE WITH TOMATOES

Yield: 6 servings

3 TABLESPOONS OLIVE OIL
2 GARLIC CLOVES, FINELY CHOPPED
1½ POUNDS ITALIAN SAUSAGE, CUT
   INTO SMALL SLICES
14 OUNCES CANNED TOMATOES *OR* 4
   FRESH TOMATOES, CHOPPED

2 TABLESPOONS CHOPPED PARSLEY
1 POUND FETTUCINE, COOKED AL DENTE
6 TABLESPOONS GRATED PARMESAN
   CHEESE

❖ Heat the olive oil in a skillet, add the garlic, and sauté just until it begins to color lightly. Add the sausage, and brown lightly. Add the tomatoes and 1 tablespoon of the chopped parsley; simmer for 20 minutes. Reheat the fettucine in a colander by placing it in very hot salted water for 1 minute. Drain thoroughly, and add to the tomato-meat mixture. Toss lightly. Top with the grated cheese and remaining parsley.

PASTA WITH PESTO

Yield: 4 servings

1 POUND LINGUINE OR FETTUCINE
¼ CUP HEAVY CREAM
1 CUP PESTO (SEE RECIPE IN CHAPTER 3)
FRESHLY GROUND BLACK PEPPER TO
   TASTE

FRESHLY GRATED PARMESAN OR
   ROMANO CHEESE TO TASTE
   (OPTIONAL)

❖ Bring 4 quarts of salted water to a boil in a large kettle or stockpot. Add the pasta; use a wooden fork or spoon to stir the pasta until all strands are under water. Boil rapidly until done to taste: tender but not mushy. Stir 2 tablespoons of the hot pasta cooking water and the heavy cream into the pesto. Drain the pasta in a colander, and return it to the hot pan. Stir in the pesto, tossing well to combine. Sprinkle with black pepper or grated cheese if desired. Serve immediately on warm plates.

MEXICAN LASAGNA

Yield: 12 servings

2 POUNDS GROUND BEEF
1 CUP CHOPPED ONIONS
1 CUP CHOPPED CELERY
15 OUNCES BOTTLED GREEN-CHILI SALSA
10 OUNCES BOTTLED MILD ENCHILADA
  SAUCE
3 OUNCES TOMATO PASTE

½ CUP SLICED BLACK OLIVES
½ TABLESPOON SALT
⅛ TEASPOON PEPPER
12 CORN TORTILLAS (6 OR 8 INCH)
3 CUPS SHREDDED AMERICAN CHEESE
1½ CUPS COTTAGE CHEESE
2 EGGS, SLIGHTLY BEATEN

❖ Cook the ground beef, onion, and celery together in a skillet until the beef is browned; drain. Stir in the green-chili salsa, enchilada sauce, tomato paste, black olives, salt, and pepper. Heat to boiling. Lower the heat, and simmer uncovered for 20 minutes, stirring occasionally. Tear the tortillas into bite-size pieces. Combine 2 cups of the shredded American cheese, the cottage cheese, and the eggs. Spread one-third of the meat mixture on bottom of 12- by 20- by 2-inch baking pan. Top with half the cheese mixture, then half the corn tortillas. Repeat the layers, ending with the meat. Sprinkle the remaining cup of shredded cheese over the top. Bake in a 375°F oven for 30 to 45 minutes, until bubbly around the edges. Let stand for 15 minutes before serving.

LINGUINE WITH WHITE CLAM SAUCE

Yield: 6 servings

¼ CUP OLIVE OIL
1 LARGE GARLIC CLOVE, FINELY
  CHOPPED
1 TEASPOON OREGANO
2 TABLESPOONS FLOUR

1 POUND CANNED CHOPPED CLAMS
SALT AND PEPPER TO TASTE
2 TEASPOONS CHOPPED PARSLEY
1 POUND LINGUINE, COOKED AL DENTE

❖ Heat the olive oil in a saucepan, add the chopped garlic and oregano, and sauté until light brown. Add the flour, and cook, stirring, for a few minutes. Add the chopped clams, and simmer for 10 minutes. Adjust the seasonings. Stir in the chopped parsley, and toss this sauce with the cooked linguine.

PENNE ALL' ARRABBIATA

Yield: 6 servings

1 PEPERONCINO, CHOPPED
½ CUP OIL
1 ONION, THINLY SLICED
8 OUNCES BACON, DICED
1 POUND CANNED WHOLE PEELED
   TOMATOES, CHOPPED

6 FRESH BASIL LEAVES, CHOPPED
SALT TO TASTE
1 POUND PENNE (RIDGED PASTA)
   COOKED AL DENTE
GRATED PARMESAN CHEESE TO TASTE

❖ Heat the peperoncino gently in the oil, add the sliced onion, and sauté until the onions are translucent. Remove from the heat. In a separate pan, fry the diced bacon until crispy; drain. Combine the peperoncino, onions, and bacon; add the tomatoes and basil. Simmer uncovered for at least 30 minutes. Add salt if needed. Serve the sauce over the hot penne, with the Parmesan cheese.

VERMICELLI CON SARI

Yield: 6 servings

½ CUP OLIVE OIL
1 GARLIC CLOVE, CRUSHED
3 POUNDS RIPE TOMATOES, PEELED,
   SEEDED, AND CHOPPED
6 LARGE FRESH BASIL LEAVES, CHOPPED
SALT AND PEPPER TO TASTE

20 PITTED BLACK OLIVES, SLICED
12 ANCHOVY FILLETS, CHOPPED
1 TABLESPOON DRAINED CAPERS
1 POUND VERMICELLI
6 TABLESPOONS GRATED PARMESAN
   CHEESE

❖ In a large saucepan, heat the olive oil, add the garlic and sauté until transparent but not brown. Add the tomatoes, and bring to a simmer. Add the chopped basil, salt, pepper, black olives, anchovies, and capers. Simmer until the sauce thickens to the desired consistency. Cook the vermicelli al dente in boiling, salted water; drain, and divide among 6 serving plates. Pour the sauce over the vermicelli, sprinkle with the grated cheese, and serve.

GNOCCHI ALLA ROMANA

Yield: 6 servings

3 CUPS PLUS 1½ TABLESPOONS WATER
½ TEASPOON SALT
¾ CUP FARINA
3 EGG YOLKS
PINCH OF CAYENNE

10 OUNCES SWISS CHEESE, DICED
  SMALL
1 TEASPOON CORNSTARCH
¼ CUP SOUR CREAM
¼ CUP GRATED PARMESAN CHEESE

❖ Boil the 3 cups of water, salt, and farina for approximately 4 to 6 minutes. Remove from the heat, cover, and let stand for 8 to 10 minutes. Blend the egg yolks and cayenne into the cooked farina; cover and chill. Stir the diced cheese into the chilled farina. Form the egg-size dumplings, and place in a buttered baking dish.

Stir the cornstarch into the 1½ tablespoons of water until smooth. Add the sour cream, and blend well. Place in the top of a double-boiler. Cook until thickened, whisking continually. Cover the dumplings with this sauce, and sprinkle with the grated Parmesan cheese. Bake in a 400°F oven for about 15 minutes or until golden brown.

POLENTA DUMPLINGS

Yield: 6 servings

6 CUPS WATER
1 TABLESPOON CHICKEN BASE*
3 CUPS YELLOW CORNMEAL
12 THIN SLICES GORGONZOLA CHEESE

12 THIN SLICES FONTINA CHEESE
½ CUP WHITE WINE
7 TABLESPOONS BUTTER, MELTED

❖ In a heavy-bottomed pan, bring the water and chicken base to a boil. When it is boiling rapidly, slowly add the yellow cornmeal in a stream, mixing constantly with a wire whisk to prevent lumps. Cook over medium heat for 30 to 45 minutes, stirring frequently with a wooden spoon. Turn out into a 9¼-by 5¼-by 2¾-inch loaf pan to cool. When cold, cut into 12 slices, approximately ¼-inch thick. Place the slices in a buttered earthenware baking dish in a single layer; top each with a slice of Gorgonzola and a slice of Fontina cheese. Sprinkle with wine and the melted butter. Bake in a 450°F oven until the wine has evaporated and the cheese has melted. Serve at once.

* For information about this base, see chapter 3.

GORGONZOLA POLENTA

Yield: 6 servings

3 CUPS MILK
3 TABLESPOONS UNSALTED BUTTER
¾ CUP CORNMEAL (NOT STONE GROUND)
3 TABLESPOONS SOUR CREAM
2½ TABLESPOONS GRATED GRUYÈRE CHEESE
2½ TABLESPOONS FRESHLY GRATED PARMESAN CHEESE

⅓ CUP CRUMBLED GORGONZOLA CHEESE
⅓ CUP GOLDEN RAISINS
PINCH OF FRESHLY GRATED NUTMEG
SALT AND FRESHLY GROUND PEPPER TO TASTE
6 THIN SLICES GORGONZOLA CHEESE, 1 INCH SQUARE
¼ CUP FINE BREADCRUMBS

❖ In a heavy-bottomed saucepan, bring the milk and butter to a boil. Add the cornmeal in a stream, whisking constantly. When the mixture begins to thicken, continue to boil, stirring constantly with a wooden spoon, until very thick and smooth, about 5 minutes. Stir in the sour cream, grated Gruyère, Parmesan, crumbled Gorgonzola, raisins, and nutmeg; heat until smooth. Remove from the heat; add salt and pepper to taste. Spoon the cornmeal mixture into six ½-cup ramekins or custard cups; tap the molds gently to settle the mixture, and smooth the tops with a spatula. Cool for at least 15 minutes.

Use a knife to loosen the polenta from ramekins, and unmold onto a generously buttered baking dish. Place a slice of Gorgonzola on top of each; sprinkle with a fine layer of breadcrumbs. Bake in a 450°F oven for 10 to 12 minutes; then broil until lightly golden. This dish goes well with game birds and whole cranberry sauce.

YORKSHIRE PUDDING

Yield: 12 servings

2 CUPS MILK
6 EGGS
1¾ CUPS ALL-PURPOSE FLOUR
¾ CUP FAT OR SHORTENING (SEE NOTE BELOW)

½ TEASPOON BAKING POWDER
SALT AND PEPPER TO TASTE

(continued)

❖ Preheat the oven to 400°F. Mix the milk, eggs, flour, ½ cup of the fat, baking powder, salt, and pepper until smooth. Grease each of 12 ramekin molds with 1 teaspoon of the remaining fat. Place the molds in the oven for 3 minutes, remove, and fill two-thirds full with the batter. Bake in a 400°F oven for 15 minutes, until fluffy and light brown.

Note: Yorkshire pudding traditionally accompanies roast beef, and the classic recipe calls for the drippings from that meat to be used as the fat.

BUTTERED NOODLES POLONAISE

Yield: 6 servings

¾ CUP BUTTER
2 CUPS BREADCRUMBS

1 POUND EGG NOODLES, COOKED
   AL DENTE

❖ Heat the butter in a skillet, add the breadcrumbs, and fry to a golden brown. Heat the noodles in boiling water for 1 minute, drain. Toss the noodles with the fried breadcrumbs.

Note: This dish can also be served as a hot dessert, sprinkled with powdered sugar.

RICE PILAF

Yield: 10 servings

¼ CUP SALAD OIL
1 ONION, FINELY DICED
1 GARLIC CLOVE, MINCED
1 POUND VERMICELLI, BROKEN
   INTO PIECES
1 POUND LONG-GRAIN RICE

1 TEASPOON SALT
½ TEASPOON WHITE PEPPER
¼ TEASPOON TURMERIC
3 BAY LEAVES
1½ QUARTS BOILING CHICKEN STOCK

❖ Heat the oil in a heavy casserole; add the onion and garlic, and brown slightly. Add the vermicelli, and brown. Add the rice, salt, pepper, turmeric, and bay leaves, and heat thoroughly. Add the boiling stock, cover the casserole, and cook over low heat until all the liquid is absorbed, approximately 20 minutes. Fluff with a fork, remove the bay leaves, and serve.

Note: For best results, place the casserole in a preheated 325°F oven, rather than on the stove, for slow steaming.

CHAPTER NINE

Vegetables

THE consumption of vegetables has increased in recent years not only because they contribute bright color, varied texture, and wonderful flavor to our meals, but also because they are valuable sources of vitamins, minerals, and fiber and are usually low in calories. Vegetables are some of the best sources of dietary fiber, and many are very high in vitamin C, vitamin A, and/or the B-complex vitamins. For vegetables to retain their nutritive value, they must be prepared properly; improper preparation can destroy vitamins. Normally, a cooked vegetable with a bright, natural-appearing, good color is a nutritious one, because the right color can be achieved only when the proper preparation methods are used.

Each vegetable has a distinctive color because it possesses certain color pigments. White vegetables contain white pigments called *flavones*, which turn white in an acid (sour) medium and yellow in a base (alkaline) one. Thus, it is acceptable to add *just a pinch* of cream of tartar (tartaric acid) to potatoes when mashing them to increase the whiteness of the final product. Never add baking soda to any white vegetable, as it will ruin the flavor.

Red vegetables, such as beets or red cabbage, are red because they contain pigments called *anthocyanins.* These pigments cause the vegetable to turn a bright red in an acid medium and a dull purple in an alkaline one. Thus, many beet recipes call for the addition of an acid, such as vinegar, as is the case when making pickled or Harvard beets. Red cabbage is often cooked with tart apples, not only to add flavor, but also to preserve the bright red color. An alkaline ingredient, such as baking soda, has a detrimental effect on the color of these products (as well as on the color of many red fruits). Never use baking soda as the leavening agent in blueberry muffins, as the blueberries will turn a dirty purple or blackish color and the appeal of the muffins will be ruined. Some red vegetables, such as tomatoes and red peppers, get their redness from pigments called lycopenes. These are not much affected by acids or alkalis. Since both vegetables are slightly acidic anyway, an acidic medium is usually best for them.

Green vegetables contain a very perishable color pigment called chlorophyll, the agent responsible not only for the green color but also for photosynthesis.

Because heat destroys chlorophyll, green vegetables should be cooked quickly, to reduce its destruction, as well as to reduce the loss of the water-soluble vitamins—vitamin C and the B-complex vitamins—in green vegetables. Some green vegetables steam well (reducing vitamin and color loss), but others, such as spinach, tend to "pack" when steamed. All vegetables should be served immediately after cooking to maintain nutrients, color, and texture. Some chefs like to blanch green vegetables in cold water to stop the cooking process and thus preserve the green color. Though this procedure does preserve color, it also results in nutrient loss. The conscientious chef today refrains from blanching and depends more upon fast service to present the vegetable in optimum condition.

Never add baking soda to a green vegetable. Although it may help to preserve the green color for a time, the use of soda destroys ascorbic acid (Vitamin C) and thiamine, nutrients necessary for good health. An alkaline reaction also destroys the texture of green vegetables, another reason soda is not recommended for use with green vegetables, or with dried beans and peas and other legumes.

Carotenes, the most stable of the plant pigments, are found in many green, yellow, and orange vegetables. They are not destroyed by either acids or bases, are relatively insoluble in water, and hold up well under heat. Vegetables that contain large amounts of carotene, such as carrots, are excellent sources of vitamin A, necessary for healthy tissues and good eyesight.

The current trend toward serving vegetables slightly undercooked rather than overcooked is positive, as the vegetables are usually more nutritious and have a better texture. The stir-fry method used in Oriental cuisines also helps preserve color and retain nutrient values.

Nutrients can be lost not only in cooking but during preparation as well. As much as possible, do not peel vegetables. If carrots, for example, are young, brush them well, rinse, and cook without peeling. This practice prevents nutrient loss and retains valuable fiber. Often more nutrients are just under the skin of a vegetable, rather than in its interior. This is especially true of potatoes, which are therefore more nutritious if served with the skins intact.

If possible, do not soak vegetables prior to cooking, especially if they are peeled. The water leaches out the nutrients, and if this water is lost, so are the nutrients. Cook vegetables in as little water as possible to retain nutrients. Potatoes, carrots, and many other vegetables steam and stir-fry well. In addition, to reduce nutrient losses resulting from prolonged storage, use vegetables as soon after purchasing as possible.

Vegetables

STUFFED ARTICHOKES

VERMONT BAKED BEANS

GREEN BEANS WITH BACON AND TOMATOES

BROCCOLI TIMBALES

BRUSSELS SPROUTS WITH BACON

GLAZED BUTTERNUT SQUASH

SWEET-AND-SOUR RED CABBAGE

FRIED CAULIFLOWER

BRAISED CELERY HEARTS

CHESTNUT STUFFING

SAUTÉED CUCUMBERS WITH DILL

EGGPLANT SOUFFLÉ

RATATOUILLE

POTATO DUMPLINGS

DUCHESS POTATOES

POTATO CAKE

POTATO PANCAKES

BAKED STUFFED POTATOES

GRATIN DAUPHINOIS

GRANNY'S GRATIN OF POTATOES

SPINACH FRITTATA

STUFFED TOMATOES WITH SPINACH

TOMATO PARMIGIANA

BAKED TOMATO AND ONION CASSEROLE

ZUCCHINI IN MARINARA SAUCE

ZUCCHINI MUSHROOM MÉLANGE

STUFFED ARTICHOKES

Yield: 4 to 6 servings

6 ARTICHOKES
1½ CUPS BREADCRUMBS (FROM ITALIAN
    OR FRENCH BREAD)
1 SMALL ONION, CHOPPED
1 TABLESPOON CHOPPED PARSLEY
3 TABLESPOONS GRATED ROMANO
    CHEESE

½ TEASPOON SALT
½ TEASPOON PEPPER
¼ CUP OLIVE OIL
2 TABLESPOONS WATER
1 ONION, QUARTERED
1 BAY LEAF

✤ Cut the stalks and tips from the artichokes, and remove some of the tough outer leaves; spread the remaining leaves open. Mix the breadcrumbs, chopped onion, parsley, cheese, salt, pepper, olive oil, and water; spread a tiny bit of this mixture on each leaf. Stand the artichokes in a pot; add boiling water to reach halfway up the artichokes. Add the quartered onion and bay leaf. Cover, and cook gently until tender, or until the leaves pull out easily, about 40 minutes. Drain and serve.

VERMONT BAKED BEANS

Yield: 8 servings

4 CUPS DRY NAVY BEANS
1½ CUPS SUGAR
⅛ TEASPOON GINGER
⅛ TEASPOON PEPPER
2 TEASPOONS DRY MUSTARD

5 OUNCES SALT PORK, CUT INTO ¾-INCH
    CUBES
⅓ CUP MOLASSES
⅔ CUP VERMONT MAPLE SYRUP

✤ Soak the beans overnight in water. Parboil according to the directions on the package. Drain and rinse. Mix 1 cup of the sugar, the ginger, pepper, and dry mustard together. Layer one-third of the mixture, one-third of the salt pork, and one-third of the beans in a crockery bean pot. Repeat twice more, using all the beans, sugar mixture, and salt pork. Pour the molasses and maple syrup on top of the beans, and add enough water to cover the beans by ½ inch. Cover, and bake, in a 350°F oven for 2 hours, adding water after the first hour if the liquid has evaporated. Reduce the heat to 300°F, add the remaining ½ cup of sugar, and continue baking until tender. (Baking time can vary greatly, depending on the beans; do not overcook and allow them to become mushy.)

GREEN BEANS WITH BACON AND TOMATOES

Yield: 6 servings

1 POUND GREEN BEANS
6 OUNCES BACON, DICED
1¼ CUPS FINELY DICED ONIONS
3 GARLIC CLOVES, MINCED

20 OUNCES CANNED TOMATOES, PEELED
   AND CHOPPED
SALT AND BLACK PEPPER TO TASTE

❖ Clean the green beans by cutting off the ends and peeling off the strings. Bring the beans to boil in salted water, and boil for 5 minutes; cool and drain. Render the bacon in large skillet, add the onions, and sauté until translucent. Add the garlic and tomatoes, and cook over low heat for 5 minutes. Add the green beans, season, and bring to a short boil. Serve.

Note: Frozen beans can be used instead of fresh, reducing the boiling time to no more than 2 minutes.

BROCCOLI TIMBALES

Yield: 5 to 6 servings

14 OUNCES BROCCOLI FLORETS,
   CHOPPED
3 TABLESPOONS BUTTER
2 TABLESPOONS MINCED SHALLOTS
3 TABLESPOONS SIFTED FLOUR
¾ CUP WARMED MILK

2 EGGS, BEATEN
1 TEASPOON GROUND MARJORAM
SALT AND PEPPER TO TASTE
¼ CUP WHITE BREADCRUMBS
6 ROUND GARLIC CROÛTONS, BUTTERED

❖ Steam the broccoli for about 8 minutes. Drain thoroughly to remove any excess moisture. Heat the butter in a saucepan, add the shallots, and sauté until translucent. Blend in the flour to make a roux. Gradually add the milk and

(continued)

beaten eggs, and cook, stirring constantly, until thickened. Add the marjoram, salt, and pepper to taste. Fold the chopped broccoli and breadcrumbs into the custard. Place the round garlic croûtons in the bottoms of well-buttered 5-ounce custard cups or timbale forms. Fill each with the broccoli custard. Place the cups in a baking dish filled with 1 inch of hot water. Bake in a 350° oven for 40 minutes, until firm. Remove from the oven and water bath, and let stand for 5 to 10 minutes. Unmold by inverting on a serving platter. Serve with hollandaise or cheese sauce.

BRUSSELS SPROUTS WITH BACON

Yield: 6 servings

2 POUNDS FRESH BRUSSELS SPROUTS
½ CUP DICED ONION

6 OUNCES BACON, DICED
SALT AND BLACK PEPPER TO TASTE

❖ Cut off the core of each sprout, and remove the upper layer of leaves. Boil in salted water for 10 minutes; drain. Sauté the onions with the bacon until translucent. Add the boiled brussels sprouts; season with salt and black pepper. Cover, and simmer over low heat for about 5 minutes.

GLAZED BUTTERNUT SQUASH

Yield: 8 servings

4 BUTTERNUT SQUASH
1 CUP BROWN SUGAR
½ TEASPOON SALT

½ TEASPOON GROUND GINGER
½ CUP BUTTER

❖ Wash the squash, halve lengthwise, and remove the seeds. Place, split side up, on a baking pan. Mix the sugar, salt, and ginger, and sprinkle over the squash. Melt the butter, and drizzle over the squash. Bake in a 350°F oven for approximately 45 minutes.

SWEET-AND-SOUR RED CABBAGE

Yield: Approximately 4 quarts

4 POUNDS RED CABBAGE, CORED AND
    THINLY SLICED
1 POUND APPLES, PEELED, CORED, AND
    THINLY SLICED
1 CUP BURGUNDY WINE
½ CUP SUGAR
1 TABLESPOON SALT
½ TEASPOON CARAWAY SEEDS

½ TEASPOON GROUND BLACK PEPPER
8 OUNCES CHICKEN FAT
1 CUP CHOPPED ONIONS
¼ CUP RED-WINE VINEGAR
3 OUNCES HAM BASE*
1½ CUPS WATER
1 TABLESPOON CORNSTARCH

❖ Combine the red cabbage, apples, Burgundy, sugar, salt, caraway seeds, and pepper, stirring together well. Marinate, covered and refrigerated, for 3 days.

Heat the chicken fat in a small skillet, and sauté the onions until lightly browned. In a large cooking pot, combine the cabbage and its marinade, the chicken fat and onion mixture, the red-wine vinegar, and the ham base. Simmer uncovered for 3 hours. Combine the water and cornstarch in mixing bowl, and slowly stir into the cabbage mixture. Bring to a boil, and cook for 5 minutes. Serve hot.

* For information about this base, see chapter 3.

FRIED CAULIFLOWER

Yield: 6 servings

2 MEDIUM CAULIFLOWER HEADS
1 LEMON, SLICED
1½ CUPS ALL-PURPOSE FLOUR
2 EGGS, SEPARATED

SALT AND WHITE PEPPER TO TASTE
1 CUP CLUB SODA *OR* BEER
1 PINT SALAD OIL

❖ Clean the cauliflower by removing the green leaves and cutting off any brown spots on the florets. Place in boiling water with the lemon slices, and cook until the stalk is barely tender, about 10 to 12 minutes. Remove, and chill under cold running water. Cut into wedges or separate into florets.

(continued)

Place 1 cup of the flour in a bowl. Add the egg yolks, salt, pepper, and club soda or beer, and mix well into a smooth batter. Beat the egg white until medium-stiff peaks form. Fold into the batter. Heat the oil in a deep fryer. Dredge the cauliflower in the remaining ½ cup of flour, then dip into the batter. Deep-fry in the hot oil until golden brown and crispy. Remove to absorbent paper. Serve hot with rémoulade or tartar sauce.

Note: If prepared as an appetizer, separate the cooked cauliflower into small, bite-sized florets, and proceed as for large pieces.

BRAISED CELERY HEARTS

Yield: 6 servings

3 YOUNG CELERY HEARTS
3 OUNCES SMOKED BACON, DICED
½ CUP FINELY CHOPPED LEEKS
½ CUP PEELED AND DICED TOMATOES
2 GARLIC CLOVES, MINCED

1½ CUPS BROWN SAUCE (SEE RECIPE IN CHAPTER 3)
SALT AND PEPPER TO TASTE
1 CUP GRATED PARMESAN CHEESE (OPTIONAL)

❖ Parboil the celery in salted water for 5 minutes; drain. Cut into finger-long pieces and arrange in a baking dish. Render the diced bacon, add the leeks and sauté until translucent. Add the tomatoes and garlic; sauté for 2 minutes. Add the brown sauce; bring to a boil, and season. Pour over the celery in the baking dish, cover, and braise in a 350°F oven for approximately 20 minutes. If cheese is used, sprinkle it over the celery for the last 5 minutes of baking time.

CHESTNUT STUFFING

Yield: Approximately 6 servings

1 CUP MILK
1 TABLESPOON CHICKEN BASE*
1 EGG
3 CUPS BREADCRUMBS (DRY BREAD MAY BE USED)
1 TEASPOON GROUND SAGE

½ TEASPOON MARJORAM
½ TEASPOON THYME
1 TEASPOON SALT
¼ CUP CHOPPED FRESH PARSLEY
1 CUP FINELY CHOPPED CHESTNUT MEATS

✤ Mix the milk, chicken base, and egg. Blend this mixture with the bread-crumbs, sage, marjoram, thyme, salt, parsley, and nutmeats. Use as a stuffing for poultry or meats, or simply bake in a greased pan at 350°F for approximately 1 hour.

* For information about this base, see chapter 3.

SAUTÉED CUCUMBERS WITH DILL

Yield: 6 servings

3 LARGE CUCUMBERS
6 TABLESPOONS BUTTER
SALT AND WHITE PEPPER TO TASTE

1 TABLESPOON LEMON JUICE
1 CUP CHOPPED FRESH DILL

✤ Peel the cucumbers, and halve lengthwise. Scoop out the seeds, and slice obliquely. Melt the butter in a sauté pan, add the cucumbers, and sauté until translucent. Stir in the salt, pepper, and lemon juice. Sprinkle with the chopped dill, and serve.

EGGPLANT SOUFFLÉ

Yield: 4 servings

2 MEDIUM EGGPLANTS
2 TABLESPOONS OLIVE OIL
SALT TO TASTE
1 TABLESPOON BUTTER
1 TABLESPOON FLOUR

½ CUP MILK
PEPPER TO TASTE
2 EGG WHITES, BEATEN TO STIFF PEAKS
¼ CUP GRATED GRUYÈRE CHEESE

✤ Preheat the oven to 400°F. Cut the eggplants in half lengthwise, and cut several slits in the cut sides. Sprinkle both sides with the oil and 1 teaspoon of

(continued)

salt. Place in an ovenproof dish, cut side down, and bake for 15 minutes. Turn them over, and bake for 10 minutes more. Remove from the oven to cool. Heat the butter in a saucepan. When it foams, add the flour, and cook, stirring constantly with a whisk, until slightly brown. Add the milk, and stir until thickened. Add salt and pepper to taste. Stir until smooth. Scoop out the eggplants, being careful not to tear the shells. Chop the pulp, and add it to the hot sauce; mix well. Fold in the stiff egg whites. Fill the eggplant shells with the mixture, sprinkle the cheese on top, and turn to the ovenproof dish. Bake in a 375°F oven until the filling puffs up and is golden brown, about 30 minutes. Remove from the oven, and serve at once.

RATATOUILLE

Yield: 6 servings

8 OUNCES EGGPLANT, PEELED AND
    SLICED LENGTHWISE INTO STRIPS
8 OUNCES ZUCCHINI, CUT INTO 1-INCH
    SLICES
1 TEASPOON SALT
7 TABLESPOONS OLIVE OIL
8 OUNCES YELLOW ONION, THINLY
    SLICED

2 GREEN PEPPERS, SLICED
2 GARLIC CLOVES, CRUSHED
SALT AND PEPPER TO TASTE
1 POUND FIRM, RIPE TOMATOES, PEELED,
    SEEDED, AND SLICED INTO STRIPS

❖ Place the eggplant and zucchini in a bowl, and toss with the salt. Let stand for 30 minutes. Drain; dry each slice with a towel.

In a 10-inch skillet, heat 4 tablespoons of olive oil. Add the eggplant in one layer, and sauté for 1 minute on each side. Remove and set aside; keep warm.

Repeat the same procedure with the zucchini, in the same oil. Pour off the oil after sautéing the zucchini. In the same skillet, cook the onions and peppers slowly in the remaining 3 tablespoons olive oil for 10 minutes, until tender but not brown. Stir in the garlic, and season to taste. Lay the tomato strips over the onions and peppers; season with salt and pepper. Cover the skillet, and cook over low heat for 5 minutes, until tomatoes have begun to render their juice.

Uncover, baste with the juice, and raise the heat. Boil for several minutes, until the liquid has almost completely evaporated. Combine the cooked zucchini and eggplant, spoon the tomato mixture over them and serve with garlic bread.

POTATO DUMPLINGS

Yield: 8 servings

9 MEDIUM POTATOES, PEELED AND
   GRATED
1 TEASPOON SALT
3 EGGS, WELL BEATEN

1 CUP FLOUR
¾ CUP BREADCRUMBS
1 TEASPOON GRATED NUTMEG

✤ Combine the grated potatoes, salt, eggs, flour, breadcrumbs and nutmeg. Shape into 1½- to 2-ounce balls, or about 3 tablespoons per ball. If sticky, add more breadcrumbs (not flour). Cook in boiling salted water for 7 to 10 minutes (test-cook one dumpling for firmness and flavor before cooking all of them).

Note: The dumplings may be made a day ahead and stored on a floured pan until ready to cook.

DUCHESS POTATOES

Yield: 8 servings

1 POUND POTATOES, PEELED
2 EGG YOLKS
1 TEASPOON SALT

½ TEASPOON WHITE PEPPER
¼ TEASPOON NUTMEG
2 TEASPOONS BUTTER

✤ Place the potatoes in a pot, cover with water, and cook until tender. Drain, and dry over low heat in the pot. Puree the potatoes in a blender or food processor. Add the egg yolks, salt, pepper, nutmeg and butter. Fill a pastry bag with large tip with the mixture. Pipe onto a sheet pan, and bake in a 325°F oven until golden brown.

Variation: Breaded Duchess Potatoes: Instead of piping out the potato mixture, shape it by packing it firmly in small buttered molds or ramekins. Remove the molded mixture from the molds, roll in breadcrumbs to coat, brush lightly with melted butter, and place on a baking sheet. Bake in a 400°F oven for 8 to 10 minutes, until lightly browned.

POTATO CAKE

Yield: 6 servings

2 POUNDS NEW POTATOES
1 CUP HEAVY CREAM
1 TEASPOON SALT
½ TEASPOON WHITE PEPPER

2 CUPS GRATED GRUYÈRE CHEESE
2 EGGS
¼ TEASPOON NUTMEG

✤ Cook potatoes in boiling salted water until tender. Drain, peel, and mash or puree. Preheat the oven to 350°F. Stir ¼ cup of the cream and the salt and pepper into the potatoes. Spread evenly in a 1½-quart soufflé pan or casserole. Mix the cheese, remaining ¾ cup of cream, eggs, and nutmeg, and pour over the potatoes. Bake for 30 to 40 minutes. Let stand for 10 minutes before serving.

POTATO PANCAKES

Yield 24 pancakes

2 POUNDS POTATOES, PEELED AND
    GRATED MEDIUM
2 EGGS, SLIGHTLY BEATEN
2 TABLESPOONS FLOUR

1 LARGE ONION, GRATED
SALT AND PEPPER TO TASTE
OIL FOR FRYING (SEE NOTE BELOW)

✤ Combine the grated potatoes, eggs, flour, onions, salt and pepper; mix well. Heat the oil in a heavy-bottomed frying pan (not a griddle). (The oil should be deep enough to come halfway up the potato pancake when it is put into the oil.) Using a tablespoon, gently drop one spoonful at a time into the oil. (If the batter is a little heavy, you may have to flatten the pancakes just a little bit.) Fry until golden brown; drain on absorbent towels before serving.

Note: Pork lard seems to be the best frying medium for German-style potato pancakes; they are best fried to order.

BAKED STUFFED POTATOES

Yield: 6 portions

3 BAKING POTATOES
3 TABLESPOONS OIL
1 TABLESPOON BUTTER
¼ CUP FINELY DICED ONION
3 TABLESPOONS FINELY DICED HAM
1 TABLESPOON CHOPPED CHIVES

SALT AND WHITE PEPPER TO TASTE
3 TABLESPOONS CREAM
3 TABLESPOONS GRATED PARMESAN
CHEESE
3 TEASPOONS BUTTER, MELTED

❖ Wash and dry the potatoes. Brush the skins with the oil, and prick well with a fork. Bake in a 400°F oven for about 1 hour, until they are easily pierced with a fork. Halve the potatoes lengthwise, and scoop out the pulp, leaving the shells intact.

In a small pan, melt the butter, add the onions and ham, and sauté for 1 minute.

Mash the potato pulp with a fork. Add the sautéed onions, ham, chopped chives, salt, and pepper; mix well. Add the cream to soften the potato mixture. Return the potato mixture to the potato shells using either a pastry tube, to make an attractive pattern, or a spatula. Trace some crisscrosses on the tops, and sprinkle with the Parmesan cheese and a few drops melted butter. Bake in a 450°F oven until lightly browned.

GRATIN DAUPHINOIS

Yield: 6 servings

1 GARLIC CLOVE
2 TABLESPOONS BUTTER
1 POUND POTATOES, PEELED AND
THINLY SLICED
½ CUP PLUS 2 TABLESPOONS GRATED
GRUYÈRE OR EMMENTAL CHEESE

1 EGG
1 CUP MILK, SCALDED
PINCH OF NUTMEG
SALT AND WHITE PEPPER TO TASTE

❖ Preheat the oven to 350°F. Rub a 2-inch-deep earthware baking dish with the garlic clove. Butter the dish with 1 tablespoon of the butter. Combine the

(continued)

potatoes and ½ cup of the grated cheese. Arrange the potato-cheese mixture in the baking dish. Beat the egg; add the milk, nutmeg, salt, and pepper. Pour over the potatoes. Sprinkle the remaining 2 tablespoons of cheese over the potatoes. Dot with the remaining tablespoon of butter. Bake for 45 to 50 minutes, until the potatoes are cooked and the top is nicely browned.

GRANNY'S GRATIN OF POTATOES

Yield: Approximately 12 servings

3 POUNDS BOILING POTATOES
   (12 MEDIUM)
4 OUNCES BUTTER
½ CUP ALL-PURPOSE FLOUR
4 CUPS HOT MILK
2 LARGE GARLIC CLOVES, PUREED
1 TEASPOON CURRY POWDER

1 TABLESPOON DIJON-TYPE MUSTARD
SALT AND PEPPER TO TASTE
HOT PEPPER SAUCE (TABASCO), TO
   TASTE
⅔ CUP COARSELY GRATED SWISS
   CHEESE

✢ Peel the potatoes, halve them, and cut into slices ⅜-inch thick; place into a pot of lightly salted water as they are sliced. Bring to a boil, cover partially, and boil for 5 to 6 minutes, until just tender. Drain.

Melt the butter in a heavy-bottomed 2- to 3-quart saucepan, blend in the flour, and stir over moderately low heat until butter and flour foam together for 2 minutes, without browning. Remove from the heat, and when the bubbling has stopped, vigorously beat in the hot milk. Beat in the pureed garlic. Combine the curry and mustard, and beat into the sauce, along with the salt, pepper, and hot pepper sauce. Bring to a boil, and boil slowly for 2 minutes, stirring with a wooden spoon. Taste, and correct the seasonings. The sauce should be quite thick; beat in spoonfuls of milk if needed.

Preheat the oven to 425°F. Grease a 3-quart baking dish, and spread a thin layer of sauce over the bottom. Reserving one-third of the sauce and one-quarter of the cheese, spread the potatoes, cheese, and sauce in layers; end with the reserved sauce and the last of the cheese. Bake in the upper-third of the preheated oven for about 30 minutes, just until bubbling hot and nicely browned on top.

Note: The potato, sauce, and cheese mixture may be prepared a day in advance and baked the following day. Cover and refrigerate until ready to bake.

SPINACH FRITTATA

Yield: Approximately 6 servings

1 POUND SPINACH (FRESH OR FROZEN)
½ TABLESPOON COOKING OIL
4 OUNCES BACON, DICED
1 TABLESPOON CHOPPED SHALLOTS
1 BUNCH SCALLIONS, CHOPPED
4 EGGS, BEATEN

12 OUNCES GRUYÈRE CHEESE, GRATED
4 OUNCES PARMESAN CHEESE, GRATED
SALT AND PEPPER TO TASTE
½ TABLESPOON POWDERED NUTMEG
3 TABLESPOONS BUTTER

❖ Steam the spinach for 10 to 15 minutes, until wilted, if using fresh; follow package instructions for frozen. Drain well, squeezing out all the water. Finely chop the spinach. Heat the oil in a skillet, add the bacon, shallots, and scallions, and sauté until tender but not brown. Add the spinach, and pour the mixture into a stainless-steel bowl. Add the beaten eggs and the cheeses; mix well. Add salt, pepper, and nutmeg; mix well.

Heat the butter in a skillet over medium heat. When it foams, add the spinach-egg mixture. Turn the heat to low, and cook until the eggs have set and only the top surface is runny. Place the skillet under the broiler to set the top, for 30 seconds to 1 minute. Remove from the pan, slice into wedges, and serve.

Note: The spinach-egg mixture will keep in a refrigerator for 3 to 4 days.

Variations: The spinach-egg mixture can also be used to stuff cherry tomatoes, zucchini, or cucumbers; bake in a 350°F oven for 10 minutes, and serve as a hot hors d'oeuvre. The mixture can also be used to stuff a large tomato; bake in a 350°F oven for about 25 minutes, and serve as a side dish (this makes a beautiful centerpiece vegetable on a vegetable plate). By adding diced cooked ham, turkey, chicken, or beef, it can be used as a filling for stuffed tomatoes or bell peppers, to serve as an entrée. It can also be baked in a well-greased pie tin and cut into wedges and served as one would serve a quiche; or it could be placed in a well-greased hotel pan and baked at 350°F for 45 minutes, until firm but not dry, cut into 2-inch squares and served as a hot hors d'oeuvre (cut into 3-inch squares and serve on a buffet line as a vegetable).

STUFFED TOMATOES WITH SPINACH

Yield: 6 servings

6 FIRM TOMATOES, CORED
2 TEASPOONS SALT
1 TABLESPOON BUTTER
1 TABLESPOON FLOUR
1 CUP MILK
8 OUNCES FROZEN SPINACH, THAWED
  AND FINELY CHOPPED

¼ TEASPOON NUTMEG
¼ TEASPOON WHITE PEPPER
3 TABLESPOONS GRATED CHEDDAR
  CHEESE

✤ Sprinkle the cored tomatoes with 1 teaspoon of the salt, and set upside down. Heat the butter, stir in the flour, and cook until bubbly and smooth, stirring constantly. Add the milk, and cook for 5 minutes, stirring constantly. Remove from the heat. Add the chopped spinach, and mix well; add the nutmeg, pepper, and remaining teaspoon of salt. Fill the cored tomatoes with the mixture; sprinkle 1 teaspoon of Cheddar cheese on top of each. Bake in a 325°F oven for 10 to 15 minutes.

TOMATO PARMIGIANA

Yield: 4 servings

2 MEDIUM TOMATOES
3 OUNCES BOURSIN CHEESE, SOFTENED
2 TABLESPOONS GRATED PARMESAN
  CHEESE
2 TABLESPOONS BREADCRUMBS
2 EGGS

½ CUP MILK
SALT AND FRESHLY GRATED WHITE
  PEPPER TO TASTE
2 TABLESPOONS FLOUR
½ CUP BUTTER
MILD PAPRIKA FOR COLOR

✤ Slice each tomato into 4 even slices. Lay the tomato slices on a flat surface. Spread the Boursin cheese on 4 of the slices. Place the plain slices on top of each covered slice, so the Boursin is in the middle, like a sandwich. Mix the Parmesan cheese and breadcrumbs together. Beat the eggs with the milk, and season. Dredge the tomatoes in the flour, dip in the eggwash, and then coat with the breadcrumb-cheese mixture. Heat the butter in a skillet, add the breaded tomatoes, and sauté until golden brown. Sprinkle with the paprika, and serve.

BAKED TOMATO AND ONION CASSEROLE

Yield: 4 servings

2 SMALL ONIONS, THINLY SLICED
1 GARLIC CLOVE, CRUSHED
1 TABLESPOON CHOPPED FRESH BASIL
1½ POUNDS TOMATOES, PEELED,
    SEEDED, AND CUT INTO ½-INCH
    SLICES

SALT AND PEPPER TO TASTE
¼ CUP BREADCRUMBS
2 TABLESPOONS BUTTER

❖ Grease a 7½- by 10½- by 2-inch casserole dish. Place the onion slices in the dish, and sprinkle with the crushed garlic and chopped basil. Place the tomato slices atop the onions. Season with salt and pepper, sprinkle with the breadcrumbs, and dot with the butter. Bake in a preheated 325°F oven for approximately 35 to 40 minutes, until the top is lightly browned.

ZUCCHINI IN MARINARA SAUCE

Yield: 8 servings

4 OUNCES SALT PORK, FINELY DICED
4 GARLIC CLOVES, MINCED
20 OUNCES CANNED PEELED TOMATOES,
    DRAINED AND CHOPPED
¼ CUP TOMATO PUREE
1 TEASPOON BASIL

1 TEASPOON OREGANO
½ TEASPOON BLACK PEPPER
4 POUNDS ZUCCHINI, CUT INTO
    ½-INCH SLICES
1 TEASPOON SALT

❖ Render the salt pork in a heavy-bottomed casserole. Add the garlic and tomatoes, and sauté for 1 minute. Add the tomato puree, basil, oregano, and pepper, and sauté for 2 minutes. Add the zucchini; mix well. Add the salt. Cover the casserole, and bake in a 350°F oven for 20 minutes, or until the zucchini is tender. Adjust the seasonings to taste, and serve.

ZUCCHINI MUSHROOM MÉLANGE

Yield: 6 servings

2 TABLESPOONS MARGARINE
1 SMALL ONION, DICED
1 MEDIUM ZUCCHINI, SLICED AND
    QUARTERED
8 OUNCES MUSHROOMS, SLICED (ABOUT
    1½ CUPS)

PEPERONI, (12 OUNCES), SLICED AND
    QUARTERED
½ TEASPOON SEASONING SALT
8 OUNCES FONTINA CHEESE, SLICED

❖ In a heavy skillet, melt the margarine; add the onions, zucchini, mushrooms, and peperoni, and sauté until the onions are translucent. Sprinkle with the seasoning salt. Cook over low heat for 15 minutes. Place the sliced cheese on top, cover, and cook for 3 minutes, until the cheese is melted.

CHAPTER TEN

Breads and Muffins

THE items in this broad category usually contribute a significant amount of starch to a meal. They are similar in some respects but vary greatly in others.

Leavening agents, essential to the production of high-quality baked products, are responsible for the increase in volume during mixing and baking. Steam, caused by the heating (and expansion) of water as the product is baked, and carbon dioxide, produced by the fermentation of yeast or by the reaction of baking powder, are the most common means used to help baked goods to rise. Air incorporated during mixing also expands as the product is warmed. In yeast breads, a small amount of sugar helps to activate the yeast, and salt is added not only for flavor, but also to help control the rate of yeast growth. Never use more of either of these ingredients than called for in a recipe. Baking powder (which contains cream of tartar, soda, and starch) is commonly used in muffins.

Yeast breads require a strong bread flour and much kneading to develop strength. Flours vary in moisture content; only experience can teach you the amount of flour to add during the kneading process. Once kneaded, yeast breads should rise in a warm, draft-free location for optimum results. Follow recipe guidelines for shaping and baking yeast breads. To test for doneness, tap the top of the bread lightly; if it sounds hollow and has pulled away from the sides of the pan, it is done.

Muffins require a flour lower in gluten and very little mixing; overmixing can result in a tough product. The liquid ingredients are incorporated with only the few swift strokes needed to moisten the dry ingredients. Muffins containing high amounts of sugar or fat can withstand slightly more mixing, as these ingredients interfere with gluten development, but mixing should still be limited to a minimum. All ingredients in a tender product such as muffins should be as cold as possible.

Batters require very little handling but often have larger amounts of liquids, and strong beating with an electric mixer is required to develop the gluten. When the dough pulls away from the sides of the bowl, it has usually been beaten enough.

Proper baking temperatures should be observed. A popover, for example, can be a total failure if the oven is not hot enough to produce steam inside early. The heat is then lowered to give the popover time to bake completely, so it will not collapse when it comes out of the oven.

Breads and Muffins

FRENCH BREAD

WHEAT BREAD

ITALIAN BREAD

RYE BREAD—PUMPERNICKEL

UNBELIEVABLE BREAD

SQUAW BREAD

BREAD AND ROLLS FROM
REFRIGERATED DOUGH

SOFT ROLLS

GRISSINI

CROISSANTS

DANISH PASTRY

MUFFINS

BLUEBERRY MUFFINS

OATMEAL MUFFINS

CARROT MUFFINS

WHOLE-WHEAT MUFFINS

BANANA NUT BREAD

DATE AND NUT LOAF

CINNAMON COFFEE CAKE

CORN FRITTERS

FRENCH BREAD

Yield: 3 loaves, 1 pound each

2 CUPS LUKEWARM WATER
2 OUNCES CAKE YEAST
1 TEASPOON SUGAR
⅓ CUP SHORTENING

1 TEASPOON SALT
7 CUPS BREAD FLOUR
1 EGG WHITE
1 TABLESPOON WATER

✤ In a mixer bowl, combine the lukewarm water, yeast, and sugar; let stand for 3 to 5 minutes. Stir with a wire whisk until the yeast is completely dissolved. Add the shortening and salt, and mix thoroughly. Begin mixing on low speed. Gradually add the flour, scraping the bowl down twice while mixing. Continue adding flour until the dough cleans the side of the mixer bowl. Mix for 5 minutes. Cover with plastic wrap and a damp towel, and place in a warm draft-free place to rise.

When the dough has doubled in bulk, punch it down, re-cover it, and let it rise again. Repeat this procedure twice more.

Divide the dough into three 1-pound pieces. Roll the dough into a rectangular shape and then roll tightly into loaves. Place on a baking sheet dusted with cornmeal. Proof for 2 hours, until double in bulk.

Bake at 375°F for 40 minutes. Combine the egg white and water, and brush the breads with this mixture. Return them to the oven for 7 minutes. Remove from the baking sheet and chill.

WHEAT BREAD

Yield: 2 loaves

1½ CUPS PLUS 1 TABLESPOON
    WHOLE-WHEAT FLOUR
3⅓ CUPS PLUS 2 TEASPOONS
    ALL-PURPOSE FLOUR
1 TABLESPOON SALT

3½ TEASPOONS INSTANT YEAST
1¾ CUPS WATER
4½ TEASPOONS HONEY
7 TEASPOONS MARGARINE

(continued)

✣ Place the two flours, salt, and yeast ingredients in a 5-quart mixer bowl. Add the water, honey, and margarine. Mix on low speed (2d speed) with a dough hook for 7 minutes. (If mixing by hand, knead the dough in a large bowl for 10 minutes.) The dough should be smooth, dry to the touch, and elastic. Remove the dough from the bowl, and divide it into two equal pieces. Place the pieces on a lightly floured countertop, cover with clear plastic wrap, and let rise for 1 hour.

Flatten each piece into a rectangle. Roll each tightly, and seal the seam using the flat of the hand. Place into 8½-by 4½-by 2½-inch greased loaf pans, seam side *down*. Brush with warm water. Allow the dough to rise until doubled in size.

With a sharp paring knife or serrated knife, score the tops of loaves with one cut down center of each loaf. Bake in a preheated 400°F oven for 10 minutes. Reduce the heat to 375°F, and bake for 25 minutes. The bread should have golden brown color and should separate easily from the loaf pan.

ITALIAN BREAD

Yield: 2 loaves

4 CUPS PLUS 2 TABLESPOONS
   ALL-PURPOSE FLOUR
1 TABLESPOON SALT
1¾ TEASPOONS OLIVE OIL

½ TABLESPOON INSTANT YEAST
1½ CUPS PLUS 1 TABLESPOON WARM
   WATER (90°–100°F)

✣ Place the flour and salt in a 5-quart mixer bowl. Add the oil, yeast, and warm water. Mix on low speed (2d speed) with a dough hook for 7 minutes. (If mixing by hand, knead the dough for 10 minutes in a large bowl.) The dough should be smooth, dry to the touch, and elastic. Remove the dough from the bowl, and divide into two equal pieces. Cover with clear plastic wrap, and let rise for 25 to 30 minutes, until doubled in size.

Flatten each piece into a rectangle. Roll each piece tightly, and seal the end seam with the flat of the hand. The loaves should be 12 inches in length. Place on a cornmeal-dusted baking sheet, seam sides down. Spray with warm water. Allow the dough to rise until double in size, 30 to 40 minutes, spraying with warm water periodically to prevent skin from forming.

With a sharp paring knife or serrated knife, score the tops of the loaves with two 20-degree-angle cuts, 3 to 4 inches in length. Place the loaves in a preheated 450°F oven. Spray the walls of the oven with water to create steam. Bake for 10 minutes. Reduce the temperature to 400°F, and bake for 20 minutes. The loaves should be golden brown, light, and sound hollow when tapped on the bottom.

RYE BREAD–PUMPERNICKEL

Yield: 2 loaves

STARTER DOUGH

1½ CUPS RYE FLOUR
5 FLUID OUNCES WARM WATER

½ TEASPOON INSTANT YEAST

❖ Place the rye flour, water, and yeast in a 2-quart plastic container, and mix until incorporated, 2 to 3 minutes. Cover with clear plastic wrap, and allow to ferment overnight (8 to 12 hours) at room temperature. Preparing this starter dough in advance will develop the sourdough taste that distinguishes this bread.

4 CUPS ALL-PURPOSE FLOUR
9 FLUID OUNCES
   WARM WATER (90°F)
4 TEASPOONS SALT

1½ TABLESPOONS MOLASSES
1 TABLESPOON VEGETABLE OIL
¼ CUP INSTANT YEAST

❖ Place the fermented starter dough and the flour, water, salt, molasses, oil, and yeast in a 5-quart mixer bowl. Mix with a dough hook for 7 minutes. (If mixing by hand, mix in a large bowl for 10 minutes). The dough should be smooth and sticky to the touch. Remove from the bowl, and divide into two equal pieces. Cover the dough with plastic wrap to prevent a skin from forming, and allow it to rest for 40 minutes on a lightly floured countertop.

Using a sharp paring knife or serrated knife, cut a cross on the top of each loaf. Let rest for 20 more minutes. Place the loaves on a baking sheet that has been sprinkled with cornmeal. Bake in a preheated 425°F oven for 10 minutes. Reduce the heat to 375°F and bake for 35 minutes. Remove from the oven, and allow to cool on cooling racks.

UNBELIEVABLE BREAD

Yield: 5 loaves

1 CUP QUICK OATS
½ CUP CORNMEAL
1 QUART BOILING WATER
¼ CUP MOLASSES
1 TABLESPOON SALT

½ CUP BUTTER
2 OUNCES DRY YEAST
1 CUP WARM WATER
9 CUPS BREAD FLOUR

✤ Stir the quick oats and cornmeal into the boiling water. Add the molasses, salt, and butter, and set aside to cool until lukewarm. Dissolve the yeast in the warm water. Add the yeast mixture and 4½ cups of the flour to the oat/cornmeal mixture, and mix well. Add the remaining 4½ cups of flour, and mix for 10 minutes. Place the dough in a lightly greased bowl, turning to oil all sides. Cover the dough with plastic wrap, and allow it to rise in a warm place for 1 to 1½ hours, until doubled in bulk.

Punch the dough down, return it to the bowl, cover with plastic wrap, and again allow to rise for about 1 hour, until doubled in bulk.

Divide the dough into five pieces, and shape into loaves. Grease five 5- by 9-inch tins, and place the loaves in the tins. Allow the loaves to rise, uncovered, in a warm place, for 45 minutes, until doubled in bulk.

Bake in a 350°F oven for 45 minutes.

SQUAW BREAD

Yield: Approximately 32 rolls

2 PACKAGES DRY YEAST
  (¼ OUNCE EACH)
1½ TEASPOONS SUGAR
2 CUPS WARM WATER (80°F)
2 TEASPOONS SALT
¾ CUP CAKE FLOUR

2½ TO 3 CUPS ALL-PURPOSE FLOUR
2 TABLESPOONS SHORTENING
1 EGG WHITE, BEATEN TO SOFT PEAKS
1 CUP CORNMEAL
OIL FOR DEEP-FRYING

✤ Dissolve the yeast and sugar in 1 cup of the water. In a large mixer bowl, combine the dissolved yeast mixture, the remaining 1 cup of water, and the salt. Add the flours, and mix with a dough hook until the dough no longer sticks to the sides of the bowl. Add the shortening, and then fold in the egg whites. Place the dough in a greased bowl, turning to oil all sides. Cover the dough with plastic wrap, and allow it to rise in a warm place until at least doubled in bulk, approximately 1 hour.

Punch the dough down. Cut it into 1-ounce pieces. Sprinkle with the cornmeal. Place on a greased baking sheet, 2 inches apart. Bake in a 400°F oven until oven-set white, about 5 to 10 minutes. Cool completely. Deep-fry at 375°F until golden brown; serve hot.

Note: After removing the rolls from the oven, they can be stored in the refrigerator for up to 3 days before deep-frying.

BREAD AND ROLLS FROM REFRIGERATED DOUGH

Yield: 4 loaves or 4 dozen rolls

¼ CUP PLUS A PINCH OF SUGAR
1¼ CUPS WARM WATER
4 PACKAGES DRY YEAST
   (¼ OUNCE EACH)
13½ OUNCES CANNED EVAPORATED MILK

⅓ CUP SHORTENING
2½ TEASPOONS SALT
2 EGGS
11–12 CUPS BREAD FLOUR

✤ Stir a pinch of sugar into the water. Sprinkle the yeast over the water, and allow it to dissolve. Add the remaining ¼ cup of sugar, evaporated milk, shortening, salt, eggs, and flour. Knead until smooth and elastic, about 10 to 12 minutes. Cover with a cloth and rest the dough for 15 minutes, then cover the bowl with plastic wrap and refrigerate for at least 4 hours (for as long as overnight).

(continued)

Make up into loaves or various-shaped dinner rolls. To form a loaf, place the dough on a floured board. Flatten it into a 9- by 18-inch rectangle. Fold cross-wise into thirds, overlapping the two sides. Roll the dough tightly toward you, beginning at one of the open ends. Press with the thumbs after each turn. Pinch the edge to seal. Seal each end, and fold ends under. Place, seam side down, in greased 9- by 5-inch pans. Allow the dough to proof for 1 hour in a warm, draft-free place. Bake in a 400°F oven for 20 to 25 minutes (for loaves) or 15 to 20 minutes for rolls.

SOFT ROLLS

Yield: 2 dozen

4⅓ CUPS ALL-PURPOSE FLOUR
2 TEASPOONS SALT
4 TEASPOONS INSTANT YEAST
1½ TABLESPOONS GRANULATED SUGAR

2 TABLESPOONS MARGARINE
1 SMALL EGG
1½ CUPS PLUS 2 TEASPOONS SKIM MILK

EGG WASH
1 EGG
1 TABLESPOON MILK

❖ Place all the dry ingredients and the margarine in a 5-quart mixer bowl. Add the small egg and skim milk. Mix with a dough hook on low speed for 7 minutes. (If mixing by hand, mix in a large bowl for 10 minutes.) The dough should be dry, smooth, and elastic. Remove the dough from bowl. Cover the dough with clear plastic wrap, and allow to rest for 30 minutes, until doubled in size, on a lightly floured countertop.

Divide the dough into four equal parts. Roll each into a 12-inch length. Slice each into six equal pieces. Place the pieces in greased muffin tins, flattening the dough to cover the bottom of the tin. Beat together the egg and milk, and brush the dough with this eggwash. Allow to rise until doubled in size, 30 to 60 minutes.

Bake in a preheated 375°F oven for 15 minutes, until the rolls feel light in weight and have an even golden brown crust. Remove from the muffin tins, and allow to cool on cooling racks. They may be brushed with melted butter or margarine for a softer, buttery-tasting product.

GRISSINI

Yield: 2 dozen

1 CUP WARM WATER
1 PACKAGE ACTIVE DRY YEAST
  (¼ OUNCE)
2 TABLESPOONS OLIVE OIL
1 TEASPOON SALT

2¼ CUPS ALL-PURPOSE FLOUR
1 EGG
1 TEASPOON WATER
2 TABLESPOONS POPPY *OR* SESAME
  SEEDS

❖ Place the water in a large mixing bowl, and sprinkle the yeast over it; let stand until the yeast dissolves, about 5 minutes. Add the olive oil, salt, and about 1 cup of the flour; beat until blended. Gradually add the remaining flour; beat until the mixture comes together to form a soft dough. Turn onto a floured surface, and knead until the dough is smooth and elastic. Place the dough in a lightly oiled bowl, turning to oil all sides. Cover loosely with wax paper, and let rise in a warm place until doubled in bulk, about 1 hour.

Punch the dough down. Divide it in half, and cut each half into twelve pieces. Roll each piece between the palms to form a stick about 6 inches long. Arrange the sticks on lightly greased baking sheet, about 1 inch apart. In a small cup, beat the egg with the water to make an eggwash. Brush the dough sticks with the eggwash. Sprinkle with the poppy or sesame seeds. Let the dough sticks rise, uncovered, until almost doubled in size, about 30 minutes. Preheat the oven to 400°F.

Bake the breadsticks for about 20 minutes, until brown. Turn off the oven, and open the door a few inches; leave the breadsticks in the oven for 10 minutes, until crisp. Remove from the oven, and transfer to a cooling rack.

CROISSANTS

Yield: 12 croissants, 1 ounce each

3¼ CUPS ALL-PURPOSE FLOUR
1 TEASPOON SALT
½ TABLESPOON GRANULATED SUGAR
1 TABLESPOON INSTANT YEAST
1⅓ CUPS WARM WATER (90°F)

9 OUNCES BUTTER OR MARGARINE,
  ROOM TEMPERATURE
2 EGGS
2 TABLESPOONS MILK

(continued)

❖ Place the flour, salt, sugar, instant yeast, and warm water in a 3-quart mixer bowl. Mix by hand or with a dough hook for 2 to 4 minutes, until smooth and moist. Place on a lightly floured baking sheet. Allow the dough to rest in the refrigerator for 20 minutes, uncovered, to dry its surface.

Place the dough on a lightly floured bread board or table. Roll into a 7- by 10-inch rectangle. Cream the butter or margarine lightly by hand until soft (not runny) but still slightly firm. Place silver-dollar-sized pieces of butter in rows over two-thirds of the dough's width, leaving an outer one-third empty.

Fold the empty third over the center (fat-covered) third. Then fold the other fat-covered third over the center, to complete the first "three fold." Now turn the folded dough one-quarter turn clockwise, and roll again into a 7- by 10-inch rectangle. Refold as above (without further incorporation of butter or margarine). Place the dough on a lightly floured baking sheet, cover it with plastic wrap, and allow it to rest in the refrigerator for 20 minutes.

On a lightly floured marble or wood surface (marble helps to maintain the cold temperature of the dough), roll the dough to a 22- by 12-inch rectangle. Divide into two equal sections of 11 by 6 inches each. Cut each strip into triangular pieces, about 4 inches wide by 6 inches long. Roll the dough into croissants by pulling slightly at the longest end while rolling the triangle base to that longest end. Curve slightly into a crescent shape. Place the croissants on parchment-lined baking sheets 3 inches apart, to allow for expansion. Allow the dough to rise in a warm place (85°F) for 20 minutes.

Beat the eggs and milk together to make an eggwash. Brush the croissants lightly with the eggwash. Allow them to rest for another 20 to 30 minutes, until double in size.

Bake in a preheated 400°F oven for 15 to 20 minutes, until light golden brown and light in weight.

DANISH PASTRY

Yield: 18 pastries, 1 ounce each

3½ CUPS ALL-PURPOSE FLOUR
1 TEASPOON SALT
1 TABLESPOON GRANULATED SUGAR
1½ TEASPOONS INSTANT YEAST
3 EGGS
1¼ CUPS WARM SKIM MILK (90°F)
12 OUNCES BUTTER OR MARGARINE
   (3 STICKS)
2 TABLESPOONS MILK
¼–½ CUP FILLING OR PRESERVES

✣ Place the flour, salt, sugar, instant yeast, 1 egg, and warm skim milk in a 3-quart mixer bowl. Mix by hand or with a dough hook for 2 to 4 minutes, until smooth and moist. Place on a lightly floured baking sheet. Allow the dough to rest in the refrigerator for 20 minutes, uncovered, to dry its surface.

Place the dough on a lightly floured bread board or table. Roll into a 7- by 10-inch rectangle. Cream the butter or margarine by hand until soft (not runny) but still slightly firm. Place silver-dollar-sized pieces of softened butter or margarine in rows over two-thirds of the dough's width, leaving an outer one-third empty.

Fold the empty third over the center (fat-covered) third. Then fold the other fat-covered third over the center, to complete the first "three fold." Now turn the folded dough one-quarter turn clockwise and roll again into a 7- by 10-inch rectangle. Refold as above (without further incorporation of butter or margarine). Repeat the procedure a third time. Place the dough on a lightly floured baking sheet, cover it with plastic wrap, and allow it to rest in the refrigerator for 20 minutes.

Roll the dough into a rectangle once more, and give it another "three fold." Place the dough in a pan, cover it with plastic wrap, and refrigerate it overnight, to allow the fat to firm and the dough to relax.

On a lightly floured marble or wood surface, roll the dough into a 10- by 18-inch rectangle, approximately ¼ to ½ inch thick. Cut the dough with a dough wheel, pizza cutter, or knife into ¾-inch-wide strips. Form each strip into a ring-shaped spiral (like a snail shell), with the end of the strip tucked underneath. The spiral should be tight but not bunched up.

Place the dough spirals on parchment-lined baking sheets at least 3 inches apart, to allow for rising and expansion. Allow the dough to rise in a warm place (85°F) for 20 minutes.

Beat the remaining 2 eggs and 2 tablespoons of milk together to make an eggwash. Brush the pastries with the eggwash. Place ½ to 1 teaspoon of the filling or preserves in the center (use less for jams, jellies, and preserves, because they spread a bit when heated). Allow the pastries to rise for 20 minutes, until almost double in size.

Bake in a preheated 375°F oven for 15 to 18 minutes, until light golden brown and light in weight.

MUFFINS

6 muffins

⅔ CUPS GRANULATED SUGAR
1 TEASPOON SALT
1 EGG
½ CUP OIL

¾ CUP BUTTERMILK
1¾ CUPS ALL-PURPOSE FLOUR
2 TEASPOONS BAKING POWDER

✤ Combine the sugar, salt, egg, oil, and buttermilk using a wire whip. Combine the flour and baking powder. Gradually add the flour mixture with a wooden spoon to the liquid mixture: *do not overmix.* Line a muffin tin with muffin papers. Fill three-quarters full with the muffin batter. Bake at 400°F until golden brown and firm in the center, and/or when a paring knife comes out clean when inserted into the center.

Variations: Fold in 1 cup of fruits, nuts, or other flavorful ingredients to the batter before filling the muffin tin. Coat the fruit in flour before adding, to prevent it from sinking to the bottom of the muffins.

BLUEBERRY MUFFINS

Yield: 14 muffins

3 CUPS ALL-PURPOSE FLOUR
1 CUP SUGAR
4 TEASPOONS BAKING POWDER
1 TEASPOON SALT
2 EGGS

½ CUP OIL
1 CUP MILK
2 CUPS BLUEBERRIES (FRESH OR FROZEN
    AND THAWED), LIGHTLY DREDGED IN
    FLOUR

✤ Sift together the flour, sugar, baking powder, and salt. Combine the eggs, oil, and milk; add to the flour mixture, blending well. Add the blueberries, and mix well. Fill greased muffin cups half full with the batter. Bake in a 400°F oven for approximately 20 minutes.

OATMEAL MUFFINS

Yield: 30 muffins, 2 ounces each

2 CUPS ROLLED OATS
2 CUPS SOUR CREAM
4 EGGS
⅔ CUP OIL
1 POUND BROWN SUGAR

2 CUPS FLOUR
2 TEASPOONS BAKING POWDER
1 TEASPOON BAKING SODA
1 TEASPOON SALT

❖ Stir the oats into the sour cream, and set aside. Beat the eggs; add the oil and brown sugar, and mix well. Stir in the oatmeal/sour cream mixture. Sift together the flour, baking powder, baking soda, and salt and mix with the oatmeal mixture until just moistened. Fill greased or papered muffin tins two-thirds full with this batter. Bake in a 400°F oven for 22 minutes.

CARROT MUFFINS

Yield: Approximately 3 dozen

1⅓ CUPS SALAD OIL
5 EGGS
3½ CUPS ALL-PURPOSE FLOUR
1 TABLESPOON BAKING POWDER
1¼ TEASPOONS BAKING SODA

½ TEASPOON SALT
¼ TEASPOON NUTMEG
2 TEASPOONS CINNAMON
2¼ CUPS SHREDDED CARROTS
½ CUP WHITE RAISINS

❖ Combine all the ingredients to make a batter. Fill papered muffin tins two-thirds full with the batter. Bake in a 400°F oven for 20 to 25 minutes.

WHOLE-WHEAT MUFFINS

Yield: 18 muffins

1 SCANT CUP SUGAR
1 CUP VEGETABLE SHORTENING
4 EGGS
2 TEASPOONS BAKING SODA
½ TEASPOON SALT
½ TEASPOON CINNAMON

1 POUND WHOLE-WHEAT FLOUR
  (APPROXIMATELY 3¼ CUPS)
2 CUPS CAKE FLOUR
2 CUPS MILK
¾ CUP RAISINS

❖ Cream the sugar, shortening, and eggs together. Sift the baking soda, salt, and cinnamon with the whole-wheat flour and cake flour. Add the flour mixture and the milk gradually to the creamed sugar mixture, and mix just until incorporated. Roll the raisins in flour, and fold into the batter. Line muffin tins with paper liners, or grease and flour the tins. Fill each two-thirds full with the batter. Bake in a preheated 425° oven for approximately 30 minutes.

BANANA NUT BREAD

Yield: 1 loaf

½ CUP BUTTER OR SHORTENING
1 CUP SUGAR
2 EGGS
1 TEASPOON BAKING SODA
2 CUPS SIFTED FLOUR

3 MEDIUM BANANAS, MASHED
3 TEASPOONS SOUR MILK OR
  BUTTERMILK
½ CUP FINELY CHOPPED WALNUTS OR
  PECANS.

❖ Cream together the shortening and sugar; add the eggs. Sift together the baking soda and flour. Add this mixture to the creamed sugar mixture. Stir in the bananas, milk, and nuts. Grease and flour a 9¼- by 5¼- by 2¾-inch loaf pan and fill with the batter. Bake in a 350°F oven for about 30 minutes; test for doneness by piercing the bread with a toothpick: if the toothpick comes out clean, the bread is done.

DATE AND NUT LOAF

Yield: 1 loaf

1 TEASPOON BAKING SODA
1 CUP CHOPPED DATES
1 CUP BOILING WATER
¾ CUP BROWN SUGAR
¼ TEASPOON SALT

1 TABLESPOON BUTTER OR SHORTENING
1 EGG
½ CUP CHOPPED NUTS
1½ CUPS SIFTED FLOUR

❖ Combine the baking soda, dates, and boiling water; set aside. Mix together the brown sugar, salt, and butter or shortening; add the date mixture. Add the egg, nuts, and flour; stir just to incorporate (do not overmix). Line a 9¼- by 5¼- by 2¾-inch loaf pan with greased parchment paper. Fill with the batter. Bake in 300°F oven for approximately 1 hour; test for doneness by piercing the bread with a toothpick: if the toothpick comes out clean, the bread is done.

CINNAMON COFFEE CAKE

Yield: 1 cake, 10 inches

½ CUP BUTTER
1⅓ CUPS GRANULATED SUGAR
2 EGGS
1 TEASPOON VANILLA
1½ CUPS ALL-PURPOSE FLOUR

1½ TEASPOONS BAKING POWDER
1 CUP SOUR CREAM
1 TEASPOON BAKING SODA
⅓ CUP BROWN SUGAR
1 TEASPOON CINNAMON

❖ Cream the butter with 1 cup of the sugar. Add the eggs one at a time, beating well after each addition. Add the vanilla. Sift together the flour and baking powder. Combine the sour cream and baking soda. Add the flour and sour cream mixtures alternately to the butter/sugar mixture. Pour the batter into a greased 10-inch round cake pan. Combine the brown sugar, cinnamon, and remaining ⅓ cup of sugar. Sprinkle the batter with the brown sugar mixture, swirling it slightly. Bake in a 350°F oven for 45 minutes, until a tester inserted in the center comes out clean.

CORN FRITTERS

Yield: 20 fritters

1 POUND FROZEN CORN KERNELS
6 OUNCES FLOUR (ABOUT 1¼ CUPS)
4 EGGS
1 TEASPOON SALT

¼ TEASPOON NUTMEG
½ TEASPOON WHITE PEPPER
OIL FOR FRYING

❖ Mix the corn, flour, eggs, salt, nutmeg, and pepper into a smooth batter. Heat a shallow layer of oil. Using a ¼-cup measuring cup, pour the batter into the hot oil, shape into pancakes, and fry both sides until golden brown.

CHAPTER ELEVEN

Desserts

Desserts run the gamut of elaborateness and skill, from simple fruit platters to delicate soufflés. They usually end a meal but can also be used as an afternoon or evening snack. As with other parts of the meal, the dessert should be appropriate to the occasion and should complement the foods that precede it. Formal meals usually close with a somewhat elaborate dessert, but plain fruit may instead be offered, especially given today's health-conscious diners.

Most desserts are sweet, the purpose being to satisfy the appetite. Some desserts are best served warm, such as bread pudding or apple pie, whereas others should be served cold. Remember that warm foods have more intense flavors than cold ones do. Thus, when preparing an item that is to be served warm, use less vanilla, for example, than when preparing a cold dessert.

This chapter contains recipes for a wide range of luscious desserts, each requiring quite different ingredients and preparation techniques. None of the recipes is extremely difficult, but it is advisable to read the recipe completely before beginning, to determine the proper procedures required. Then assemble the necessary ingredients and utensils. Good success should follow if the recipe is followed *exactly*. In the preparation of bakery products, do not stray too far from the recipe, as you might do in making nonbakery dishes, where imagination can sometimes be a reward. Precision is essential to successful bakery products, and your reward comes when the recipe is followed closely without experimentation. These products are often too delicately balanced to permit much variation.

FLOUR

Flour is a basic ingredient in many desserts. The kind used and its treatment in preparation and baking are often critical to product quality.

There are three different kinds of wheat flour: bread (hard), cake (soft), and all-purpose. All-purpose flour can be used in place of either bread or cake flour, but it never can produce quite the same results in certain products. Hard flour is used for breads and certain pastries, when a strong structure is desired, whereas soft flour is used for tender products, such as cookies and cakes. The difference between two flours is in the amount and type of gluten and the amount of starch they contain.

Hard flour has a high gluten content (about 16 percent) and a high ratio of gluten to starch. Cake flour contains only about 8 percent gluten and a larger percentage of starch. The gluten in hard flour is strong and tough, whereas that in cake flour is more tender and delicate.

Gluten is like gum: the addition of moisture and movement makes it sticky and imparts a stronger structure to the product. Warmth helps gluten stick more quickly. Thus some pastry dough are kept cold and minimally worked to produce a tender structure rather than a tough one. For example, pie dough should be mixed very little, so it will be tender; a bread dough is mixed considerably, to depend the gluten.

When heated, gluten coagulates, firms up, and thus forms the basic structure of the product. Cakes and cookies have a delicate structure, whereas breads have a stronger one. Some pastries have delicate structures because of the flour used and the way it is handled, while others, such as strudel dough, have a firm but flaky texture. It's all in the kind of flour used and how it is handled.

Other factors also influence the texture and quality of desserts. Shortening can surround the gluten particles in flour, which tends to prevent them from sticking together. Shortening thus "shortens" the product, which is desirable in cookies, cakes, and some pastries such as piecrusts. Sugar also acts as a tender-izer, but the results are not as good as those achieved with shortening. A cake or cookie high in both shortening and sugar is a very tender product, not only because of the flour used and the handling of the product, but also because of these two ingredients. The addition of shortening and sugar allows a dough or batter to be mixed more vigorously without developing the gluten. For example, a cake can be mixed a great deal, while a muffin, with much less shortening and sugar, cannot.

The starch in flour helps to produce a desirable texture. When flour is heated in the presence of moisture, the starch gelatinizes, thickening and firming the product. It is the starch in flour that helps to thicken some puddings and other desserts. Sometimes cornstarch is used instead of flour as the thickening agent, often producing a smoother product.

Gluten absorbs moisture slowly. Thus a pie dough is often allowed to rest in a refrigerator for about 15 minutes or more to enable the gluten to absorb moisture, making the dough more tender. This slight rest makes rolling out the pie dough easier and also tends to decrease shrinkage during baking.

PIE CRUSTS

The secrets to making a good piecrust are to be sure that the proportion of shortening to flour is correct and to mix the dough correctly. The best general ratios of shortening to flour are found in the accompanying table. Many recipes do vary slightly, but the basic ratios remain the same.

Three kinds of basic pie doughs are used in pie making. One is a mealy dough, which can be used for double-crust pies and pies in which a filling is baked, such as pumpkin or custard pie. The second is a flaky dough, good for single-crust pies in which the crust is baked and then the filling poured in and allowed to set, such as banana cream and lemon meringue. The third is an all-around crust, used for either kind of pie.

The ratio of flour to shortening and the way the shortening is worked into the dough differentiate the three crusts. To make a mealy crust, use less shortening and work the shortening well into the flour. This coats the flour particles, causing them to be more tender in the end product. This coating also helps to prevent moisture in the filling from soaking into the crust. An all-purpose crust has a higher ratio of shortening to flour, and the shortening is cut to the size of peas. Thus, it is worked into the flour less than it would be for a mealy crust. A flaky dough has the most shortening (about a one-to-one ratio of flour-to-shortening by weight) and is cut only into pieces about the size of walnuts. This dough should also be worked as little as possible. Let the dough rest after adding the moisture, and then roll the dough out lightly and fold it over. This spreads the shortening pieces out into layers between the paste. When the dough is heated, the shortening melts and forms a pool; steam forms as the moisture heats, swelling the crust. The shortening then crisps up the crust, producing a flaky dough that looks as if it has blisters. These blisters are the spots raised in the baking by the steam and crisped up by the shortening. A flaky crust is often a bit tougher than the others and also tends to soak up moisture more quickly. Pies with flaky crusts are only at their best for a day: if left to stand (always under refrigeration), the crust tends to become soggy.

PIE CRUST FORMULAS				
CRUST	FLOUR *	SHORTENING	COLD WATER	SHORTENING TREATMENT
Mealy	1 cup	5 tbsp.	2–3 tbsp.	Well-worked
All-purpose	1 cup	6⅓ tbsp.	3–4 tbsp.	Pea size
Flaky	1 cup	9 tbsp.	3–4 tbsp.	Walnut size

* Use all-purpose flour for mealy and all-purpose crusts; hard flour replaces some of the all-purpose flour for flaky crusts. Use ¼ teaspoon of salt per cup of flour.

Sometimes crumb-type crusts, made from graham crackers or ground nuts, are used. Meringue is also sometimes used to make a crust. Moreover, tarts, and even some pies, use a crust that contains eggs and sugar, resembling cookie dough more than typical piecrust.

EGGS

Eggs can be temperamental products in cooking, and care must be taken to ensure they are handled properly. They can be used in desserts as binders to hold ingredients together, as in cakes or cookies, as aerators, as in a soufflé, or as thickeners, as in a custard.

Eggs hold or bind ingredients together by combining with them, as in cakes and cookies. For this type of use, their handling is relatively straightforward, and no special care is needed.

When eggs are used as aerators, however, care must be taken. Eggs help make products light when air is incorporated into the foam of the egg; by blending this foam into the product and baking it, lightness is introduced into the product. The first secret of success is to select the right kind of egg. The freshest egg, actually, does not produce the best foam, as a newly laid egg has a firm yolk and white, which tend to hold firmly together and resist air incorporation. Slightly older eggs are better. It often helps to warm egg whites before beating them to a foam (also, the egg yolk and white are more easily separated when the egg is slightly warm). A bit of cream of tartar, lemon juice, or other acidic product can help make the egg foam more easily. Also, remember that even the slightest trace oil or grease in the whites will prevent beating them into a good foam. Even a small bit of yolk (which has fat in it) will inhibit the foam.

Never overbeat an egg white to be used as an aerator, as it will coagulate, resulting in a foam that cannot swell when heated. The foam will collapse, along with the product. Thus, while egg whites can be beaten until stiff, they should remain slightly moist, not dry. In this way, the air in the foam cells can expand without bursting the foam and will hold the product up. Sometimes products aerated by egg foam are beautiful as they come out of the oven, but as soon as cold air strikes, they collapse. To prevent this from happening, it is critical to follow the recipe *exactly*. Sometimes a bit of starch is introduced to help thicken the product and thus help hold it up after baking, as is done in the making of a soufflé. High heat can also be an enemy to a baked egg foam, so recommended temperatures should be carefully followed.

Eggs can also be temperamental when they are used as thickeners, as in custards. An egg in such a mixture joins with liquids such as milk, increasing the amount of moisture with which the egg must bind when it thickens or coagulates. If too much moisture is introduced, the egg fails to bind it all, and a broken custard results. If the heat is too high, the egg may expel excess moisture, and again a curdled custard results. Low temperatures are always recommended when eggs are cooked as thickeners. Custards should be cooked in pans of water so the heat is gentle as it enters the mixture.

When eggs are used to thicken a mixture such as a stirred custard in a sabayon, remember to keep the heat *low* and to stir *constantly*, moving the whisk or spoon into all areas, so no accumulation of the mixture occurs in one spot over a period of time. Cooking for too long can also cause a stirred custard to break or curdle; when the foam on a stirred custard disappears or when it is thick enough to coat a spoon, remove it from the heat. It is also wise to stir a cooked custard for a short time after removing it from the heat to prevent overcooking as a result of the heat retained by the pan and by the custard itself.

Desserts

PIE DOUGH

CHOCOLATE CREAM PIE

CHOCOLATE SILK PIE

LEMON CHIFFON PIE

LEMON SPONGE PIE

GANACHE TORTE WITH PECAN CRUST

WALNUT AND CHOCOLATE TORTE

LINZER TORTE

FRUIT TORTE

SPONGE CAKE WITH AMARETTO
AND CHOCOLATE

CHARLOTTE ROYALE

APPLE STRUDEL

ALSACE LORRAINE GUGELHUPF

CHOCOLATE CHIP COOKIES

ICEBOX OATMEAL COOKIES

ALMOND STAR COOKIES

CHOCOLATE MOUSSE

WILLIAMS PEAR MOUSSE WITH
CHOCOLATE SABAYON

(continued)

Desserts (continued)

CRÈME BRÛLÉE

VANILLA SAUCE

BREAD PUDDING WITH BRANDY SAUCE

SALZBURGER NOCKERL

CRÊPES À LA RITZ

CRÊPES NORMANDY

OMELETTE STEPHANIE

CALIFORNIA FRUIT OMELET

SOUFFLÉ ROTHSCHILD

CRANBERRY NUT SOUFFLÉ

BIERER'S PEARS

PINEAPPLE AND BANANA FLAMBÉ

STRAWBERRIES AND CREAM

COUPE YVONNE

HAWAIIAN ICE CREAM BOMBE

PIE DOUGH

Yield: 2 two-crust pie shells or 4 one-crust pie shells, 9 inches each

4 CUPS PASTRY OR CAKE FLOUR
2 TEASPOONS SALT
1¾ CUPS SHORTENING

½ CUP PLUS 2 TABLESPOONS ICE-COLD
WATER

✤ In a mixing bowl, combine the flour and salt, mixing well. Cut the shortening into the flour mixture using a pastry blender or two forks. Mix until crumbly; *do not overmix*, or the dough will become tough. Add the cold water, mixing just until the flour is moistened and forms a soft dough; *do not overmix.* Cover the dough with plastic wrap, and store under refrigeration until ready to use.

Note: The dough will keep in the refrigerator for at least a week if wrapped tightly. For longer storage, store well-wrapped pie dough in the freezer for up to 2 months.

CHOCOLATE CREAM PIE

Yield: 2 pies, 9 inches each

4 OUNCES BAKING CHOCOLATE
¼ CUP BUTTER
1½ CUPS GRANULATED SUGAR
4 CUPS MILK
3 WHOLE EGGS
3 EGG YOLKS
¼ TEASPOON SALT

2½ OUNCES CORNSTARCH
2 TEASPOONS VANILLA EXTRACT
3 EGG WHITES
2 PREBAKED PIE SHELLS, 9 INCHES EACH
    (SEE RECIPE LATER IN THIS CHAPTER)
2 CUPS WHIPPED CREAM FOR TOPPING
CHOCOLATE SHAVINGS FOR GARNISH

✤ Combine the baking chocolate and butter in a heavy-bottomed stainless-steel saucepan. Heat until melted, stirring occasionally. Gradually add ¾ cup of the granulated sugar to the melted chocolate mixture, beating constantly with a wire whisk. Heat to boiling, stirring occasionally with a wire whisk. Gradually add 3 cups of the milk to the melted chocolate mixture, beating constantly with a wire whisk. Heat to boiling, stirring occasionally with a wire whisk.

Combine the eggs, egg yolks, salt, cornstarch, vanilla extract, and remaining cup of milk; mix well with a wire whisk. Strain the mixture through a mesh strainer. Stir some of the hot chocolate sauce into the egg mixture. Gradually add the tempered mixture to the boiling chocolate sauce, mixing constantly with a wire whisk. Cook over medium heat for approximately 5 minutes, until the mixture has thickened, stirring constantly. Remove from the heat.

Beat the egg whites until stiff but not dry. Gradually add the remaining ¾ cup of sugar, and beat until stiff. Fold into the chocolate custard. Divide the filling evenly between the baked pie shells. Cover the tops of the pies with waxed paper. Refrigerate until firm. Cover the top of each pie with whipped cream, then decoratively pipe whipped cream along the edge. Sprinkle with the shaved chocolate.

CHOCOLATE SILK PIE

Yield: 1 pie, 9 inches

1½ POUNDS UNSALTED BUTTER,
    SOFTENED
1½–2 CUPS POWDERED SUGAR
4 EGGS
2 TEASPOONS VANILLA

1 POUND SEMISWEET CHOCOLATE,
    MELTED
½ CUP ROASTED AND CHOPPED PECANS
    OR ALMONDS
1 9-INCH GRAHAM CRACKER CRUST

❖ Beat the butter and sugar until very fluffy. Add the eggs one at a time; add the vanilla. Add the melted chocolate and nuts, and whip until blended well. Pour into the crust, and refrigerate until set.

LEMON CHIFFON PIE

Yield: 1 pie, 9 inches

¼ OUNCES GELATIN
¼ CUP COLD WATER
5 EGG YOLKS
⅔ CUP SUGAR
⅓ CUP LEMON JUICE

2 TEASPOONS GRATED LEMON ZEST
PINCH OF SALT
5 FRESH EGG WHITES
PREBAKED 9-INCH PIE SHELL

❖ Combine the gelatin and cold water in a mixing bowl, and mix thoroughly; set aside for 3 to 5 minutes. Combine the egg yolks, ⅓ cup of sugar, lemon juice, lemon zest, and salt in a heavy-bottomed stainless-steel saucepan or steam-jacketed kettle. Heat the mixture to a simmer, stirring constantly with a wire whisk. Cook and stir for approximately 5 minutes, until the mixture thickens. Add soaked gelatin, and mix until all the gelatin dissolves. Chill until the mixture begins to set.

Beat the egg whites with a wire whisk until stiff but not dry, gradually adding the remaining ⅓ cup of sugar while beating. Gently fold the beaten egg whites into cooked lemon mixture. Pour the filling into the baked pie shell. Chill until firm. Pipe the edge of the pie with whipped cream, and decorate the top with lemon twists if desired.

LEMON SPONGE PIE

Yield: 6 servings

1 CUP SUGAR
2 TABLESPOONS BUTTER
3 TABLESPOONS FLOUR
½ TEASPOON SALT
JUICE AND ZEST OF 1 LEMON

2 EGG YOLKS, BEATEN
1 CUP MILK
2 EGG WHITES, STIFFLY BEATEN
1 UNBAKED 9-INCH PIE SHELL

❖ Cream the sugar and butter together. Mix in the flour and salt. Combine the lemon juice and zest, beaten egg yolks, and milk, and add to above the sugar/butter mixture. Fold in the beaten egg whites. Pour into the pie shell, and bake at 350°F for 30 minutes.

GANACHE TORTE WITH PECAN CRUST

Yield: 1 cake, 10 inches

7 OUNCES PECAN NUTS, FINELY
  CHOPPED (APPROXIMATELY 2 CUPS)
½ CUP SUGAR
3½ TABLESPOONS BUTTER, MELTED

1 POUND BAKING CHOCOLATE, CUT INTO
  PIECES
1 EGG YOLK
1 PINT HEAVY CREAM, HEATED

❖ Combine the pecans, sugar, and melted butter. Press into a 10-inch spring-form pan. Bake in a 325°F oven for 20 minutes. Cool.

Melt the chocolate in a double-boiler or microwave oven. Remove from the heat, and stir in the egg yolk. Gradually whisk in the heavy cream. Pass the mixture through a strainer into the pecan crust. Chill for 4 hours.

SAUCE
½ CUP UNSALTED BUTTER
⅓ CUP PLUS 1 TABLESPOON SUGAR

1 CUP HEAVY CREAM, HEATED

(continued)

✤ Melt the butter in a heavy-bottomed saucepan, add the sugar, and caramelize. Whisk in the heavy cream. Transfer to a stainless-steal bowl, and cool to room temperature. Pour 2 tablespoons of the sauce on each serving plate, and top with a slice of the torte in the center.

WALNUT AND CHOCOLATE TORTE

Yield: 1 cake, 10 inches

2 CUPS SHELLED WALNUTS
½ CUP SUGAR
6 OUNCES BAKING CHOCOLATE, CUT
   INTO SMALL PIECES

1½ TABLESPOONS ORANGE ZEST
1 TEASPOON LEMON ZEST
5 EGG YOLKS
6 EGG WHITES

✤ Place the walnuts and ¼ cup of the sugar in a food processor, and grind to a fine crumb. Add the chocolate pieces and orange and lemon zests, and continue to process until the chocolate is roughly ground. Whip the remaining ¼ cup of sugar with the egg yolks to a pale cream, and add to the walnut mixture. Beat the egg whites to stiff peaks, and very gently fold into the walnut mixture. Pour into a greased 10-inch round baking pan, and bake in a 350°F oven for approximately 30 minutes, until a toothpick inserted in the center comes out dry.

LINZER TORTE

Yield: 1 torte, 10 inches

1⅓ CUPS FLOUR
1 CUP GROUND ALMONDS (SEE NOTE
   BELOW)
⅓ CUP SUGAR
⅓ CUP BUTTER
¼ TEASPOON CINNAMON

DASH OF GROUND CLOVES
DASH OF SALT
1 EGG
1 CUP RED RASPBERRY PRESERVES
POWDERED SUGAR FOR DUSTING

❖ In a medium bowl, combine the flour, almonds, sugar, butter, cinnamon, nutmeg, cloves, salt, and egg until well mixed. Set aside 1½ cups of dough. Press the remaining dough into the bottom and up the sides of a 10-inch springform pan. Preheat the oven to 350°F. Spoon the red raspberry preserves over the dough in the pan. Roll the reserved dough into 9-inch-long ropes. Carefully arrange the dough ropes into a lattice pattern over the red raspberry preserves. Bake for 30 to 40 minutes, until golden. Cool on a wire rack. Sprinkle with powdered sugar.

Note: Grind unblanched almonds to a fine powder with a nut grinder or blender.

FRUIT TORTE

Yield: 1 torte, 10 inches

1 VANILLA GÉNOISE, 10 INCHES (RECIPE FOLLOWS)
PASTRY CREAM (RECIPE FOLLOWS)
9 CANNED PEACH HALVES
7 LARGE FRESH STRAWBERRIES, HALVED

1 KIWI, SLICED
1 CANNED-PINEAPPLE RING
9 FRESH RASPBERRIES
½ CUP APRICOT GLAZE
2 CUPS WHIPPED CREAM

❖ Slice the génoise in half; place one génoise layer in the bottom of a 10-inch quiche dish. Spread cooled vanilla pastry cream on top, about ¼ inch thick. Then lay a ring of peach halves (slightly fanned, if desired) around the outside perimeter, followed by a ring of strawberries inside the peach border, a ring of kiwi slices inside the strawberry border, and a pineapple ring in the center, filled with raspberries. Add fresh raspberries between the peach halves. Glaze the torte with apricot glaze. Slice and serve with the whipped cream.

VANILLA GÉNOISE

5 OUNCES ALL-PURPOSE FLOUR (1¼ CUPS)
5 OUNCES CORNSTARCH (1 CUP PLUS 3 TABLESPOONS)
5 EGGS

5 OUNCES GRANULATED SUGAR (½ CUP PLUS 2 TABLESPOONS)
½ TEASPOON VANILLA EXTRACT
2 OUNCES WARM MELTED BUTTER (¼ CUP)

(continued)

❖ Sift together the flour and cornstarch. Place the eggs and sugar in mixer bowl; using a wire-whisk mixer attachment, beat until stiff. Remove the bowl from the mixer; add the vanilla extract, and slowly fold in the flour/cornstarch mixture with a rubber spatula. After the flour has been incorporated, fold in the warm melted butter. Fill a paper-lined 10-inch layer cake tin with the batter. Bake immediately in a 350°F oven for about 30 minutes. Turn upside down on paper, remove the tin, and cool.

PASTRY CREAM

1 OUNCE CAKE FLOUR (ABOUT ¼ CUP)   3 EGG YOLKS
2 TABLESPOONS CORNSTARCH   1 TABLESPOON BUTTER
SCANT ½ CUP SUGAR   ½ TEASPOON VANILLA EXTRACT
2½ CUPS MILK

❖ In a small mixing bowl, combine the flour, cornstarch, ¼ cup of the sugar, 5 fluid ounces of the milk, and the egg yolks. Whisk until smooth. Bring the remaining 15 fluid ounces of milk and ¼ cup of sugar to a boil. Slowly pour the egg/flour mixture into the boiling milk, and stir with a wire whisk until the cream thickens (about 1 minute). Remove from the heat. Blend in the butter and vanilla extract. Pour into mixing bowl, and whisk until cool.

SPONGE CAKE WITH AMARETTO AND CHOCOLATE

Yield: 1 cake, 9 inches

⅔ CUP SUGAR   3 CUPS WHIPPING CREAM
7 EGGS   1 TEASPOON VANILLA EXTRACT
¾ CUP ALL-PURPOSE FLOUR   6 OUNCES SEMISWEET CHOCOLATE
3 TABLESPOONS CORNSTARCH   CHIPS
2 TEASPOONS GRATED LEMON ZEST   ¼ CUP AMARETTO LIQUEUR

❖ In a bowl mix the sugar and eggs. Heat over hot water to 115°F, beating until doubled in volume. Sift the flour and cornstarch together three times. Carefully fold the flour, cornstarch, and lemon zest into the egg mixture. Pour into a greased and floured 9-inch cake pan. Bake at 425°F until set and springy, about 15 minutes. Remove and cool on a cake rack.

Heat the cream to 180°F. Stir in the vanilla extract and chocolate chips. Remove from the heat. Stir to melt the chocolate; then chill overnight.

Split the cake into two layers. Place the lower half on a cake pan, and sprinkle with half the Amaretto (2 tablespoons). Whip the chocolate cream mixture until stiff. Spread one-quarter of the chocolate cream on the cake. Add the top layer of the cake, and sprinkle with the remaining Amaretto. Spread the top and sides of the cake with the chocolate cream, reserving some of it to pipe through a pastry bag for finishing decoration.

CHARLOTTE ROYALE

Yield: 8 to 10 servings

JELLY ROLL

8 EGG YOLKS
½ CUP SUGAR
¼ TEASPOON SALT (OPTIONAL)
¼ TEASPOON GRATED LEMON ZEST (OPTIONAL)
4 EGG WHITES

¾ CUP ALL-PURPOSE FLOUR, SIFTED TOGETHER
¼ CUP CORNSTARCH
2 CUPS RASPBERRY PRESERVES OR ORANGE MARMALADE

❖ Whisk the egg yolks with 2 tablespoons of the sugar, salt, and lemon zest until stiff, not foamy. Beat the egg whites with the remaining 6 tablespoons of sugar until stiff. Fold the yolk mixture into the meringue (egg whites). Sift together the flour and cornstarch, and fold into the batter. Spread the batter evenly on three parchment-covered baking sheets; the third sheet will be only half covered. Bake in a 450°F oven for 4 minutes.

Spread each sponge with a layer of jelly, and roll tightly into a 1½-inch-diameter cylinder.

BAVARIAN CREAM

1¼ OUNCES GELATIN
1 QUART MILK
8 OUNCES SUGAR (1¼ CUPS)

12 EGG YOLKS
½ TABLESPOON VANILLA EXTRACT
1 QUART CREAM, WHIPPED

(continued)

❖ Soak the gelatin in 1 cup of the milk for 5 minutes. Bring the remaining 3 cups of milk and the sugar to a boil. Add the soaked gelatin. Beat the egg yolks until they form a ribbon when dripped from the beater. Pour the hot sweet milk slowly into yolks, whisking constantly. Heat to 175°F, stirring constantly. Remove from the heat, and let cool, stirring occasionally to prevent a skin from forming. Add the vanilla. Fold in the whipped cream.

To assemble the charlotte, cut the jelly roll into thin slices. Line a 2½-quart bombe or charlotte mold completely with the jelly roll slices. Pour in the Bavarian cream. Chill until firm. Unmold onto a serving platter. The charlotte may be brushed with hot apricot glaze and garnished with whipped cream before serving.

APPLE STRUDEL

Yield: 10 servings

10 APPLES, PEELED AND CORED (ROME
   BEAUTY RECOMMENDED)
JUICE OF 1 LEMON
1 CUP SUGAR
½ CUP RAISINS
½ CUP CHOPPED WALNUTS
DASH OF CINNAMON
DASH OF NUTMEG
1 POUND PHYLLO DOUGH
1 CUP MELTED BUTTER
½ CUP POWDERED SUGAR

❖ Slice the apples, and pour the lemon juice over slices. Add the sugar, raisins, walnuts, cinnamon, and nutmeg, and toss together. Set aside.

Arrange several layers of the phyllo dough on a table. Brush each layer of dough with melted butter; overlap the dough layers slightly to make a longer and wider strudel. Continue to overlap and lay the phyllo dough sheets, brushing each layer with butter, until all the sheets are used. Spoon the sugar/apple mixture in a log down the center of the dough. Roll up the phyllo dough to make a long strudel. Seal the seam and ends by pressing with fingers. Brush the outside of the dough with butter. Bake in a 350°F oven for approximately 45 minutes, until golden brown. Remove from the oven, dust with powdered sugar, and serve warm.

ALSACE LORRAINE GUGELHUPF

Yield: 1 ring, 10 inches

26 OUNCES BUTTER, ROOM
   TEMPERATURE
2½ CUPS SUGAR
2 TEASPOONS VANILLA EXTRACT
ZEST FROM 2 LEMONS, GRATED
¼ TEASPOON SALT
6½ CUPS ALL-PURPOSE FLOUR

4 TEASPOONS BAKING POWDER
12 EGGS, ROOM TEMPERATURE
7 OUNCES GERMAN SWEET CHOCOLATE,
   CUT INTO SMALL PIECES
¾ CUP ALMONDS, PEELED AND SLICED
6 TABLESPOONS DARK RUM

❖ Preheat the oven to 350°F. Combine the butter, sugar, vanilla, lemon zest, and salt; beat until fluffy. Sift the flour and baking powder together. Alternately add one egg and a spoonful of the flour mixture to the butter mixture, beating after each addition. Fold in all the remaining flour, chocolate, almonds and rum with a wooden spoon. Pour the batter into a greased tube mold. Bake on a rack for about 35 to 45 minutes, until a pick inserted in the center comes out clean.

CHOCOLATE CHIP COOKIES

Yield: Approximately 50 cookies

½ CUP BUTTER
1½ CUPS FIRMLY PACKED BROWN
   SUGAR
1⅔ CUPS GRANULATED SUGAR
2 LARGE EGGS
1 TEASPOON HOT WATER
1 TEASPOON VANILLA EXTRACT

1½ CUPS BREAD FLOUR
1 TEASPOON BAKING POWDER
½ TEASPOON BAKING SODA
1½ CUPS ROLLED OATS
14 OUNCES SEMISWEET CHOCOLATE
   CHIPS

❖ Cream the butter and the sugars. Add the eggs gradually, continuing to beat as they are added. Add the water, vanilla, flour, baking powder, baking soda, and oats, and mix well. Gently stir in the chocolate chips. Spoon rounded teaspoons of dough onto parchment-lined or greased and floured baking sheets. Bake in a 350°F oven for about 10 to 15 minutes.

ICEBOX OATMEAL COOKIES

Yield: 25 cookies, 2 ounces each

⅓ CUP GRANULATED SUGAR
1½ CUPS FIRMLY PACKED BROWN
   SUGAR
5 OUNCES BUTTER
¼ CUP LARD
2 EGGS
1 CUP ROLLED OATS
½ CUP BROKEN PECANS

1 POUND BREAD FLOUR (ABOUT
   3¾ CUPS)
1 TEASPOON BAKING SODA
1 TEASPOON CINNAMON
PINCH OF SALT
1 CUP RAISINS, SOAKED TO SOFTEN,
   AND DRAINED

✤ Cream the sugars, butter and lard. Add the eggs one at a time, while beating. Add the oats, pecans, flour, baking soda, cinnamon, salt, and raisins; mix well.

Mold the dough into cylinders about 2½ inches thick. Square off the ends, wrap in wax paper, and refrigerate. When the dough is cold and firm, cut the cylinders into ¼-inch-thick slices. Place on greased and floured or silicone-paper-lined baking sheets, and bake at 350°F for about 15 minutes. Do not overbake.

ALMOND STAR COOKIES

Yield: 4 dozen

1½ POUNDS ALMOND PASTE
7 OUNCES CONFECTIONERS' SUGAR

10 LARGE EGG YOLKS

✤ Mix the almond paste and sugar. Add one yolk at a time; do not whip. Using a pastry bag with a #3 star tip, pipe the dough onto parchment paper. Let dry for 8 hours. Bake in a 450°F oven until brown, about 10 minutes.

CHOCOLATE MOUSSE

Yield: 6 servings

5 OUNCES MILK CHOCOLATE
5 OUNCES SEMISWEET CHOCOLATE
2 EGG YOLKS, BEATEN
1 EGG
⅓ CUP SUGAR
2 TABLESPOONS MILK, ROOM
  TEMPERATURE

2 TABLESPOONS KIRSCHWASSER
2 EGG WHITES
1¼ CUPS HEAVY CREAM, WHIPPED
1 PINT MINT SAUCE (RECIPE FOLLOWS)

❖ Melt both chocolates together in a double-boiler. Add the beaten egg yolks, whole egg, and half (8 teaspoons) of the sugar. Cook in the double-bouler over medium heat until thick, stirring constantly. Add the milk and Kirschwasser, and mix. Remove from the heat, and refrigerate until lukewarm. Beat the egg whites with the remaining sugar (8 teaspoons) to stiff peaks. Fold the beaten egg whites and the whipped cream into the chocolate mixture. Line a 1-quart mold or loaf pan with plastic wrap, and pour in the mousse. Refrigerate for 6 hours. Slice into ½-inch-thick pieces, and serve with the mint sauce.

MINT SAUCE

Yield: 1 pint

3 EGG YOLKS
5 TEASPOONS SUGAR
¾ CUP HEAVY CREAM

2 TABLESPOONS GREEN CRÈME DE
  MENTHE
¾ CUP HEAVY CREAM, WHIPPED

❖ Combine the egg yolks, sugar, heavy cream, and crème de menthe. Cook in a double-boiler over medium heat, stirring constantly, until the mixture coats a spoon. Chill. Fold the whipped cream into the mint mixture, and chill.

WILLIAMS PEAR MOUSSE WITH CHOCOLATE SABAYON

Yield: 8 servings

4 FRESH PEARS, PEELED, CORED, AND
    CHOPPED
¾ CUP PLUS 1 TABLESPOON SUGAR
1¼ CUPS WHITE WINE
3 EGG YOLKS
1 TABLESPOON GELATIN, DISSOLVED IN
    ¼ CUP COLD WATER

1 CUP HEAVY CREAM, WHIPPED
PEAR BRANDY TO TASTE
1 CUP CHOCOLATE SABAYON (RECIPE
    FOLLOWS)

✢ In a saucepan, cook the pears, ¼ cup of the sugar, and the white wine for 10 minutes, until tender. Pour into a blender, and puree the mixture. Strain the puree through a sieve. Over a hot-water bath, whisk the egg yolks and remaining sugar until warm, and then beat with an electric mixer until cool. Add the pear puree to the egg yolk mixture, and whip until cold and creamy. Stir in the dissolved gelatin. Fold in the whipped cream, and add brandy to taste. Chill, and serve topped with the chocolate sabayon.

CHOCOLATE SABAYON

Yield: Approximately 1 cup

4 EGG YOLKS
SCANT ½ CUP SUGAR
1 TABLESPOON COCOA

¾ CUP MILK
DARK CRÈME DE CACAO TO TASTE

✢ Combine egg yolks, sugar, cocoa, and milk over a hot-water bath; whisk until warm. Add the crème de cacao, and beat with an electric mixer until cold.

CRÈME BRÛLÉE

Yield: 8 servings

3 CUPS HEAVY CREAM
1 CUP MILK
2 TEASPOONS VANILLA EXTRACT
PINCH OF SALT

1 CUP GRANULATED SUGAR
7 EGG YOLKS
½ CUP FIRMLY PACKED BROWN SUGAR

❖ Warm the cream and milk in heavy saucepan. Add the vanilla extract and a pinch of salt. Combine the granulated sugar and egg yolks, pour in heavy cream and milk, and mix well. Pour the mixture into custard cups. Place in a warm-water bath, and cook in a 300°F oven for 30 minutes. Remove from the oven, and cool for 30 minutes. Sieve the brown sugar over tops of the custards. Glaze under boiler for 12 seconds to caramelize the brown sugar.

VANILLA SAUCE

Yield: 1 quart

⅓ CUP SUGAR
1 TABLESPOON ALL-PURPOSE FLOUR
PINCH OF SALT
2 CUPS WHIPPING CREAM

6 EGG YOLKS
1 TEASPOON VANILLA EXTRACT
2 CUPS VANILLA ICE CREAM

❖ Combine the sugar, salt, and flour, mixing well. Pour the cream into a heavy saucepan, add the sugar/flour/salt mixture, and heat until almost boiling. In a separate mixing bowl, beat the egg yolks until fluffy. Add a small amount of the hot liquid to the egg yolks, continuing to beat. Pour the tempered egg yolks into the hot liquid, continuing to beat. Cook this mixture until it begins to thicken slightly, whisking constantly while cooking. When the mixture begins to thicken, remove it from the heat, add the vanilla extract, and mix into the ice cream. Keep the sauce warm in a bain-marie or warm-water bath until ready to serve. Serve over crêpes, soufflés, or bread pudding.

BREAD PUDDING WITH BRANDY SAUCE

Yield: 12 servings

6 EGGS
1 CUP SUGAR
1 QUART MILK
1 CUP LIGHT CREAM
1 TEASPOON VANILLA EXTRACT
½ TEASPOON NUTMEG

1 TEASPOON CINNAMON
¼ CUP BUTTER, MELTED
½ CUP SEEDLESS RAISINS
10 SLICES DAY-OLD BREAD, BROKEN
 INTO PIECES

❖ Whip the eggs and sugar together. Add the milk, cream, vanilla, nutmeg, cinnamon, melted butter, and raisins. Mix well. Butter a 2½-quart baking pan. Place the bread in the pan, and pour the custard mixture over it. Mix lightly until well blended. Bake in a 1-inch-deep water bath for approximately 1 hour.

BRANDY SAUCE

Yield: 2 cups

3 EGG YOLKS
¾ CUP SUGAR
1 TEASPOON VANILLA EXTRACT
1½ CUPS MILK

1 TABLESPOON MINOR'S SAUCE/SOUP
 THICKENER*
2 TABLESPOONS WATER
1½ TABLESPOONS BRANDY

❖ Beat the egg yolks until light and lemon colored. Add the sugar, vanilla, and milk, and blend well. Cook over medium heat, stirring constantly, until the liquid simmers. Blend the thickener and water until smooth. Add to the simmering liquid, stirring constantly. Simmer for 3 to 4 minutes. Add the brandy, mix well, and serve over the bread pudding.

* For information about this thickener, see chapter 3.

SALZBURGER NOCKERL

Yield: 2 to 3 servings

4 EGG WHITES
¼ CUP CONFECTIONERS' SUGAR
1 TABLESPOON FLOUR
ZEST OF 1 LEMON, GRATED

1 TEASPOON VANILLA EXTRACT
3 EGG YOLKS, BEATEN
1 TABLESPOON MELTED BUTTER
¼ CUP LIGHT CREAM

✤ Beat the egg whites until stiff. Gradually beat in the confectioners' sugar until the mixture has the consistency of a heavy meringue. Combine the flour, lemon zest, and vanilla extract, add to the beaten egg yolks, and mix well. Carefully fold together the two mixtures. Combine the melted butter with the light cream; fold into the egg mixture. Pour into a well-buttered 1-quart ovenproof glass dish. Dust with granulated sugar, and bake at 450°F for 15 minutes. Serve with sauce anglaise (vanilla sauce—see recipe earlier in this chapter).

CRÊPES À LA RITZ

Yield: Approximately 16 crêpes, 6 to 8 servings

CRÊPES
2 EGGS
1 CUP MILK
¾ CUP FLOUR

½ TEASPOON SALT
1 TEASPOON SUGAR

✤ Place the eggs, milk, flour, salt, and sugar in a blender, and mix for 2 minutes at medium speed. Let set for 20 to 30 minutes. Brush a heated crêpe pan with oil. Add 2 to 2½ tablespoons of batter, and tilt the pan to coat it evenly. Cook until light brown and done; remove from the pan. Continue making crêpes until all the batter is used.

FILLING
1 CUP WATER
1 CUP SUGAR
¼ CUP FLOUR
JUICE AND ZEST OF 4 LEMONS
1 TABLESPOON BUTTER
4 EGG WHITES

POWDERED SUGAR AS NEEDED
¾ TO 1 CUP RASPBERRY SYRUP,
    (2 TABLESPOONS PER PORTION)

(continued)

❖ Bring the water, sugar, flour, and lemon juice and zest to a boil, stirring constantly until smooth and pastelike. Remove from the heat and stir in the butter. Beat the egg whites until stiff, and fold into the mixture. Fill the crêpes with the mixture, and fold. Place together on a serving platter, sprinkle with the powdered sugar, and glaze under a broiler. Serve immediately with fresh raspberry syrup.

CRÊPES NORMANDY

Yield: 20 crêpes

1 POUND MCINTOSH APPLES, CORED, PEELED, AND MEDIUM-DICED
½ CUP GRANULATED SUGAR
2 TABLESPOONS ALL-PURPOSE FLOUR
¼ TEASPOON GROUND CINNAMON
2 TABLESPOONS BUTTER

¼ CUP RAISINS
½ CUP DICED WALNUTS
½ CUP WATER
1 TABLESPOON LEMON JUICE
20 CRÊPES (SEE THE PRECEDING RECIPE FOR CRÊPES À LA RITZ)

❖ Combine the apples, sugar, flour, cinnamon, butter, raisins, walnuts, water, and lemon juice, mixing well. Cook over medium heat for approximately 4 minutes, until the apples are tender but not mushy. Chill the mixture, and use for stuffing crêpes.

OMELETTE STEPHANIE

Yield: 6 servings

6 EGG YOLKS
½ CUP GRANULATED SUGAR
ZEST OF ½ LEMON, GRATED
FEW DROPS VANILLA EXTRACT
9 EGG WHITES
½ CUP FLOUR, SIFTED
2 TABLESPOONS BUTTER, MELTED
3 TABLESPOONS HEAVY CREAM

1 TABLESPOON CLARIFIED BUTTER
1 CUP DICED FRESH FRUIT, DRAINED
3 TABLESPOONS RASPBERRY OR OTHER JAM
2 TABLESPOONS ORANGE OR HAZELNUT LIQUEUR
POWDERED SUGAR FOR DUSTING

❖ Preheat the oven to 325°F. Beat the egg yolks and ¼ cup of the sugar until creamy; add the zest and vanilla. Beat the egg whites, adding the remaining ¼ cup of sugar gradually, until firm but not dry; fold into the yolks. Fold in the flour; add the butter and cream—*do not overmix*. Heat the clarified butter in a 12-inch ovenproof skillet. Pour in the omelet batter, and tilt the pan to spread the batter evenly. Place in the oven, and bake for approximately 18 minutes, or until firm in center. While the omelet bakes, warm the fruit with the jam; add the liqueur. Remove the omelet from the oven, pour the fruit over half of it, fold the other half over the fruit, and turn out onto a serving platter. Dust with powdered sugar, and serve immediately (cut into servings tableside).

CALIFORNIA FRUIT OMELET

Yield: 6 servings

6 EGGS, SEPARATED
1 TEASPOON GRATED LEMON ZEST
6 TABLESPOONS BUTTER, MELTED
¼ CUP FLOUR
2 TABLESPOONS ORANGE LIQUEUR

4 TEASPOONS SUGAR
3 CUPS CANNED FRUIT COCKTAIL
2 TABLESPOONS TRIPLE SEC
POWDERED SUGAR FOR DUSTING

❖ Preheat the oven to 375°F. Mix the egg yolks with the grated lemon zest, melted butter, flour, liqueur, and sugar. Beat until foamy. Beat the egg whites until soft peaks form, then carefully fold together the two mixtures. Spoon the omelet batter into 6-inch-diameter circles (like pancakes) on a well-buttered baking sheet. Bake for approximately 8 minutes, until lightly browned. As the omelets bake, heat the canned fruit in its own syrup, and then drain. Remove the omelets from the oven, and loosen the omelet carefully from the pan with a spatula. Place the omelets on a warm platter. Top with the heated fruit, then drizzle with Triple Sec. Fold each omelet once. Dust with powdered sugar, and serve at once. Garnish with whipped cream if desired.

SOUFFLÉ ROTHSCHILD

Yield: 6 servings

½ CUP FLOUR
¼ CUP BUTTER
¼ CUP SUGAR
1½ CUPS MILK
½ TEASPOON VANILLA EXTRACT
6 EGG YOLKS
8 EGG WHITES

¾ CUP GRANULATED SUGAR
6 LADYFINGERS, CRUSHED
2 TABLESPOONS CURAÇAO
½ CUP DICED CANDIED FRUIT
POWDERED SUGAR FOR DUSTING
1 PINT FRESH HULLED STRAWBERRIES

❖ In a bowl mix the flour, butter, and sugar into a paste. In a saucepan, bring the milk and vanilla to a boil; remove from the heat. Add the flour mixture, stir until smooth, and return to the heat. Cook for 2 minutes, and remove from the heat. Add the egg yolks, one by one, stirring briskly. Set aside.

In another bowl, beat the egg whites and sugar with a clean whisk until soft peaks form: add the sugar gradually, beating constantly, until you get a firm, but not dry, meringue. Fold the meringue into the egg mixture very gently, taking care not to overmix. Mix the ladyfingers with the Curaçao. Fold the candied fruit and soaked ladyfingers into the soufflé batter. Pour into buttered and sugared soufflé dishes. Dust the top heavily with powdered sugar. Bake in 400°F oven for 10 to 15 minutes until firm. Garnish the rim with the fresh strawberries, and serve immediately.

CRANBERRY NUT SOUFFLÉ

Yield: 8 servings

6 TABLESPOONS BUTTER OR MARGARINE
4½ CUPS FRESH CRANBERRIES
¼ CUP FIRMLY PACKED BROWN SUGAR
¾ CUP CHOPPED WALNUTS OR PECANS

2 LARGE EGGS
7 TABLESPOONS SUGAR
⅔ CUP ALL-PURPOSE FLOUR
¼ TEASPOON SALT

✤ Melt the butter or margarine. Brush enough of the butter on a soufflé dish to coat thoroughly. Wash, clean, and pat dry the cranberries; place them on the bottom of the buttered soufflé dish. Sprinkle with the brown sugar and chopped nuts. Beat the eggs and sugar until fluffy. Fold in the flour, salt, and the rest of the melted butter. Spread the batter evenly over the cranberries. Bake in a preheated 375°F oven for 20 to 25 minutes. Increase the heat to 425°F, and bake for about 10 to 15 minutes, until firm. Serve warm with beaten cream or vanilla ice cream.

BIERER'S PEARS

Yield: 5 servings

10 CANNED PEAR HALVES
2½ TO 3 CUPS VANILLA ICE CREAM
2 CUPS FLOUR
1½ CUPS BEER (12 FLUID OUNCES)
DASH OF SALT

4 EGG YOLKS
2 TEASPOONS SALAD OIL
OIL FOR DEEP-FRYING
6 EGG WHITES
3 TABLESPOONS GRANULATED SUGAR

✤ A day or more before serving, scoop out most of the center of each pear half, creating shells. Freeze until solid. Fill the shells with the vanilla ice cream; press two halves together; continue until all halves are used. Insert a round toothpick vertically, halfway down the neck of each pear. Stand up the pears and freeze until rock solid.

One hour before serving, combine the flour, beer, salt, egg yolks, and salad oil to make a batter; it should have the consistency of pancake batter. (If too thick, add a bit of beer or water, but do not let it become too runny.) Heat the oil in a deep-fryer to 425°F. Whip egg whites until stiff, adding the sugar gradually as you whip. Fold into the batter. Dip each pear in the batter, holding it by the toothpick. Then lower into deep-fryer, let go of toothpick, and fry until golden brown, approximately 2 to 3 minutes.

PINEAPPLE AND BANANA FLAMBÉ

Yield: 2 servings

1 FRESH PINEAPPLE
2 TEASPOONS BUTTER
⅓ CUP BROWN SUGAR
DASH OF GROUND CINNAMON
2 MEDIUM BANANAS, CUT IN QUARTERS
  LENGTHWISE

2 TABLESPOONS DARK RUM
1 TABLESPOON BANANA LIQUEUR
2 LARGE SCOOPS PINEAPPLE SHERBET

❖ Melt the butter in a skillet or chafing dish. Add the brown sugar and cinnamon, then add the bananas and pineapple cubes. Sauté lightly, stirring as little as possible. Add the rum and liqueur. When heated, flame the mixture. Place a large scoop of pineapple sherbet into each pineapple boat. Spoon the fruit mixture over the sherbet immediately after flaming, and serve.

Prepare two pineapple boats by cutting the fresh pineapple in half lengthwise, *with* the foliage. Carefully hollow out the shells. Cut the fruit into ½- to ¾-inch cubes, and reserve. Chill the shells until ready to fill.

STRAWBERRIES AND CREAM

Yield: 4 to 6 servings

1 PINT FRESH STRAWBERRIES
1½ OUNCES GRANULATED SUGAR
  (ABOUT 3 TABLESPOONS)

2 TABLESPOONS PORT WINE OR GRAND
  MARNIER
1 PINT WHIPPING CREAM

❖ Wash and hull the strawberries. Cut each berry in half or in fourths. Mix the strawberries with the sugar and port or Grand Marnier. Macerate for 30 minutes. Whip the cream, and fold into the strawberries.

COUPE YVONNE

Yield: 6 servings

3 PINTS STRAWBERRIES, WASHED, DRIED,
STEMMED, AND HALVED
1½ CUPS SUGAR
3 CUPS BRISTOL PORT WINE

6 SCOOPS ORANGE SHERBET, 2½ TO
3 OUNCES EACH
¼ CUP GRAND MARNIER
18 STRAWBERRIES, UNIFORM SIZE

❖ Place the strawberry halves in a large bowl. Combine the sugar and port wine, mixing well. Pour over the strawberries, mix well, cover, and refrigerate for 2 hours. Place the orange sherbet in well-chilled dessert bowls. Sprinkle 2 teaspoons of Grand Marnier over each serving of sherbet. Top each with 1 cup of the strawberry mixture. Garnish each with 3 whole strawberries.

HAWAIIAN ICE CREAM BOMBE

Yield: 10 to 12 servings

1 PINT CHOCOLATE ICE CREAM
1 PINT VANILLA ICE CREAM
12 EGG YOLKS
1¾ CUPS SUGAR
2 TABLESPOONS KIRSCHWASSER

1 TABLESPOON FRESHLY SQUEEZED
LEMON JUICE
8 OUNCES FRESH PINEAPPLE, CHOPPED
1 PINT WHIPPING CREAM

❖ Line a 1½-quart cylindrical container (such as a bombe mold or cottage cheese bucket) with a ½-inch-thick layer of the chocolate ice cream; freeze. Add a ½-inch-thick layer of the vanilla ice cream; freeze. Whisk the egg yolks and 1¼ cups of the sugar in a 3-quart stainless-steel bowl over a double-boiler until thick and light in color; whisk off the heat until cold. Add the Kirschwasser and lemon juice. In a small saucepan, cook the pineapple and remaining ½ cup of sugar until syrupy; cool. Add to the egg yolk mixture. Whip the cream, fold in the egg yolk mixture, and pour into the ice cream–lined container. Freeze for 24 hours. Unmold the bombe, and shape like a pineapple. Garnish with chocolate leaves and almond star cookies (see recipe earlier in this chapter).

Nutrition

Food is needed to maintain life processes and growth. Research indicates a strong connection between the food one eats and general health. Nutritional habits affect physical appearance, mental and physical performance, and well-being. In some cases poor life-long eating habits may lead to the onset of certain diseases.

Good nutrition is eating the right kinds of foods in the proper amounts. A well-balanced diet provides the required amounts of key nutrients, including carbohydrates, fats, proteins, vitamins, and minerals. No one food source satisfies all nutritional needs. Foods vary in the type and amount of nutrients they contain. Moreover, for some nutrients to be most effective, other nutrients must also be consumed. For all these reasons, food variety is a most important factor in daily menu planning.

A DAILY FOOD GUIDE	
FOOD GROUP	SUGGESTED SERVINGS
Vegetables: At least 1 dark green or yellow vegetable daily, dried beans, peas, and starchy vegetables such as potatoes, corn, beets	3 to 5 servings; 1 serving equals 1 cup of raw leafy green vegetables, ½ cup of other kinds
Fruits: Citrus, melons, berries, apples, bananas, and others	2 to 4 servings; 1 serving equals 1 medium-size fruit, ½ cup of diced fruit, ¾ cup of juice
Breads, cereals, rice, and pasta: Choose from a variety of grains, such as wheat, rice, oats, and corn; select whole-grain breads and cereals	6 to 11 servings; 1 serving equals 1 slice of bread, ½ bun or bagel, 1 ounce of dry cereal, ½ cup of cooked cereal, pasta, or rice
Milk, yogurt, and cheeses: Skim or low-fat milk and fat-free yogurt	2 to 3 servings; 1 serving equals 1 cup of milk or yogurt, 1½ ounces of cheese
Meats, poultry, fish, dry beans and peas, eggs, and nuts: Trim fat from meats; substitute dry beans and peas for meat occasionally; limit use of egg yolks and organ meats; use lean beef and chicken without skin	2 to 3 servings; 1 serving equals 3 ounces

A simple way to ensure nutritional variety is to choose foods every day from the five major food groups shown in the preceding table. Most people should have at least the minimum number of servings indicated.

DIETARY GUIDELINES FOR AMERICANS

First issued in 1980 by the U.S. Department of Agriculture and the U.S. Department of Health and Human Services, these guidelines are basic principles for developing and maintaining a healthy diet. The guidelines, updated in 1990, reflect the recommendations of nutrition and health authorities, who agree that there is enough evidence to link diet and health "to encourage certain dietary practices by Americans."

The average American diet is rich in calories, fat, cholesterol, and sodium. It is low in complex carbohydrates and fiber. Vitamin and mineral deficiency diseases are rare, but often people get only minimal amounts of calcium and iron.

The new guidelines emphasize the important role life-style plays in achieving good health. Diet, exercise, alcohol intake, and smoking are the controllable factors that affect health, whereas heredity, environment, and health care are more difficult to control. Moderation is the key: avoid extremes in any diet.

DIETARY GUIDELINES

Eat a Variety of Foods

Essential nutrients are vitamins, minerals, amino acids from protein, certain fatty acids from fat, and sources of calories (protein, carbohydrates and fat).

- Fruits and vegetables are good sources for vitamins A and C, folic acid, minerals and fiber.
- Breads and cereals are rich in B vitamins, iron, and protein. Whole grains are high in fiber.
- Milk provides calcium, protein, B vitamins, vitamins A and D, and phosphorus.
- The meat group supplies protein, B vitamins, iron, and zinc.
- People who are trying to lose weight should limit food intake to the lower-calorie foods with high nutritional value and eat less of the high-calorie, low-nutrient foods, such as fats and oils, sugars, and alcoholic beverages.

Maintain a Healthy Weight

A "healthy" weight depends on how much of one's weight is fat, where the fat is located, and if weight-related medical problems are involved. The accompanying table shows recommended weights based on height, including higher values for those over age thirty-five, because research suggests that people can be a little heavier as they grow older without added health risk.

SUGGESTED WEIGHTS FOR ADULTS		
HEIGHT[1]	WEIGHT IN POUNDS[2]	
	19–34	35 +
5′ 0″	97–128	108–138
5′ 1″	101–132	111–143
5′ 2″	104–137	115–148
5′ 3″	107–141	119–152
5′ 4″	111–146	122–157
5′ 5″	114–150	126–162
5′ 6″	118–155	130–167
5′ 7″	121–160	134–172
5′ 8″	125–164	138–178
5′ 9″	129–169	142–183
5′10″	132–174	146–188
5′11″	136–179	151–194
6′ 0″	140–184	155–199
6′ 1″	144–189	159–205
6′ 2″	148–195	164–210
6′ 3″	152–200	168–216
6′ 4″	156–205	173–222
6′ 5″	160–211	177–228
6′ 6″	164–216	182–234

1. Without shoes.
2. Without clothes. The higher weights in the ranges generally apply to men, who tend to have more muscle and bone; the lower weights more often apply to women, who have less muscle and bone.

SOURCE: Derived from National Research Council, 1989.

To maintain weight, energy input should equal energy output. Food energy is measured in calories. All foods are made up of various amounts of carbohydrates, proteins, and fats. One gram of carbohydrates provides four calories, one gram of protein provides four calories, and one gram of fat provides nine calories. When the body takes in more calories than it consumes, the excess energy is stored as body fat. Calories are spent (metabolized) via basic body processes and exercise. Logically, weight reduction occurs when calorie intake (food) is lowered and exercise is increased. Exercise also speeds up the body's calorie consumption (metabolism) so calories are burned at a faster rate.

The new guidelines advise not to lose weight too fast. A loss of one-half to one pound per week is generally safe. Avoid crash weight-loss diets that severely restrict the variety of foods or calories.

Children need calories to grow and develop normally. Reduction diets are not usually recommended for them. For weight loss, it is better to focus on increased exercise and healthy diet.

To decrease calories, eat a variety of foods that are low in calories and high in nutrients. Eat less fat and fatty foods. Eat more fruits, vegetables, breads, and cereals—without adding fats and sugars. Eat less sugars and sweets and drink few or no alcoholic beverages. Eat smaller portions, and limit second helpings.

Choose a Diet Low in Fat, Saturated Fat, and Cholesterol

A diet low in fat makes it easier to include more kinds of nutritious foods without exceeding a calorie limit, because fat contains more calories than carbohydrates or proteins do. Some fat is necessary for the absorption of vitamins A, D, E, and K and is the source of some essential fatty acids. A high-fat diet—especially in saturated fats and cholesterol—causes increased blood cholesterol levels and a greater risk of heart disease.

The following are cooking tips for a diet low in fat, saturated fat, and cholesterol:

FATS AND OILS

- Use fats and oils sparingly in cooking.
- Use small amounts of salad dressings and spreads, such as butter, margarine, and mayonnaise. One tablespoon of most of these spreads provides 10 to 11 grams of fat.
- Choose liquid vegetable oils over solids because they usually contain less saturated fat.
- Check labels on foods to learn how much fat and saturated fat are in a serving.

MEAT, POULTRY, FISH, DRY BEANS, AND EGGS

- Eat two or three servings from this group daily, for a total of about 6 ounces. Three ounces of cooked lean beef or chicken (without skin)—the size of a deck of cards—provides about 6 grams of fat.
- Trim fat from meat; remove skin from poultry.
- Have cooked dry beans and peas instead of meat occasionally.
- Moderate the use of egg yolks and organ meats.

MILK AND MILK PRODUCTS

- Have two or three servings daily (a serving is 1 cup of milk or yogurt or about 1½ ounces of cheese).
- Choose skim or low-fat milk and fat-free or low-fat yogurt and cheese most of the time. One cup of skim milk has only a trace of fat, 1 cup of 2 percent milk has 5 grams of fat, and 1 cup of whole milk has 8 grams of fat.

The average American consumes too much fat. The American Heart Association recommends that only 30 percent of daily calorie intake come from fats and oils, with only 10 percent from saturated fats. To calculate the actual amount of fat that can be consumed to meet this guideline, determine the total calories required in a day, 2,000 for example. Multiply by .30 (or divide by 30): 30 percent of the calories in a 2,000-calorie diet would be 600; these are the calories to be ingested from fat sources. Nine calories are in 1 gram of fat, so divide 600 by 9 to learn the total number of grams of fat that can be ingested: 67 grams.

Eat Plenty of Vegetables, Fruits, and Grains

Three servings of vegetables, two servings of fruit, and six servings of grain products are recommended daily. These foods contribute complex carbohydrates, dietary fiber, vitamins, and minerals. Complex carbohydrates are starches, contained in breads, cereals, pasta, dry beans, and vegetables such as potatoes and corn.

Fiber is important to keep the digestive tract healthy. Again, it is best to eat a variety of foods, since each contributes a different type of dietary fiber. Fiber should come from foods, rather than from supplements, which increase the risk of intestinal problems and decrease absorption of some minerals.

Use Sugars in Moderation

Sugars and many sweet foods supply many calories but limited nutrients. They therefore should be used in moderation by healthy people, sparingly by the calorie conscious. Sugars also contribute to tooth decay.

In addition to the common sugars—granulated sugar, brown sugar, corn syrup solids, honey, and syrup—sugars also occur naturally in fruits, vegetables, and milk, which are rich sources of other nutrients. The sugar added for sweetness to a recipe can often be decreased: use ½ cup of sugar per cup of flour in cakes, 1 tablespoon of sugar per cup of flour in muffins or quick breads, and 1 teaspoon of sugar per cup of flour in yeast breads. Small amounts of cinnamon, nutmeg, or vanilla will enhance flavor when sugar is reduced.

Diets high in sugar have not been shown to cause diabetes. The most common type of diabetes occurs in overweight adults, and avoiding sugars alone will not correct an overweight condition.

Consume Salt and Sodium in Moderation

Americans eat three to five times more salt than they need. Table salt contains sodium and chloride, both essential in the diet. Everyone needs some sodium to help regulate water balance in body tissues, to maintain blood volume, and to transmit nerve impulses. However, too much sodium may contribute to high blood pressure. For those who suffer from high blood pressure, limiting sodium consumption will often cause blood pressure to fall. Those who do not have high blood pressure may reduce the risk of getting it by eating less salt. (Many factors affect blood pressure, including heredity, obesity, and excessive alcohol intake.)

Fresh (that is, unprocessed) foods, such as meats, poultry, fish, fruits, vegetables, and grains, such as rice, barley, and pasta, contain small amounts of natural sodium. These amounts easily meet body requirements; extra sodium from table salt is unnecessary. Processed foods, which often contain huge amounts of some form of sodium, and table salt are largely responsible for the excessive amount of salt in American diets.

To moderate the use of sodium and salt:

- Use salt sparingly, if at all, in cooking and at the table. Instead of seasoning with salt, use more herbs and spices, wine, lemon juice, and more savory vegetables, such as onions, celery, and carrots. Salt is not needed in the cooking water of rice, pasta, hot cereals and vegetables.
- Use fresh or plain frozen vegetables, rather than canned, which are high in sodium. Frozen prepared entrées are usually high in sodium as well (read labels for sodium content).
- Salty condiments include catsup, mustard, pickles, olives, and soy and other bottled sauces.
- Sodium is contained in the leavening agents baking powder and baking soda. Some reduction of these ingredients will still produce a quality product. For example:
  –Use ¼ teaspoon of salt per cup of flour in *yeast* breads. (Salt is necessary because it helps to control the action of yeast.)
  –Use only half the amount of salt called for in baked products other than yeast breads.
  –Use 1¼ teaspoons of baking powder per cup of flour in biscuits, muffins, and waffles.
  –Use 1 teaspoon of baking powder per cup of flour in cakes.
- Check labels for the amount of sodium in foods. Choose those lower in sodium most of the time.

Drink Alcoholic Beverages in Moderation
Alcoholic beverages supply calories but little or no nutrients. They provide no health benefit, only health problems.

---

* The information in this appendix was adapted from *Dietary Guidelines*, Third Edition (1990), prepared by the U.S. Department of Agriculture and the U.S. Department of Health and Human Services. For more information, contact the Human Nutrition Information Service, USDA, Room 325-A, 6505 Belcrest Road, Hyattsville, MD 20782.

How to Work a Recipe

THE best approach to duplicating a recipe successfully in this, or any other, cookbook is as follows:

1. Read the recipe from beginning to end several times. You can thus picture in your mind's eye the processes involved in the recipe.
2. Assemble all ingredients.
3. Assemble all tools, utensils, and equipment.
4. Preheat the oven if necessary.
5. Weigh and measure all ingredients, and place in plastic bags, bowls, or cups. Measure accurately.
6. Combine and cook the measured ingredients according to the recipe.

APPENDIX THREE

Garnishes

GARNISHES for food items can be very personal and creative works of art. The following suggestions may be helpful in attractively decorating food items.

- Do not overdecorate: keep garnishes simple and neat.
- Do not overuse parsley. While it is appropriate for some items, it is not necessarily always the best choice.
- Fresh herbs make attractive garnishes—simple but often elegant. Use them sparingly.
- Simple carved vegetables are easy to make and add a special touch. Examples include radish roses, pickle fans, and carrot curls.
- Fruits are also effective garnishes. Try a strawberry fan or a lemon or lime twist combined with a fresh sprig of mint.
- Watercress is an appropriate garnish for roast beef, beef steak, or chopped steak.
- For fish, chicken, or egg dishes, pot pies, or saucy or creamy items such as stews, parsley is most appropriate.
- Use applesauce, crab apples, sautéed or poached apple rings, or apple fritters with a touch of parsley for roast pork or pork chops.
- For fruit salads and dessert-type gelatins, sprigs of fresh mint are far more appropriate than parsley is.
- Try a small bunch of white grapes nestled in a few leaves of chicory to accompany sautéed or broiled fish and roast or sautéed chicken.
- An apple ring placed on lettuce leaves, topped with a half of a canned apricot, works nicely with roast pork, pork chops, and roast or broiled chicken.
- A garnish made of endive, sliced plum tomatoes, and a sprig of fresh basil may be perfect for a light-colored pasta dish, as well as for roast beef, lamb, pork, chicken, or fish.
- For sautéed or broiled fish (not fried), try a garnish made with red-leaf lettuce, a slice of lemon topped with capers, and a sprig of parsley.
- An orange cup filled with cranberries, accented with fresh mint, is a nice holiday accompaniment for beef, pork, and lamb.

A P P E N D I X   F O U R

Cookware and Utensils

KNIVES

Stainless Steel

Stainless steel is a hard, strong metal but is not quite as strong as super stainless. If properly maintained, a stainless steel knife will not rust, stain, or transfer metal taste to foods. It is difficult to sharpen and must be ground at regular intervals.

Super Stainless

This material is so hard that it cannot be sharpened. It is used for household knives that supposedly never need sharpening and will last for life.

Carbon versus Stainless Steel

Knives of both materials are steel, but the critical difference is the alloy's higher carbon content; stainless steel has more chromium and nickel.

The Steel and How to Use It

A steel's purpose is to maintain straight edges on knives, not to sharpen knives. To steel your knife after prolonged use, follow the procedure below (see the illustration on page 260):

1. Hold the steel by the handle beneath the guard collar with your arm outstretched in front of you.
2. Crisscross the steel and the knife at about a 60-degree angle. Then angle the knife blade at approximately 20 degrees on the steel.
3. Move the knife in an arc along the steel from the heel to the tip of the knife. The concentrated magnetism at the tip of the steel will attract all particles.
4. Repeat step 3 about four to six times, changing the edge with each movement. Then wipe the blade clean.

STOCKPOT

SAUTOIR

COLANDER (*PASSOIRE*)

STEW PAN (*MARMITE*)

MARMITE WITH SPIGOT

BRAISING PAN

SAUCEPAN

1 GALLON MEASURE

ROASTING PAN

FRYING PAN (*POÊLE À FAIRE*)

STEW PAN (*RONDEAU*)

SALMON KETTLE

SAUCEPAN (*RUSSE*)

SAUCEPAN (*SAUTOIR*)

ROASTING PAN (*RÔTISSOIRE*)

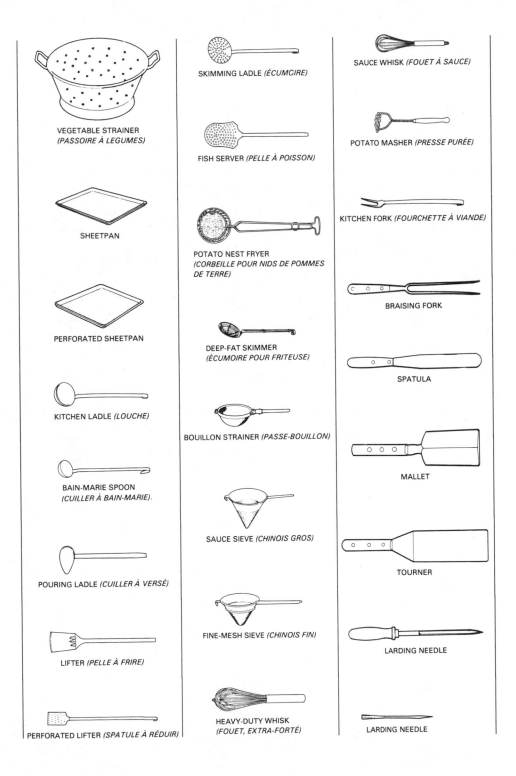

VEGETABLE STRAINER
(PASSOIRE À LEGUMES)

SHEETPAN

PERFORATED SHEETPAN

KITCHEN LADLE (LOUCHE)

BAIN-MARIE SPOON
(CUILLER À BAIN-MARIE)

POURING LADLE (CUILLER À VERSÉ)

LIFTER (PELLE À FRIRE)

PERFORATED LIFTER (SPATULE À RÉDUIR)

SKIMMING LADLE (ÉCUMCIRE)

FISH SERVER (PELLE À POISSON)

POTATO NEST FRYER
(CORBEILLE POUR NIDS DE POMMES
DE TERRE)

DEEP-FAT SKIMMER
(ÈCUMOIRE POUR FRITEUSE)

BOUILLON STRAINER (PASSE-BOUILLON)

SAUCE SIEVE (CHINOIS GROS)

FINE-MESH SIEVE (CHINOIS FIN)

HEAVY-DUTY WHISK
(FOUET, EXTRA-FORTÉ)

SAUCE WHISK (FOUET À SAUCE)

POTATO MASHER (PRESSE PURÉE)

KITCHEN FORK (FOURCHETTE À VIANDE)

BRAISING FORK

SPATULA

MALLET

TOURNER

LARDING NEEDLE

LARDING NEEDLE

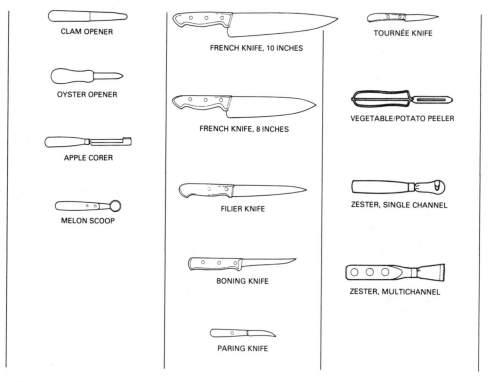

CLAM OPENER

OYSTER OPENER

APPLE CORER

MELON SCOOP

FRENCH KNIFE, 10 INCHES

FRENCH KNIFE, 8 INCHES

FILIER KNIFE

BONING KNIFE

PARING KNIFE

TOURNÉE KNIFE

VEGETABLE/POTATO PEELER

ZESTER, SINGLE CHANNEL

ZESTER, MULTICHANNEL

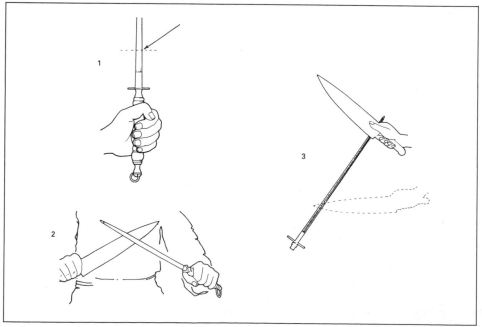

Weights and Measures

TEASPOONS

⅛ teaspoon = a few grains
1 teaspoon = 60 drops
1 teaspoon = 5 milliliters
1 teaspoon = ⅓ tablespoon
3 teaspoons = 1 tablespoon

TABLESPOONS

1 tablespoon   = 3 teaspoons
1 tablespoon   = ½ fluid ounce
2 tablespoons   = 1 fluid ounce
4 tablespoons   = ¼ cup
4 tablespoons   = 2 fluid ounces
5⅓ tablespoons   = ⅓ cup
8 tablespoons   = ½ cup
10⅔ tablespoons = ⅔ cup
12 tablespoons   = 6 ounces
16 tablespoons   = 1 cup
16 tablespoons   = 8 fluid ounces

DRY VOLUME MEASURE

2 cups   = 1 pint
2 pints   = 1 quart
4 quarts   = 1 gallon
2 gallons = 8 quarts
8 quarts   = 1 peck
4 pecks   = 1 bushel

LIQUID MEASUREMENTS

1 pint	= 2 cups liquid
2 pints	= 1 quart liquid
1 tablespoon	= ½ fluid ounce
1 cup	= 16 tablespoons = 8 fluid ounces
2 cups	= 1 pint = 16 fluid ounces
4 cups	= 2 pints = 1 quart = 32 fluid ounces = 64 tablespoons
1 liter	= 66⅔ tablespoons = 33⅓ fluid ounces

CUPS

⅛ cup	= 1 fluid ounce = 2 tablespoons
¼ cup	= 2 fluid ounces = 4 tablespoons
⅓ cup	= 5⅓ tablespoons
⅜ cup	= 3 fluid ounces = 6 tablespoons
½ cup	= 4 fluid ounces = 8 tablespoons = ¼ pint = 1 gill
⅝ cup	= 5 fluid ounces = 10 tablespoons
⅔ cup	= 10⅔ tablespoons
¾ cup	= 6 fluid ounces = 12 tablespoons
1 cup	= 8 fluid ounces = 16 tablespoons = ½ pint = 2 gills
2 cups	= 1 pint = 16 fluid ounces
4 cups	= 1 quart = 32 fluid ounces
16 cups	= 1 gallon = 64 fluid ounces

OVEN TEMPERATURES

Very low oven	250°–275° F	121°–133° C
Low oven	300°–325° F	149°–163° C
Moderate oven	350°–375° F	177°–190° C
Hot oven	400°–425° F	204°–218° C
Very hot oven	450°–475° F	232°–246° C
Extremely hot oven	500°–525° F	260°–274° C

Metric Conversions

LENGTH

1 inch		25.4 millimeters
12 inches	1 foot	30.5 centimeters
3 feet	1 yard	0.9 meters
1,760 yards	1 mile	1.6 kilometers
1 millimeter		0.04 inch
10 millimeters	1 centimeter	0.39 inch
10 centimeters	1 decimeter	3.93 inches
10 decimeters	1 meter	1.1 yards
1,000 meters	1 kilometer	0.62 mile

WEIGHT

1 ounce		28.34 grams
16 ounces	1 pound	0.45 kilogram
100 pounds	1 hundredweight	45.35 kilograms
2,000 pounds	1 short ton	1.01 megagrams
1 gram		0.035 ounce
10 grams	1 dekagram	0.35 ounce
100 dekagrams	1 kilogram	2.2 pounds
1,000 kilograms	1 megagram	1.1 short tons

LIQUID VOLUME

1 ounce		29.5 milliliters
16 ounces	1 pint	0.47 liter
2 pints	1 quart	0.95 liter
4 quarts	1 gallon	3.79 liters
31.5 gallons	1 barrel	119.24 liters
1 milliliter		0.034 ounce
1,000 milliliters	1 liter	1.06 quarts
1,000 liters	1 kiloliter	264.18 gallons

DRY VOLUME

1 pint		0.55 liter
2 pints	1 quart	1.1 liters
8 quarts	1 peck	8.81 liters
4 pecks	1 bushel	35.24 liters
1 liter		0.91 quart
100 liters	1 kiloliter	28.38 bushels

METRIC CONVERSION

The key figure in the center column can be read as either metric or American measure, thus: 1 pint = 0.568 liter, 1 liter = 1.761 pints.

PINTS		LITERS	OUNCES		GRAMS	POUNDS		KILOGRAMS
1.761	1	0.568	0.035	1	28.350	2.205	1	0.454
3.521	2	1.136	0.071	2	56.699	4.409	2	0.907
5.282	3	1.704	0.106	3	85.049	6.614	3	1.361
7.043	4	2.272	0.141	4	113.398	8.819	4	1.814
8.804	5	2.840	0.176	5	141.748	11.023	5	2.268
10.564	6	3.408	0.212	6	170.097	13.226	6	2.722
12.325	7	3.976	0.247	7	198.447	15.432	7	3.175
14.086	8	4.544	0.282	8	226.796	17.637	8	3.629
15.847	9	5.112	0.317	9	255.146	19.842	9	4.082

Ingredient Equivalents

Apples, fresh	1 pound = 3 cups sliced, approximately 3 apples
Baking powder	1 ounce = 2½ tablespoons
Baking soda	1 ounce = 2 tablespoons
Bananas	1 pound = 2½ cups sliced, about 3 medium bananas
Berries (strawberries, blueberries)	1 quart = about 3½ cups, picked over and cleaned
Butter or margarine	¼-pound stick = ½ cup; 1-pound bar = 2 cups
Cake crumbs	1 cup = 3 ounces
Chocolate, grated	4 tablespoons = 1 ounce
Cinnamon, ground	1 ounce = 4½ tablespoons
Cocoa, sifted	1 pound = 4½ cups
Cornstarch	1 tablespoon = ½ ounce; 7 ounces = 1 cup
Cream of tartar	1 ounce = 3 tablespoons
Eggs, fresh	4 to 5 eggs = 1 cup; 2 cups of eggs = 1 pound
Egg whites	8 to 10 = 1 cup
Egg yolks	12 to 14 = 1 cup
Flour, all purpose (sifted)	4 cups = 1 pound
Flour, cake (sifted)	4½ to 4¾ cups = 1 pound
Flour, whole-wheat	3½ cups = 1 pound
Honey	1 cup = 12 ounces
Lemon juice	2 tablespoons = 1 ounce
Lemon rind, grated	4 tablespoons = 1 ounce
Milk, liquid	1 cup = 8 ounces
Milk, powdered	1 cup = 4 ounces; 1 cup of powdered milk mixed with 4 cups of water = 1 quart of milk
Molasses	1 cup = 12 ounces
Nuts, shelled (pecans, walnuts, almonds)	1 cup = 4 ounces
Oil, vegetable	1 cup = 8 ounces

Orange rind	1 medium orange = 2 tablespoons grated rind
Orange juice	1 medium orange = $\frac{1}{3}$ cup juice
Raisins	1 pound box = 3 cups, approximately
Salt	2 tablespoons = 1 ounce
Shortening	2½ cups = 1 pound
Spices (allspice, cloves, mace, nutmeg)	4 tablespoons = 1 ounce
Sugar, brown	3 cups = 1 pound
Sugar, confectioners'	3½ cups = 1 pound
Sugar, granulated	2½ cups = 1 pound
Vanilla	2 tablespoons = 1 ounce
Water	8 ounces = 1 cup
Yeast, compressed, fresh	1 small cake = ½ ounce
Yeast, dried	1 package dissolved = ½ ounce of compressed yeast

Common Can Sizes

6 ounces	Used principally for frozen concentrated juices, as well as regular single-strength fruit and vegetable juices	Approximately ¾ cup or 6 fluid ounces
8 ounces	Distributed principally in metropolitan areas, used for most fruits and vegetables as well as for ripe olives	Approximately 1 cup, or 8 ounces (7¾ fluid ounces)
No. 1 (picnic)	Used principally for condensed soups, and some fruits, vegetables, meat, and fish products	Approximately 1¼ cups, or 10½ ounces (9½ fluid ounces)
No. 300	For specialty items, such as beans with pork, spaghetti, macaroni, chili con carne, date and nut bread, and clams, as well as a variety of fruits, including cranberry sauce and blueberries	Approximately 1¾ cups, or 15½ ounces (13½ fluid ounces)
No. 303	Used more extensively than any other, for a complete range of vegetables, plus fruits such as sweet and sour cherries, fruit cocktail, applesauce	Approximately 2 cups, or 1 pound (15 fluid ounces)
No. 2	Used for all vegetable items, plus a wide range of fruits and fruit and tomato juices	Approximately 2½ cups, or 1 pound 4 ounces (18 fluid ounces)
No. 2½	Used principally for fruits, such as peaches, pears, plums, and fruit cocktail, plus vegetables such as tomatoes, sauerkraut and pumpkin	Approximately 3½ cups, or 1 pound 13 ounces (26 fluid ounces)
46 ounces (No. 3 cylinder)	Used almost exclusively for vegetable and fruit juices, and for whole chicken	Approximately 5¾ cups, or 46 ounces (46 fluid ounces)
No. 10	So-called institutional or restaurant-size container in which most fruits and vegetables are packed; not ordinarily available in retail stores	Approximately 12 cups, or 6 pounds 9 ounces (96 fluid ounces)

SUBSTITUTING CAN SIZES

1 no. 10 can = 7 no. 303 cans   1 no. 10 can = 4 no. 2½ cans

1 no. 10 can = 5 no. 2 cans   1 no. 10 can = 2 no. 3 cylinder cans

APPENDIX NINE

Pasta

The artwork in this appendix is supplied courtesy of the National Pasta Association.

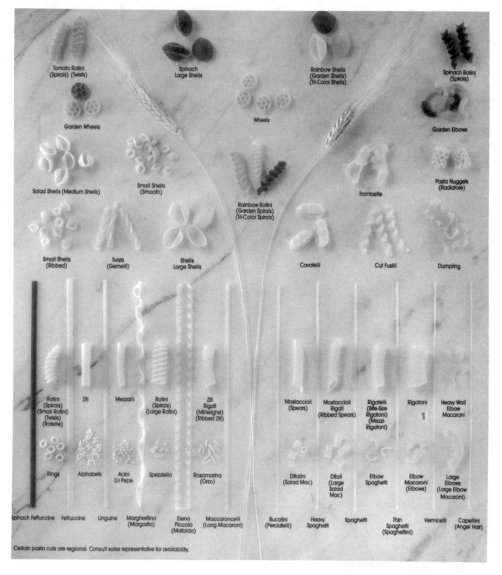

Tomato Rotini (Spirals) (Twists) · Spinach Large Shells · Rainbow Shells (Garden Shells) (Tri-Color Shells) · Spinach Rotini (Spirals)

Garden Wheels · Wheels · Garden Elbows

Salad Shells (Medium Shells) · Small Shells (Smooth) · Rainbow Rotini (Garden Spirals) (Tri-Color Spirals) · Trombette · Pasta Nuggets (Radiatore)

Small Shells (Ribbed) · Twists (Gemelli) · Shells Large Shells · Cavatelli · Cut Fusilli · Dumpling

Rotini (Spirals) (Small Rotini) (Twists) (Rotelle) · Ziti · Mezzani · Rotini (Spirals) (Large Rotini) · Ziti Rigati (Millerighe) (Ribbed Ziti) · Mostaccioli (Spears) · Mostaccioli Rigati (Ribbed Spears) · Rigatelli (Bite-Size Rigatoni) (Mezzi-Rigatoni) · Rigatoni · Heavy Wall Elbow Macaroni

Rings · Alphabets · Acini Di Pepe · Spezziella · Rosamarina (Orzo) · Ditalini (Salad Mac) · Ditali (Large Salad Mac) · Elbow Spaghetti · Elbow Macaroni (Elbows) · Large Elbows (Large Elbow Macaroni)

Spinach Fettuccine · Fettuccine · Linguine · Margheritina (Margarita) · Elena Piccola (Matalda) · Maccaroncelli (Long Macaroni) · Bucatini (Perciatelli) · Heavy Spaghetti · Spaghetti · Thin Spaghetti (Spaghettini) · Vermicelli · Capellini (Angel Hair)

Certain pasta cuts are regional. Consult sales representative for availability.

266

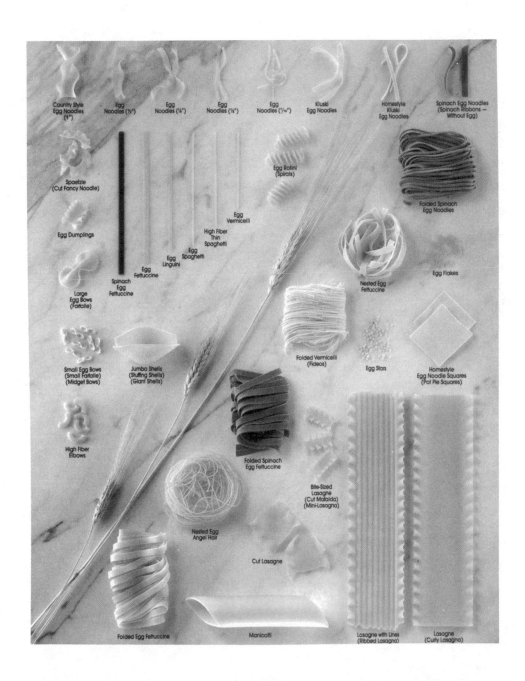

Country Style Egg Noodles (¼")

Egg Noodles (½")

Egg Noodles (¼")

Egg Noodles (⅛")

Egg Noodles (¹/₁₆")

Kluski Egg Noodles

Homestyle Kluski Egg Noodles

Spinach Egg Noodles (Spinach Ribbons — Without Egg)

Spaetzle (Cut Fancy Noodle)

Egg Dumplings

Large Egg Bows (Farfalle)

Spinach Egg Fettuccine

Egg Fettuccine

Egg Linguini

Egg Spaghetti

High Fiber Thin Spaghetti

Egg Vermicelli

Egg Rotini (Spirals)

Folded Spinach Egg Noodles

Nested Egg Fettuccine

Egg Flakes

Small Egg Bows (Small Farfalle) (Midget Bows)

Jumbo Shells (Stuffing Shells) (Giant Shells)

Folded Vermicelli (Fideos)

Egg Stars

Homestyle Egg Noodle Squares (Pot Pie Squares)

High Fiber Elbows

Folded Spinach Egg Fettuccine

Bite-Sized Lasagne (Cut Malalda) (Mini-Lasagna)

Nested Egg Angel Hair

Cut Lasagne

Folded Egg Fettuccine

Manicotti

Lasagne with Lines (Ribbed Lasagna)

Lasagne (Curly Lasagna)

Herbs and Spices

The chart and artwork in this appendix are supplied courtesy of the American Spice Trade Association.

SPICE	APPETIZERS	SOUPS	PASTAS	SEAFOOD AND POULTRY
ALLSPICE	liver pâté	pepperpot	Middle Eastern tomato sauce	Caribbean chicken
BASIL	Italian tomato toasts	minestrone	pesto	shellfish stew
BAY LEAVES	Marinated mushrooms	bean	tomato-meat sauce	marinades for barbecuing
CARAWAY SEEDS	Liptauer cheese spread	cabbage		chicken paprikash
CELERY SEEDS	tomato juice cocktail	chicken chowder		chicken salad
CHILI POWDER	bean dips	corn chowder	Southwestern chicken & tomato sauce	oven-fried chicken
CINNAMON	sugared nuts	pumpkin	noodle pudding	Moroccan chicken stew
CLOVES	fruit juices	split pea		poached fish
CORIANDER SEEDS		lentil		curried chicken
CUMIN SEEDS	guacamole dip	bean	fettucine primavera	Mexican seafood stews
CURRY POWDER	deviled eggs	mulligatawny	tomato & meat sauces	creamed shellfish
DILL WEED & SEEDS	sour cream & yogurt dips	cream of vegetable	egg noodles	herbed butters
FENNEL SEEDS	pickled shrimp	pasta & bean	Italian tomato sauces	bouillabaisse
GARLIC	cheese dips	vegetable	all tomato-based sauces	roast chicken
GINGER	Oriental shrimp	carrot	lo mein noodles	Chinese stir-fries

MEATS	POTATOES AND GRAINS	VEGETABLES AND BEANS	SALADS AND DRESSINGS	DESSERTS
Jamaican pot roast	baked rice	honey-glazed winter squash	creamy fruit-salad dressing	baked pears
Italian beef roulades	polenta	stewed tomatoes	sliced tomatoes & onions	
skewered grilled lamb or beef	Middle Eastern pilaf	steamed peas & lettuce		
pork or veal stew	roasted potatoes	sauerkraut	potato salad	spice cookies
meat pies	buttered steamed potatoes	poached celery wedges	cabbage & carrot slaw	
cornmeal-topped stews	baked stuffed potatoes	baked beans	sour cream or yogurt dressing	
Greek lamb stew	couscous	mashed yams	sugared sliced tomatoes	fruit pies, cakes, puddings
beef stew with dumplings		beets with orange sauce	fruit salad dressing	poached apples
pork kebabs	Indian rice pilaf	coriander butter for winter squash	yogurt dressing for fruit	coffee cake
chilis and currries	brown rice	black beans	vinaigrette	
hamburgers	rice pilaf	baked winter squash	fruit dressing	
Scandinavian veal meatballs	boiled new potatoes	green beans	marinated cucumbers	
beef stew		braised celery	seafood salad	
roast lamb	mashed potatoes	sautéed spinach	creamy Italian dressing	
pot roast	Chinese fried rice	carrots	sweet potato & apple salad	poached winter fruits

(continued)

SPICE	APPETIZERS	SOUPS	PASTAS	SEAFOOD AND POULTRY
ITALIAN SEASONING	spinach quiche	mushroom	all tomato-based sauces	fish florentine
MARJORAM	clam dip	split pea	seafood sauces	poultry stuffings
MINT	pineapple juice	chilled fruit		
MUSTARD	pork pâté	Cheddar cheese		broiled salmon
NUTMEG	chicken kebabs	cream of onion	delicate cream sauces	creamy seafood sauces
ONION	cream-cheese spreads	fish chowder	pasta with artichokes	French country chicken with herbs
OREGANO	vegetable juices	bean	Neapolitan pizza sauce	broiled fish
PAPRIKA	baked stuffed clams	potato-onion	baked ziti with ricotta	crab cakes
RED PEPPER	seafood cocktail sauce	seafood bisque	southern Italian tomato sauce	Szechuan stir-fries
ROSEMARY	marinated artichokes	lentil	vegetable lasagna	chicken sauté with olives
SAGE	cheese sticks	bean	browned butter sauce for ravioli	chestnut stuffings
SESAME SEEDS	herbed biscuits	sprinkled over carrot-orange	linguine tossed with sesame oil	red snapper with sesame butter
TARRAGON	marinated mushrooms	shrimp gumbo	tarragon butter for noodles	chicken breasts with wine
THYME	cheese-stuffed mushrooms	vegetable beef	pork-filled cannelloni	shrimp creole

About Black Pepper: So versatile is the flavor of our most important spice that it can be added to most dishes, including corrector, just before serving.

MEATS	POTATOES AND GRAINS	VEGETABLES AND BEANS	SALADS AND DRESSINGS	DESSERTS
Italian meatballs	baked sliced potato & onion casserole	grilled vegetables	Italian oil & vinegar dressings	
veal stew	roasted new potatoes	vegetable & bean stews	vegetable salads	
roast lamb	Greek rice	steamed carrots	creamy fruit dressing	chilled summer fruits
baked ham	potatoes au gratin	green beans with mustard sauce	vinaigrette dressings	
veal meatballs	risotto	creamed spinach	Waldorf salad	apple bread pudding
meat loaf	mashed potatoes	stewed tomatoes	marinated beans	
Greek lamb stews	lemon roasted potatoes	crumb-topped green beans	mixed vegetable salads	
beef paprikash	scalloped potatoes	corn pudding	macaroni salad	
hot pepper sauce for lamb chops	rice pilaf	stewed tomatoes	tomato salad dressing	lemon ice
lamb kebabs	sautéed potatoes	grilled tomatoes	warm lamb & bean salad	wine-poached fruits
sautéed liver	stuffed peppers	baked lima beans & tomatoes		
sesame burgers	coating for potato puffs	topping for vegetables	toasted, over fruit salad	baked bananas
stuffed veal chops	rice & vegetable casserole	green beans & onions	chicken & vegetable salad	poached pears
boeuf bourguignon	wild rice	yellow & red pepper sauté	tabbouleh	

some desserts, such as spice cookies and cakes, strawberries, and poached pears. Pepper can also be used as a seasoning

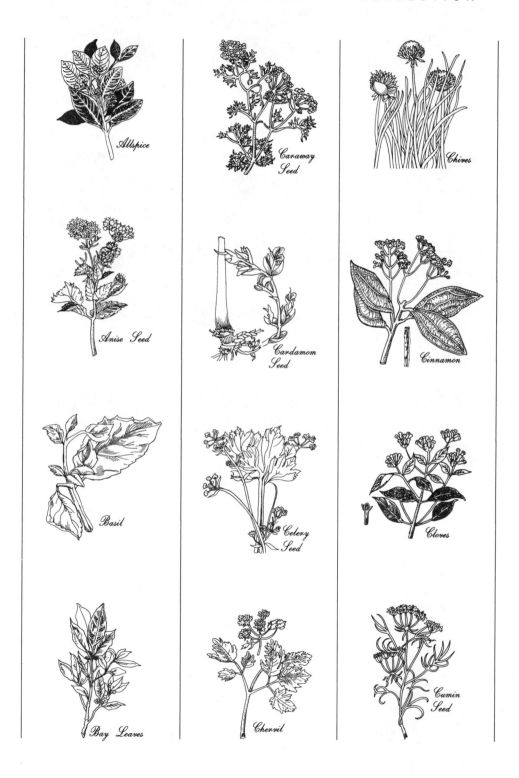

Allspice

Caraway Seed

Chives

Anise Seed

Cardamom Seed

Cinnamon

Basil

Celery Seed

Cloves

Bay Leaves

Chervil

Cumin Seed

Dill

Marjoram

Oregano

Fennel Seed

Mint

Paprika

Garlic

Mustard

Parsley

Ginger

Nutmeg/Mace

Pepper

Red Pepper

Saffron

Tarragon

Sweet Pepper

Sage

Thyme

Poppy Seed

Savory

Coriander Seed/Cilantro

Rosemary

Sesame Seed

Turmeric

Vegetable and Potato Cuts

CUTTING AND PREPARING POTATOES

Straw potatoes *(pailles)*: Shred or fine-cut julienne. Soak in cold water to remove starch, drain, pat dry, deep-fry until crisp and golden color.

Matchstick potatoes *(allumettes)*: Cut into matchstick size; follow same procedure for straw potatoes.

French-fries *(frites)*: Cut into ½-inch-thick and 3-inch-long sticks; follow procedure for straw potatoes.

Steak fries *(Pont-Neuf)*: Cut twice as thick as *frites*; follow procedure for straw potatoes.

Carré potatoes: Cut into a ⅓-inch dice; blanch in slightly salted water, drain, and fry *à la minute*.

Ridged or waffle potato chips *(gaufrettes)*: Cut on the serrated plate of the mandoline; soak in cold water, drain, pat dry, deep-fry until crisp and golden brown.

Potato chips: Cut into very thin slices, follow same procedure as ridged chips.

Château potatoes: Cut approximately 2 inches long, shaped with a knife to have seven corners; the classical preparation calls for slow browning in butter.

Noisettes and *parisienne* potatoes: Scoop out small balls with a melon baller; blanch, brown in butter *à la minute*.

THE DIFFERENT CUTS AND SHAPES OF POTATOES

Pailles	Chips
Allumettes	Château
Mignonnettes	Noisettes
Frites	Parisienne
Pont-Neuf	Fondant
Carré	Olivettes
Gaufrettes	

THE DIFFERENT CUTS AND SHAPES OF VEGETABLES

Brunoise (fine dice)   Chiffonnade
Jardinière   Julienne
Macédoine   Bâtonnets
Mirepoix   Vichy
Paysanne   Tourner

Retail Cuts of Beef, Pork, Lamb, and Veal

The charts in this appendix are supplied courtesy of the National Live Stock and Meat Board.

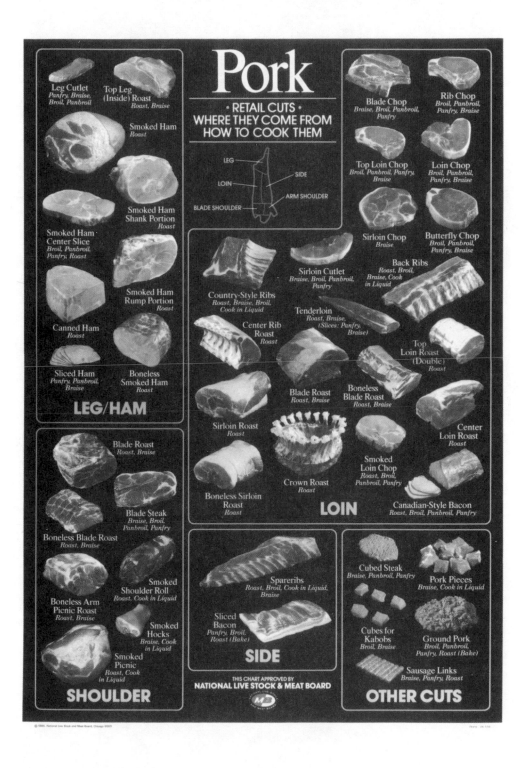

Pork
• RETAIL CUTS •
WHERE THEY COME FROM
HOW TO COOK THEM

LEG
LOIN
SIDE
ARM SHOULDER
BLADE SHOULDER

LEG/HAM

Leg Cutlet
Panfry, Braise, Broil, Panbroil

Top Leg (Inside) Roast
Roast, Braise

Smoked Ham
Roast

Smoked Ham Shank Portion
Roast

Smoked Ham Center Slice
Broil, Panbroil, Panfry, Roast

Smoked Ham Rump Portion
Roast

Canned Ham
Roast

Sliced Ham
Panfry, Panbroil, Braise

Boneless Smoked Ham
Roast

SHOULDER

Blade Roast
Roast, Braise

Blade Steak
Braise, Broil, Panbroil, Panfry

Boneless Blade Roast
Roast, Braise

Boneless Arm Picnic Roast
Roast, Braise

Smoked Shoulder Roll
Roast, Cook in Liquid

Smoked Hocks
Braise, Cook in Liquid

Smoked Picnic
Roast, Cook in Liquid

LOIN

Blade Chop
Braise, Broil, Panbroil, Panfry

Rib Chop
Broil, Panbroil, Panfry, Braise

Top Loin Chop
Broil, Panbroil, Panfry, Braise

Loin Chop
Broil, Panbroil, Panfry, Braise

Sirloin Chop
Braise

Butterfly Chop
Broil, Panbroil, Panfry, Braise

Country-Style Ribs
Roast, Braise, Broil, Cook in Liquid

Sirloin Cutlet
Braise, Broil, Panbroil, Panfry

Back Ribs
Roast, Broil, Braise, Cook in Liquid

Center Rib Roast
Roast

Tenderloin
Roast, Braise, (Slices: Panfry, Braise)

Top Loin Roast (Double)
Roast

Sirloin Roast
Roast

Blade Roast
Roast, Braise

Boneless Blade Roast
Roast, Braise

Center Loin Roast
Roast

Boneless Sirloin Roast
Roast

Crown Roast
Roast

Smoked Loin Chop
Roast, Broil, Panbroil, Panfry

Canadian-Style Bacon
Roast, Broil, Panbroil, Panfry

SIDE

Spareribs
Roast, Broil, Cook in Liquid, Braise

Sliced Bacon
Panfry, Broil, Roast (Bake)

OTHER CUTS

Cubed Steak
Braise, Panbroil, Panfry

Pork Pieces
Braise, Cook in Liquid

Cubes for Kabobs
Broil, Braise

Ground Pork
Broil, Panbroil, Panfry, Roast (Bake)

Sausage Links
Braise, Panfry, Roast

THIS CHART APPROVED BY
NATIONAL LIVE STOCK & MEAT BOARD

© 1986, National Live Stock and Meat Board, Chicago 60611

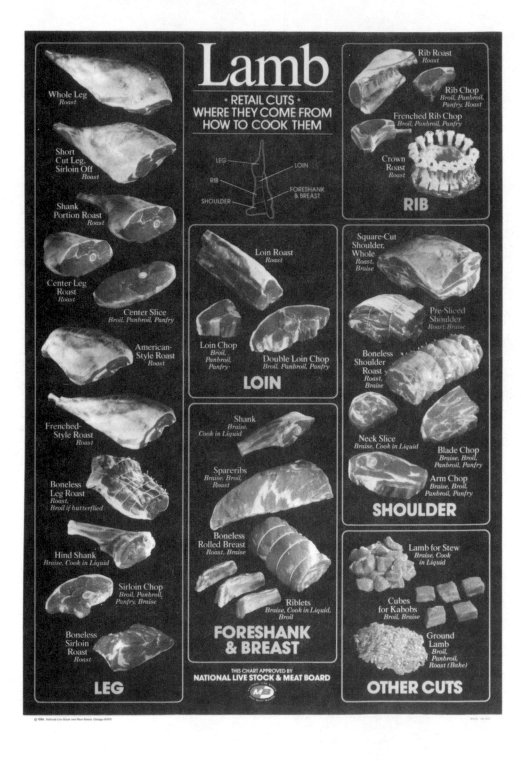

Lamb

· RETAIL CUTS ·
WHERE THEY COME FROM
HOW TO COOK THEM

LEG

LOIN

RIB

FORESHANK & BREAST

SHOULDER

Whole Leg
Roast

Short Cut Leg, Sirloin Off
Roast

Shank Portion Roast
Roast

Center Leg Roast
Roast

Center Slice
Broil, Panbroil, Panfry

American-Style Roast
Roast

Frenched-Style Roast
Roast

Boneless Leg Roast
Roast, Broil if butterflied

Hind Shank
Braise, Cook in Liquid

Sirloin Chop
Broil, Panbroil, Panfry, Braise

Boneless Sirloin Roast
Roast

LEG

Loin Roast
Roast

Loin Chop
Broil, Panbroil, Panfry

Double Loin Chop
Broil, Panbroil, Panfry

LOIN

Shank
Braise, Cook in Liquid

Spareribs
Braise, Broil, Roast

Boneless Rolled Breast
Roast, Braise

Riblets
Braise, Cook in Liquid, Broil

FORESHANK & BREAST

THIS CHART APPROVED BY
NATIONAL LIVE STOCK & MEAT BOARD

Rib Roast
Roast

Rib Chop
Broil, Panbroil, Panfry, Roast

Frenched Rib Chop
Broil, Panbroil, Panfry

Crown Roast
Roast

RIB

Square-Cut Shoulder, Whole
Roast, Braise

Pre-Sliced Shoulder
Roast, Braise

Boneless Shoulder Roast
Roast, Braise

Neck Slice
Braise, Cook in Liquid

Blade Chop
Braise, Broil, Panbroil, Panfry

Arm Chop
Braise, Broil, Panbroil, Panfry

SHOULDER

Lamb for Stew
Braise, Cook in Liquid

Cubes for Kabobs
Broil, Braise

Ground Lamb
Broil, Panbroil, Roast (Bake)

OTHER CUTS

© 1984, National Live Stock and Meat Board, Chicago 60611

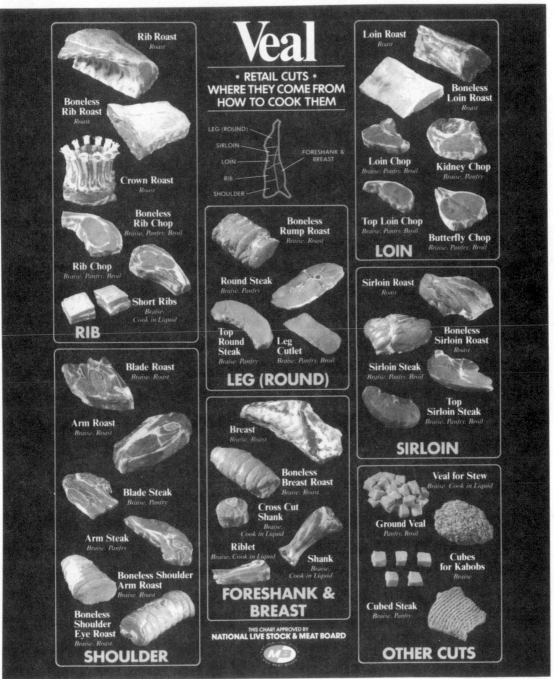

Veal

• RETAIL CUTS •
WHERE THEY COME FROM
HOW TO COOK THEM

LEG (ROUND)
SIRLOIN
LOIN
RIB
SHOULDER
FORESHANK & BREAST

Rib Roast
Roast

Boneless Rib Roast
Roast

Crown Roast
Roast

Boneless Rib Chop
Braise, Panfry, Broil

Rib Chop
Braise, Panfry, Broil

Short Ribs
Braise, Cook in Liquid

RIB

Blade Roast
Braise, Roast

Arm Roast
Braise, Roast

Blade Steak
Braise, Panfry

Arm Steak
Braise, Panfry

Boneless Shoulder Arm Roast
Braise, Roast

Boneless Shoulder Eye Roast
Braise, Roast

SHOULDER

Boneless Rump Roast
Braise, Roast

Round Steak
Braise, Panfry

Top Round Steak
Braise, Panfry

Leg Cutlet
Braise, Panfry, Broil

LEG (ROUND)

Breast
Braise, Roast

Boneless Breast Roast
Braise, Roast

Cross Cut Shank
Braise, Cook in Liquid

Riblet
Braise, Cook in Liquid

Shank
Braise, Cook in Liquid

FORESHANK & BREAST

THIS CHART APPROVED BY
NATIONAL LIVE STOCK & MEAT BOARD

Loin Roast
Roast

Boneless Loin Roast
Roast

Loin Chop
Braise, Panfry, Broil

Kidney Chop
Braise, Panfry

Top Loin Chop
Braise, Panfry, Broil

Butterfly Chop
Braise, Panfry, Broil

LOIN

Sirloin Roast
Roast

Boneless Sirloin Roast
Roast

Sirloin Steak
Braise, Panfry, Broil

Top Sirloin Steak
Braise, Panfry, Broil

SIRLOIN

Veal for Stew
Braise, Cook in Liquid

Ground Veal
Panfry, Broil

Cubes for Kabobs
Braise

Cubed Steak
Braise, Panfry

OTHER CUTS

586100   06-409

GLOSSARY

A

abaisse   A piece of pastry dough rolled to the required size.

abatis   Poultry trimmings, such as wing tips and giblets.

abricot   Apricot.

agiter   To stir.

agneau   Lamb.

aiglefin   Haddock.

aiguillettes   Meat or fish cut into fine strips.

ail   Garlic.

airelle rouge   Cranberry.

à la   In the style of, e.g., *à la française.*

à la carte   A list of food items, each priced separately.

à la mode   In the fashion of.

al dente   To the bite, referring to pasta or vegetables cooked only until firm or crunchy, not soft.

allumettes   Matchstick-size cut, usually for potatoes.

aloyau   Sirloin of beef (contre-filet).

anchois   Anchovy.

ancienne (à l')   Old-fashioned style.

anglais (à l')   English style, plainly cooked or breaded and fried food.

anguille   Eel.

anis   Aniseed.

annoncer   To announce (to call out orders).

antipasto   (Italian) Appetizer.

Argenteuil   Garnished with asparagus, from the district in France famous for that vegetable.

aromates   Herbs, spices, and flavorings.

arrowroot   Powdered starch obtained from the roots of the arrowroot plant, used as a flour or thickener.

artichaut   Artichoke.

asperge   Asparagus.

aspic   A clear jelly made from concentrated liquid in which meat, poultry, or fish was cooked.

assiette   Plate or dish.

assiette anglaise   Dish of assorted cold meats.

aubergine   Eggplant.

au bleu   A method of cooking fish, such as trout, in which the fish is killed just before being plunged in boiling court-bouillon with vinegar.

au four   In the oven, baked.

au jus   With natural juice.

B

baba — Small yeast-raised cake, soaked in rum-flavored syrup and topped with whipped cream.

bain-marie — A double-boiler insert for slow cooking, when direct boiling is to be avoided. Also, a steam table in which smaller pans and their contents are kept hot.

ballotine — Stuffed, rolled boneless game or domestic bird.

bar — Sea bass.

barbeau — Barbel.

barbue — Brill.

barder — To cover meats with slices of salt pork or bacon.

baron — Of mutton or lamb, the saddle with legs.

barquette — A small boat-shaped pastry shell or mold.

basilic — Basil.

baste — To moisten meat in the oven, to prevent drying.

bâton, bâtonnet — Shaped like a small stick (commonly denotes a small stick-shaped garnish).

batter — A liquid dough thin enough to pour.

batterie de cuisine — Kitchen equipment.

bécasse — Woodcock.

bécassine — Snipe.

béchamel — Basic white sauce made of milk and roux, one of the foundation sauces.

beignets — Fritters.

betterave — Beetroot.

beurre — Butter.

beurre manié — Butter kneaded with flour, used for thickening sauces.

bien cuit — Well or thoroughly cooked.

bisque — A thick cream soup, often made from shellfish, e.g., *bisque d'homard* (lobster bisque).

blanc — Water with flour and lemon juice, used to cook vegetables, particularly artichokes, to keep them white.

blanc d'oeuf — Egg white.

blanchir — To blanch, that is, to immerse food in cold water, bring to boil, drain, and refresh by returning to cold water.

blanquette — Ragout or stew made of veal or lamb in a rich velouté sauce.

bleu — Blue, applied to very rare broiled meat. *see also* au bleu.

boeuf — Beef.

bombe	Ice cream dessert layered in a special mold.
bordure	Border, usually applied to rice (ring of rice).
bouchée	Small puff pastry.
boudin noir	Blood sausage or black pudding.
bouillabaisse	A fish stew, a specialty of southern France.
bouillir, bouilli	To boil, boiled.
bouillon	Reduced meat stock.
boulanger	Baker.
bouquet garni	A bunch of kitchen herbs, such as bay leaf, thyme, and parsley, tied with celery or leek, used to flavor soups and sauces.
bourgeoise (à la)	Family style, used for braised meats garnished with carrots, onions, and diced bacon.
Bourgogne	Burgundy (wine).
boutons (de Bruxelles)	Buttons (of Brussels), poetic menu term for brussels sprouts.
braiser	To braise.
braisière	Braising pan or stewing pan.
breme	Bream.
brider	To truss, to tie poultry or meat.
brioche	Pastry or bread made from yeast-leavened sponge dough containing butter and eggs.
brochette	Skewer, used for broiling or grilling kebabs.
brunoise	Vegetables cut into a fine dice.
brut	Coarse.
bruxelloise (à la)	In the Brussels style, used for dishes garnished with brussels sprouts, braised endive, and château potatoes.

C

cabillaud	Fresh cod.
caille	Quail.
canapés	Pieces of toasted bread, garnished, and served as appetizers or snacks.
canard	Duck.
canard sauvage	Wild duck.
caneton	Duckling (male).
cantaloup	Melon.
caramel	Melted sugar cooked until brown and syrupy.
caramelizer	To caramelize, to cook sugar until it turns brown.
carbonnade	Braised steak.
carcasse	Carcass; the bone structure of meat or poultry without the meat on it.

carpe — Carp.

carré — Rack of veal or lamb.

carrelet — Sand dab.

cartouche — Greased round of paper, used to cover meat dishes during cooking.

casserole — Ovenproof dish, or dishes cooked and served in a casserole.

cassis — Black currant (and black currant liqueur).

cassoulet — Stew of beans with pork, mutton, goose, or duck, in an earthenware pot.

cayenne — A very hot red chili pepper.

céleri — Celery.

céleri-rave — Celeriac or celery root, a turniplike rooted celery.

Cèpe — Edible fungus, a kind of yellowish flap mushroom.

cerfeuil — Chervil.

cerise — Cherry.

cervelles — Brains.

champignon — Mushroom.

chanterelles — Mushrooms (*Cantharellus* species).

Chantilly — Whipped cream sweetened with sugar.

chapelure — Brown breadcrumbs.

chapon — Capon (castrated cock).

charcutier — Butcher and sausage maker.

charcuterie — Prepared meat, especially pork, including such meat specialties as sausages, ham, rillettes, galantines, and pâtés.

chateaubriand — Double steak cut from the center of the beef fillet.

chaud-froid — Cooked food coated with cold white sauce, served cold.

chef de cuisine — Chef in charge, or executive chef.

chef de partie — Chef in charge of a shift or section of the kitchen (e.g., *chef garde-manger*).

chevreuil — Venison.

chicorée — Chicory, including endive.

chiffonnade — Leaf vegetables shredded or cut into thin ribbons.

chinois — Cone-shaped fine strainer or sieve, also called a china cap.

chipolata — Small sausage flavored with chives.

chou — Cabbage.

choucroute — Sauerkraut, cabbage pickled with salt and fermented.

chou de mer — Sea kale.

chou-fleur — Cauliflower.

chou-frisé — Savoy cabbage.

choux (pâte de) — Dough used for cream puffs, éclairs, profiteroles, and similar pastries.

choux de bruxelles — Brussels sprouts.

clarifier — To clarify or clear liquids (e.g., consomme, aspic) with ground beef, egg whites, and seasonings.

clouter — To stud; *oignon clouté* is an onion studded with cloves.

cocotte — A small ovenproof dish.

coeur — Heart (e.g., *coeur de laitue,* heart of lettuce.

colin — Hake.

commis — An apprentice in the kitchen or dining room.

compote — Stewed fruit.

concasser — To chop roughly (commonly applied to tomatoes).

concombre — Cucumber.

confiture — Jam.

congre — Conger eel.

contre-filet — Sirloin that faces the tenderloin.

coq au vin — Chicken stewed in wine sauce.

coquille — (1) Shell-shaped dish.
(2) Cooked and served in a shell.

coquille Saint-Jacques — Scallop.

corbeille — Basket.

cornet — Cone-shaped slice of meat or pastry, often filled.

corser — To flavor and enrich.

côte — A cut of meat, usually a rib or chop.

côtelette — Cutlet.

coulibiac — Oval pie filled with layers of salmon or other fish, rice or kasha, herbs, mushrooms, and onions; from the Russian *kulibyaka.*

couper — To cut.

coupe — Small bowl used to serve cream, compote, or ice cream.

courge — Marrow.

courgette — Zucchini.

court-bouillon — Stock composed of water, vinegar and/or wine, herbs, and seasoning, used for poaching fish, sweetbreads, and other foods.

crabe — Crab.

crème — Cream.

crème pâtissière — Pastry cream.

crêpes — Thin pancakes.

crépine — Pig's caul (intestinal membrane) used as casing for sausage and forcemeat.

crépinettes — Individual portions of meat, chicken, or pork enveloped in crépine or breaded and sautéed or baked.

crevette — Shrimp.

croissant — Crescent-shaped French roll layered like puff pastry.

croquette — Chopped meat or vegetables bound with a sauce, molded, breaded, and deep-fried.

croustade — Pastry crust used to hold savory fillings.

croûte au pot — A beef broth, popular in France, garnished with vegetables and dried bread crusts.

croûtons — Fried pieces of bread of various sizes and shapes, served as accompaniments to soups or used as socle (a base for other foods).

cru — Raw.

cuire — To cook.

cuisinier — Cook.

cuisse, cuissot — Drumstick or leg.

cuit — Cooked.

culotte — Rump of beef.

D

dariole — Small cylindrical mold.

darne — A thick middle-cut slice of a fish steak.

débarrasser — To clear away.

débrider — To remove trussing string after cooking.

décorer — To decorate as for platters, cakes.

déglacer — To deglaze, to dilute roasting plaque (with liquid).

dégraisser — To skim grease from stews, sauces.

demi-glace — Reduced brown sauce.

demi-tasse — Literally, a half cup; also a small cup of black coffee.

dépouiller — To remove scum from surface of a liquid during cooking.

des — Dice.

désosser — To bone poultry or fish.

diablotins — Small gnocchi or croûtons topped with grated cheese and browned.

dinde — Turkey.

dindonneau — Young turkey.

dredge — To coat food, such as with flour, by rolling or sprinkling.

dresser — To plate food for service.

du jour — Of the day (*soup du Jour*—soup of the day).

duxelles — Chopped shallots and mushrooms slowly cooked in butter to a paste.

E

échalote	Shallot.
éclair	Choux pastry baked in thick fingers, filled with cream or pastry cream, and iced with fondant or chocolate.
écrévisse	Crayfish.
égoutter	To drain, strain off liquid.
émincer	To mince, to chop as finely as possible.
en	In, served in.
en papillote	Mode of cooking (particularly fish) in greased paper.
en tasse	In a cup (consommé en tasse).
entrecôte	Steak cut from the sirloin of beef, literally "between the ribs."
entrée	In the United States, the main course.

entremetier	Cook who prepares vegetables and egg dishes.
entremets	Sweets, desserts.
envelopper	To wrap.
épaule	Shoulder.
éperlan	Smelt.
épinard	Spinach.
escalope	Thin slice or scallop of meat or fish.
escargot	Edible snail.
espagnole	Basic brown sauce.
estouffade	Brown meat stock; also, a dish cooked slowly, covered, with minimum additional liquid.
estragon	Tarragon.
esturgeon	Sturgeon.
étuver	To cook slowly under cover with a minimum of added liquid.

F

fagot	Faggot, bouquet garni.
faisan	Pheasant.
farce	Stuffing or forcemeat.
farcir (farci)	To stuff (stuffed).
faux-filet	Boned sirloin.
fécule	Cornstarch or flour used for thickening liquids.
fenouil	Fennel.
feuilletage	Puff pastry.
filet	Fillet; a thin cut of meat or poultry or the skinless flesh of fish removed from the bone.
filet mignon	Small steak cut from tenderloin of beef, veal, lamb, or other meat.
fines herbes	A mixture of fresh chopped herbs (often parsley, tarragon, chervil, and chives) used for seasoning.

flamber	To flame.
flan	Open tart; in Spanish, a caramel cream custard.
flanchet	Flank.
flétan	Halibut.
fleurons	Small crescent-shaped puff pastry, used as a garnish.
foie	Liver.
foie gras	Fat goose liver.
foncer	To line the bottom of a dish with bacon or pastry.
fondant	Thick liquid sugar icing.
fond blanc	White stock.
fond brun	Brown stock.
fonds de artichaut	Artichoke bottoms.
fonds de cuisine	Basic stocks or essences.
fondue	Melted cheese with wine into which pieces of bread are dipped; also, special sauces into which sautéed cubes of meat are dipped.
fontaine	The well or hole made in the dry flour and other dry ingredients before adding liquid to make pastry.
fouetter	To whip or whisk.
fraise	Strawberry.
framboise	Raspberry.
frangipane	A custardlike pastry cream flavored with almonds.
frappé	Iced.
frapper	To ice.
friandises	Small confections, petits fours.
fricandeau	Veal braised until very tender.
fricassée	Stew of white meat in a white sauce.
frire	To fry.
frit	Fried.
friture	Deep-fat frying.
fumer (fumé)	To smoke (smoked).
fumet	Concentrated stock or essence from fish or shellfish.

G

galantine	Stuffed boned chicken or veal in the form of a large roll, usually glazed with chaud-froid sauce and decorated for cold buffets.
garbure	A thick vegetable soup.
garde-manger	Cold kitchen; also, the chef who is in charge of the garde-manger.
garnir (garni)	To garnish (garnished), to decorate.
garniture	The garnish: starches and/or vegetables served with the main course.

gâteau — Cake.

gelée — Jelly, aspic.

génoise — Sponge cake.

gibier: — Game.

gigot d'agneau — Leg of lamb.

glacé — Frozen or glazed.

glace de poisson — Fish glaze or extract, made by reducing stock or fumet to the consistency of syrup.

glace de viande — Meat glaze or extract, usually made by reducing meat stock to a dark, thick jelly.

glacer — (1) To freeze or chill. (2) To cook in such a way as to produce a shiny surface. (3) To color food under a salamander or hot oven broiler.

gnocchi — Dumplings of semolina, flour, choux paste, or potatoes.

goujon — Gudgeon—meat or fish cut into small strips, roughly of gudgeon size; also small freshwater fish.

granité — Water ice.

gratin — Browned surface of foods cooked in a hot oven or under a salamander.

gratiner — To brown a dish sprinkled with crumbs and grated cheese under a salamander or in the oven.

griller (grillé) — To grill, to broil (grilled, broiled).

groseille — Currant.

H

hacher — To chop finely.

hachis — Hash.

hareng — Herring.

haricot blanc — White bean.

haricot vert — Green bean.

hatelet — Decorative silver skewer used in buffet pieces.

homard — Lobster.

hors d'oeuvre — The first course of appetizer: canapés and other finger foods served hot or cold at the beginning of a meal.

huître — Oyster.

J

jambon — Ham.

jardinière — Fresh mixed vegetables cut into small dice or julienne.

jarret — Knuckle or hock.

jaune d'oeuf	Egg yolk.	jus	The natural juice of meat, vegetables, or fruits.
julienne	Meat or vegetables cut into fine strips.	jus lié	Thickened juice.

K

kromeski	A type of meat croquette.	

L

laitue	Lettuce.	laurier	Bay leaf.
lamproie	Lamprey.	liaison	A thickening or binding agent, commonly egg yolk and cream, used to thicken soups and sauces.
langouste	Spiny lobster.		
langue	Tongue.		
lapin	Rabbit.		
lard	Bacon, salt pork, or rendered pork fat.		
larder	To lard, to insert strips of fat with a larding needle into lean meat.	lié	Slightly thickened.
		lier	To thicken (usually with starch or egg).
lardons	Strips of salt pork or bacon used for larding.	lièvre	Hare.
		limande	Lemon sole.

M

macédoine	Diced, mixed vegetables or fruits.	marinade	Blend of liquids and flavorings in which food is steeped to flavor, moisten, and soften it.
maigre	Lean, suitable for fast days as prescribed by the Roman Catholic Church.		
mais	Maize, sweet corn.	marmite	Stockpot.
maître d'hôtel	Restaurant manager.	marmite, la petite	A type of consommé cooked and served in a small earthenware pot.
maquereau	Mackerel.		

marron	Chestnut.
masquer	To coat or mask with sauce or jelly before serving.
médaillons	Round pieces of meat.
mélanger	To mix two or more ingredients together.
menthe	Mint.
merlan	Whiting.
merluche	Hake.
meunière (à la)	A method of cooking in which the meat of fish is dredged in flour and shallow-fried in butter.
mignonnette	Coarsely ground whole peppercorns; also, médaillons.
mirepoix	Diced vegetables and herbs sautéed in bacon fat, used as flavoring for soups and sauces.
mise en place	Literally, "put in place"; organizing and completing in advance all preliminary tasks involved in meal preparation (such as chopping, slicing, peeling) before cooking begins, as well as in service before guests arrive.
moelle	Beef marrow.
mollet	Soft-cooked egg.
monter	To beat cream or egg whites, to supply volume; also, to enrich, as *monter au beurre,* enrich with butter.
morue	Salt cod.
moule	Mussel.
moulin	Hand mill (pepper grinder).
mousse	Sweet or savory dish consisting of a puree lightened with beaten egg whites or cream.
mouton	Mutton.
mulet	Gray mullet.
mûr	Ripe.
mûre	Blackberry.

N

napper	To coat with sauce, aspic, sugar, etc.
navarin	A brown mutton stew.
navet	Turnip.
noisette	Hazelnut; in reference to meat, a round piece of veal or lamb tenderloin; also, small potato balls.
noques	Flour dumplings.
nouilles	Noodles.

O

oeuf	Egg.	oignon	Onion.
oie	Goose.	oseille	Sorrel.

P

pailles	Straws.	paysanne (à la)	Peasant or country style, served with vegetables and diced bacon.
paillettes	Pastry straws.		
panade	Flour or bread cooked in milk, water, or stock, used to bind forcemeats or stuffings.		
		pêche	Peach.
		perche	Perch.
		perdreau	Partridge.
paner (pané)	To coat with breadcrumbs (breaded).	persil	Parsley.
		persillé	Sprinkled with chopped parsley.
pannequets	Pancakes.	petits fours	Small fancy cakes or biscuits, dipped in icing and decorated.
papillotes	Cooking in paper wrapping (en papillote).		
paprika	Hungarian red pepper.	piccata	Small veal cutlets.
		pièce montée	Centerpiece on a platter or buffet.
parer	To trim meat or fish.	pied	Foot.
parfumer	To impart bouquet by adding aromates.	pilaw, pilaf	Rice sauteéd in butter, then steamed in stock.
parures	Trimmings, cooked or raw.		
		piment	Capsicum pepper.
passer	To strain through a tammy cloth or sieve.	pintade	Guinea hen.
		piquer	To insert small pieces of fat into lean meat with a special needle.
pastillage	Sugar pastes used in molding.		
pâte	Paste or pastry.		
pâté	Rich pastelike forcemeat, often baked in pastry (en croûte).	plaque à rôtir	Roasting plaque or drippings.
		plat	Plate or dish.
		plat du jour	Dish of the day (speciality of the day).
paupiettes	Thin flattened slices of meat, stuffed and rolled.		
		plie	Plaice.

pocher	To poach, to cook gently in simmering liquid.	**pot-au-feu**	Rich soup with meats and vegetables.
poêler	To cook with a bit of butter in a tightly closed pot just large enough to hold the meat.	**potiron**	Pumpkin.
		poularde, poulardine	Young, fat chicken—a roaster.
		poule	Stewing hen.
		poulet	Young chicken—a broiler or fryer.
pointe	Tip (of a knife or of asparagus).	**poulet d'Inde**	Young turkey.
		poussin	Young, immature chicken.
poire	Pear.		
poireau	Leek.	**praline**	Toasted almonds or other nuts in carmelized sugar.
poitrine	Chest, breast, or brisket.		
poivrade	Flavored with pepper.	**printanière (à la)**	Spring style: garnished with spring vegetables.
poivre	Pepper.		
pojarski	A minced cutlet of veal in the shape of a cutlet.	**profiteroles**	Small or medium-sized balls made of choux paste, filled with pastry or whipped cream or with savory fillings.
pomme	Apple; also used in menus and in kitchen as short for *pomme de terre*.		
pomme de terre	Potato.	**prune**	Plum.
		puree	Food that is mashed or sieved until smooth.
porc	Pork.		
potage	Soup.		

Q

quartier	Quarter; to divide or cut into quarters.	**quiche lorraine**	Custard of eggs, cream, bacon, and Gruyère cheese in a thick pie dough.
quenelles	Dumplings made of meat, poultry, fish or game forcemeat.		

R

radis	Radish.	**raifort**	Horseradish.
ragoût	A rich brown stew of meat or poultry.	**ramequin**	A savory tartlet or earthenware dish

	in which food is baked and served.
ravioli	Small pasta squares filled with cheese, spinach, or meat.
réchauffé	Reheated or made with leftovers.
réchauffer	To reheat.
reduction	A thickened concentrated liquid created by boiling.
revenir	To fry quickly to brown.
ris	Sweetbreads.
risotto	Italian rice dish, made by cooking rice in butter and then gradually adding stock.
rissole	Deep-fried small turnover.
rissoler	To brown.
rognon	Kidney.
rognonnade (de veau)	Saddle (of veal) complete with kidneys.
romaine	Cos lettuce.
Roquefort	A "blue" semi-soft French cheese made from sheep's milk.
rôtir (roti)	To roast (roasted).
rôtisseur	Roast cook.
rouget	Red mullet.
roux	Thickening agent made of flour and melted butter or other fat, used to thicken soups and sauces.
royale	Unsweetened molded custard, cut into various shapes and used as a garnish.
russe	Stew pan.

S

sabayon	French name for *zabaglione*; dessert made of whipped eggs, sugar, and wine.
saignant	Rare.
saisir	To sear.
salé	Salted.
salpicon	A mixture of finely diced meat and vegetables bound with a sauce.
saucisses	Fresh sausage.
sauge	Sage.
saumon	Salmon.
sauter	Literally, to jump: to cook by tossing in small amounts of hot fat (sauté).
sauteuse	Shallow pan with sloping sides.
sautoir	Round shallow heavy pan with straight walls and a long handle.
savarin	Ring-shaped baba, filled with cream or fruit.
selle	Saddle.
sorbet	Frozen mixture of fruit juice and sugar, sometimes with gelatin and Italian meringue.

Soubise	A thick sauce made with pureed onions stewed in butter.		that expands when baked.
soufflé	A sweet or savory dish that puffs because of air, beaten into egg,	sous chef	Assistant to chief cook.
		suprême	The best part of meat, game, or poultry.

T

table d'hôte	The set menu for the day at a fixed price.	tournedos	Small steaks from the center cut of beef tenderloin.
tasse	Cup.	tourner	To turn, to shape vegetables or potatoes.
terrine	Earthenware casserole; also a term for a pâté cooked in a terrine.	tranche	A slice.
		trancher	To carve or slice.
		trancheur	Carver.
		travailler	To work, to manipulate or knead.
tête de veau	Calf's head.		
thon	Tuna.	truffe	Truffle, a pungent black or white fungus that grows underground in northern Italy and France.
timbale	A straight-sided 2-inch-deep dish or mold.		
tomate	Tomato.		
topinambour	Jerusalem artichoke.	truite	Trout.

V

veau	Veal.	viande	Meat.
velouté	Literally, "velvet"; white stock thickened with roux to make a sauce, or a soup made with this sauce.	viennoise (à la)	Viennese style, coated with egg, breaded, fried, and garnished with lemon, capers, olives, and hard-cooked eggs.

| vol-au-vent | Puff-pastry shell in which sweet or | | volaille | savory fillings are served. Poultry. |

Z

| zeste | Zest, the outer rind of citrus fruit. | |

INDEX